SECRET OF IMMUNITY

by
Toru Abo, M.D.

and

HEALING YOUR HEALING POWER

by
Kazuko Hillyer Tatsumura,
Ph.D., O.M.D.

KOKORO PUBLISHING
NEW Y0RK

Gaia Holistic, Inc.
Kokoro Publishing Company
20 West 64th Street, Suite 24E
New York City, NY - 10023
Tel. No. (212) 799-9/11 Fax. No. (212) 799-1661
Email: kazuko@gaiaholistic.com
www.gaiaholistic.com

The exercises and practices in *Secret of Immunity* are not intended to replace the services of your physician or to provide an alternative to professional medical treatment. The Immune System Revolution offers no diagnosis of or treatment for any specific medical problem that you may have. Where it suggests the possible usefulness of certain practices in relation to certain illnesses or symptoms, it does so solely for educational purposes—either to explore the possible relationship of natural breathing to health, or to expose the reader to alternative health and healing approaches.

Printed in the United States of America

ISBN: 9798693095038

Designed by Dede Cummings & Daniel Damkoehler Redesign
Edited by Ellen Keelan & Jim Luce

Cover art concept by Kazuko Hillyer Tatsumura
The cover design represents the planet earth ("Gaia"), with the top representing blue sky and sunlight, the middle section representing brown trees and the earth itself, and the red representing the magma beneath the ground.

This edition is printed on acid-free paper that meets the American National Standards Institute 39.48 Standard.

Ki (Chi) - Life Force Energy
Calligraphy by Masato Nakagawa

Kokoro – Mind-Heart
Calligraphy by Masahiro Oki

Acknowledgments

My deepest appreciation to the following people in making this book a reality:

- To Dr. Abo for letting us translate his marvelous work and share his valuable knowledge with people on this side of the world.
- To my spiritual teachers: His Holiness the 14th Dalai Lama of Tibet and Mother Theresa.
- To my masters: the late Masahiro Oki and the late Masato Nakagawa, Sr.
- To the late Tomeko Mitsui for her tireless work in holistic healing and in writing the original version of this book, entitled You Can Cure Cancer with ONNETSUKI.
- To Reimi Takeuchi for assisting me in translating the book.
- To Kodansha International, especially Mr. Mitsuru Tomita and Ms. Ayako Akahagi for their generosity in allowing us to publish this translated version in the U.S.
- To Takarajima Publishing for letting us use the illustrations.
- To Reiko Hillyer, Mary Carney, Karen Ferraro, and Rosalie Prinzivalli for their assistance with my writing
- To Dede Cummings and Ellen Keelan for the difficult task of designing and editing the first edition of this book.

Gasshou

With deepest gratitude,
Kazuko Hillyer Tatsumura, September 2020

Preface

Dr. Toru Abo is Japan's leading immunologist, and one that the nation is proud to share with the world. Dr. Abo has practiced medicine for many years and discovered many facts and new theories in the field of immunology. However, after uncovering the true mechanism of our immune system, he has become an ardent spokesperson against the Western medical establishment, speaking out in particular against the blindness of today's three major cancer treatments. His first book, *Immune Revolution*, published in 2003 by Kodansha International, caused a sensation among readers both for and against his theories. In the field of traditional Eastern and holistic medicine, the book was considered groundbreaking because it presented scientific proof for years of traditional belief for the first time. For the general public, who had never been exposed to such theories, the book was an eye-opener. It became the pioneering text of holistic thinking toward medicine. Until that point, the medical establishment had not been questioned. The physician was blindly considered to be always right—the only and ultimate authority. Dr. Abo's text opened the door for a new trend of holistic approach to Western medicine and has been on the best-seller list ever since. Today, Dr. Abo continues to announce new discoveries and theories, to publish highly interesting and informative books, and to give lectures on a variety of health subjects. We are most privileged to be able to publish his first book in English and to introduce his theory on the immune system to the West for the first time.

This book is the second in a series of nine books on health and spirituality being published by KOKORO Publishing. The series includes the following titles:

- *Overcoming Cancer and Other Diseases in a Holistic Way*, by Tomeko Mitsui & Kazuko Tatsumura (published in 2000, second edition in 2007, and latest edition 2020)
- *Your Immune Revolution and Healing Your Healing Power*, by Toru Abo & Kazuko Tatsumura (published in 2007 and 2020)
- *Joy of Yoga*, by Masahiro Oki
- *Deep Breath Changes Your Body and Mind/Spirit*, by Osamu Tatsumura
- *The Mystery of the Body's Relation Points and Corrective Exercises*, by Fernando & Paula Mototo

I hope you will enjoy these books, and please send us comments. Contact Gaia Holistic Health at *www.gaiaholistic.com* or (212) 799-9711 or *Kazuko@gaiaholistic.com* for more information about upcoming books and how to purchase them.

Contents

Secret of Immunity

by Toru Abo, M.D.

INTRODUCTION

Why Modern Medicine Can't Cure Disease

It's often said that boosting your immune system can cure or prevent disease. Not a day goes by that I don't see advertisements in newspapers or magazines for folk medicines that are said to improve the immune system. It's especially common to hear that immunotherapy works for today's difficult diseases such as cancer, atopic dermatitis (eczema), and collagen diseases.

But when people talk about types of treatments and their effectiveness, they're basing their discussion on results alone. They rarely have the knowledge or understanding that underlies the theory of how a boosted immune system helps prevent disease. Conversely, in medical schools that study immunology, the main focus is on scientific research and analysis of the mechanism of the immune system, with little understanding of the processes and systems that cause illnesses to occur, and how to really cure them. So, in the eyes of ordinary people, immunity and the study of immunity seem to be totally separate subjects, even though they share the word "immunity."

It seems that modern medicine has not been very effective in curing disease, despite all the attention immunotherapy has received. It's been successful in analyzing the subjects of DNA, genome, and albuminoidal molecule studies, which look at the very detailed systems of the human body. But only rarely have these studies been applied directly to medical treatment. So, it's understandable that people criticize modern medicine for being unable to cure illness.

STRESS IS THE TRUE CAUSE OF DISEASE

Even today, immunology, like other medical research, is focused on analysis. But in the twenty-five years that I've been studying immunology, I've conducted my own research with the specific goal of understanding the fundamental mystery of disease more holistically and making good use of this understanding for true healing. In the 1990s, I discovered the principle of white blood cells and their dominant influence over the autonomic nervous system. With this understanding, I began to recognize the general mechanism that underlies human disease, and at the same time I began to grasp the problems of modern medicine and why it can't cure disease. I also began to recognize the vicious cycle by which modern medical science and its treatments contribute to the worsening of disease, particularly cancer, allergy, collagen diseases, and others that affect an increasing number of patients.

The autonomic nervous system is composed of the sympathetic and parasympathetic nervous systems, which function in balance. Mental or physical stress can upset this balance by causing extreme tension in the sympathetic nervous system, resulting in an imbalance of white blood cells and a corresponding malfunction of the immune system, which I'll discuss in more detail in this text. If we understand this mechanism, we can theorize and prove that the stress of our modern lifestyle can cause the immune system to decline, resulting in disease. Stress alone creates the underlying conditions that support the outbreak of disease. In other words, if you don't manage stress, you can't cure disease. Even if you suppress symptoms temporarily with medication, the root of the disease won't vanish as long as you're stressed. On top of this, the chemicals in the strong medications prescribed today put additional stress on your body.

The successes of Minkanryo-ho Tekina (folk) and Daitaiiryo (Alternative) immunotherapy have been clear from treatment outcomes, but there's been no real understanding of the mechanism that causes these effects. I suspect that, in the absence of a clear, logical theory or scientific proof, the doctors and patients involved in these treatments lack confidence in their commitment. Once they better understand the healing mechanism, however, doctors will be able to recommend and apply these treatments with more confidence and patients will comply more effectively so that a real cure can occur. Not only will this lead to more successful results, it will also encourage people to develop a lifestyle that creates and supports a healthy body that's immune to disease.

In the following chapters, I will discuss lymphocytes, the

mechanism of the immune system in relation to the autonomic nerves, and healing methods for a number of diseases. First, however, I'd like readers to have a basic grasp of why modern medical science can't cure disease, and how disease can be healed through immunity.

A RATHER NEW HISTORY OF IMMUNOTHERAPY

Immunology came to rise in the late nineteenth and early twentieth century. In the 1860s and 1870's, Louis Pasteur discovered that infectious diseases are caused by bacteria, and that if an animal survives after being infected, it sometimes gains resistance to that bacteria. This was the beginning of the development of immunology. (In fact, Edward Jenner had previously discovered a vaccine that prevented smallpox, but although vaccinations were conducted, there was no further commitment to the study of immunology because there was no theory at the time that bacteria actually caused disease.) The second great accomplishment in immunology was Robert Koch's discovery of the tuberculosis bacillus. He discovered that an animal or person who has had an infectious disease caused by bacteria can develop antibodies in their serum to fight the disease and can recover with less severe symptoms if re-infected.

Since these discoveries, research and study of the immune system and immunocytes has been slow to develop. In the late 1890s, it was determined that immunocytes such as T and B cells were created in the thymus and bone marrow. But the study of lymphocytes' influence on the immune system did not begin until the 1960s. Previous research emphasized serology over immunology, focusing primarily on finding an immune serum. The discovery in the 1960s of the relationship between lymphocytes and the immune system opened up a whole new horizon for immunology. Various lymphocytes have been detected since the discovery of T and B cells, such as the NK cell. In the 1990s, my colleagues and I found a T cell that differentiates and is produced in areas other than the thymus. Around that time, we also learned that within T cells there are helper T cells that support B cells in producing antibodies by finding antigens, and cytotoxic T cells that eliminate antigens. We also began to realize that there are Th1 and Th2 cells within the helper T cells.

In addition to categorizing the many types of lymphocytes, research has expanded to include study of the proteins that interact with antigens used by the lymphocytes, and the genes that produce lymphocytes. Susumu Tonegawa, who received the Nobel Prize for solving the problem of diversification of antibodies, is part of this research. There has also been major advancement in the study of lymphocytes and cytokines, important signaling compounds that transfer substances for lymphocytes.

IMMUNOLOGY FACES DANGER OF COMPLACENT SELF-INDULGENCE

When I began researching immunology about twenty-five years ago, I attended an immunology conference in Japan with only about 500 researchers, requiring only two or three conference rooms. Now that conference is ten times larger, with between 7,000 and 8,000 participants. Due to the large number of researchers, the conference has become divided into different fields of research. At a large conference today, there might be about fifteen specialties meeting in different rooms. Moreover, research subjects have become extremely focused. Although the attendees are all "immunologists," they're unable to communicate with each other when they visit other conference rooms dedicated to different fields. Each researcher is busy conducting his own specific self-indulgent research, and only a few immunologists study with the goal of understanding the whole picture. That's why most immunologists are able to discuss their findings only with their fellow researchers in a small group.

As I observe this change, my doubts grow stronger and stronger. Is this really the right way? Textbooks on immunology for medical students are usually written by several people, each in charge of a different subject, because no one scholar can comprehend every matter. When I do find a textbook written solely by one scholar, it's usually a researcher from long ago. In today's textbooks, information in one chapter may be contributed by someone who's very precise about their own specialty but can't explain how this specialty relates to the subjects in other chapters. I believe that this problem results from an overemphasis on analytical research.

Rarely has this specialized immunology actually helped

develop medical treatments that result in immunity from cancer, autoimmune disease, or allergies. In fact, I can't think of a single case. While the field of clinical immunology seems focused, in reality there's no practical connection between research and actual clinical application, because they're totally separate matters. Researchers are entirely devoted to analysis. Doctors who manage clinical treatments merely apply these results to temporarily manage the problem. Meanwhile, the number of patients with cancer, autoimmune diseases, and allergies is increasing drastically. But the progress of medical research is not reflected in relief of their symptoms.

SEARCHING FOR IMMUNOLOGY THAT GRASPS TOTALITY OF BODY, LIFE

I've been faithful in my research to find a study that will lead to the genuine healing of disease. And I've approached my study of immunology in a way that grasps the functions of a living body as a whole, rather than through the lens of analytical research. One major reason I decided to move in this direction is that I understood the principle of the white blood cells' dominance over the autonomic nervous system. With this discovery, I felt that I grasped the whole picture of the immune system, and I began to see the real cause of disease. But I didn't accomplish this on my own. My research builds on the study of biological binary notation by the late Dr. Akira Saito, an instructor at Tohoku University. It also includes principles included in the study of atmospheric pressure and infectious diseases by Dr. Minoru Fukuda, whom I met in Nigata. As my research advanced further in this direction, I began to see clearly the cause of many persistent diseases that had formerly been considered mysteries.

THE REAL CAUSE OF CANCER, EXPOSED WITH IMMUNOLOGY

If you understand the immunological theories that our research group is studying, the cause of cancer will become clear to you. Cancer is produced as a result of an extreme strain. That strain can be physical, caused by overworking, for example, or an extremely unstable lifestyle, or mental, stemming from worry or sorrow. The factors may vary. But when we look at the big picture, we can see that cancer is a product of stress that has exhausted patients mentally and physically.

TESTIMONIAL 1

Recovery From Stage III Thyroid Gland Cancer Through Autonomic Immunotherapy

"I was diagnosed with cancer about two years ago, in April. While at a prefectural hospital to have interferon treatment for viral hepatitis type C, it was discovered that I also had a thyroid gland tumor. I was transferred to another hospital for surgery.

"I was diagnosed with Stage I cancer during an examination before the surgery. 'You don't need to worry, because your five-year survival rate is 95 percent,' the doctor said very confidently. Trusting him that I would be fine once I had the surgery, I had one of my thyroid glands removed at the beginning of May. After the surgery, I had a few concerns. First, the surgery lasted two hours longer than the scheduled four. Second, looking in the mirror I found both horizontal and vertical cuts, although I had been told there would be just a horizontal cut.

When I asked the doctor, he said, 'Well, the surgical knife slipped.' I began to doubt him, and I felt that something was wrong.

"Three weeks later, I received the pathological diagnosis from the biopsy. Surprisingly, I was told that my cancer had already reached Stage III and had spread to the lymph nodes. The doctor said there was no choice but to take out the other thyroid gland and the lymph node to which the cancer had spread.

"Despite this situation, I must have subconsciously been seeking a way to cure my disease. One day, still feeling down, I left the hospital for a walk and went to a bookstore, where I found a book written by Dr. Minoru Fukuda, in cooperation with Professor Toru Abo. I became eager to have his autonomic nervous system immune treatment. In February, I traveled to Kyushu to visit a surgery clinic run by Dr. Keisuke Tajima, who practiced this treatment method.

"I was very encouraged and empowered to hear Dr. Tajima say, 'You will get better if you receive this treatment and change your lifestyle.' Since my case was a rather serious one, he suggested that I seek advice and treatment from Dr. Fukuda. I found myself on a plane to Nigata a few days later.

"As a matter of fact, the treatment was already improving my health. On my trip to the Tajima clinic, my body was so exhausted that I could barely sit up on the train. But after receiving Dr. Tajima's treatment, I felt so well that I had no problem sitting on the airplane the whole time.

"During the examination, Dr. Fukuda said, 'I wonder how you even manage to move around.' He diagnosed a very serious congestion in my head. I said, 'That may be because I barely took a bath while I was in the hospital.' But his reply was, 'You wouldn't have this congestion just from that.' He put needles all over my body, especially on my head, and a thick, sticky blood came out. Surprisingly, I did not feel any pain from the needles. After Dr. Fukuda and Dr. Tajima consulted on my situation, I began visiting the Tajima clinic twice a week, making the two-day trip from the other prefecture.

"In about three months, the congestion in my head was gone. As it began to dissipate, I started to feel a sharp pain, something I had never had before when needles were applied. I suspected that my sympathetic nerve was tenser than that of most people due to the interferon treatment I'd had. Around this time, I began to believe that I would recover.

"When we began treatment, I felt my body warming up and my sight getting brighter whenever the needles were applied. After about three months, I started to perspire during treatment. This was a sign that my energy was getting stronger. Whenever I had a treatment, my body felt better and I felt a livelier energy.

"Another dramatic result is that the scars from the thyroid surgery began to disappear. In autonomic nervous system immune treatment, the effectiveness of the treatment is determined by an increase or decrease in the number of lymphocytes. My total white blood cell count is around 3,000, and the number of lymphocytes hasn't dramatically increased, probably because one of my thyroid glands is missing. It's natural that the number won't increase much: my immunity is lower than most people because of the viral type C hepatitis and the interferon treatment I had before my cancer surgery. But it's obvious that my health is improving, I haven't returned to my Job yet, since it's very physical, but my home life is now that of a normal, healthy person, not of someone who's sick. I feel I'm enough recovered to take an office job if I have the opportunity, even if it's not possible to return to my old job yet.

"Since I started the autonomic nervous system immune treatment, my life has changed. As for diet, I eat mainly brown rice, vegetables, and seaweed, which have abundant fiber. As a result, I suppose, there's an obvious difference in my stool. It used to sink under the water, but now it floats. According to the doctors, this shows that my immune system is becoming normal, and I'm quite happy.

"Drs. Fukuda and Tajima say that stress is the main cause of cancer, and I think this was indeed the case for me. Until I suffered from cancer, I had a tendency to focus too much on work. I had a problem with needing to be in control and I couldn't let others handle a job, so I used to work too hard, especially when I had a big job. It wasn't uncommon for me to work twenty-four hours straight, and I had no hesitation working late at night. I believe that this kind of overwork and stress caused my cancer. Today, I'm trying to live my life joyfully, without stress. I also massage my nails three times a day, applying pressure next to my nails to stimulate my parasympathetic nervous system. And I massage my body with a towel after a bath in the morning and at night.

"I no longer have anything to do with so-called modern medicine. I have no reason to rely on it after they gave up on me. Since the autonomic nervous system immune treatment improved my health so much, I'd like to continue this treatment from now on. During the treatment, I met other people going through the same treatment for difficult diseases like mine. Some of them pave up and left after a short period because they didn't experience any dramatic effects. In my case, it took about three months to see a clear increase in lymphocytes. But immunity disorders like viral hepatitis type C don't improve fast because it's difficult to increase lymphocytes. It's up to you to decide whether it's worth trying this treatment or not. I understand that cancer patients feel restless without immediate results, because they think they have no time to waste. But autonomic nervous system immune treatment helped me recover to the point that I can live a normal life after being diagnosed with a very difficult cancer that the doctors had given up on. There's no doubt about that."

Until today, medical science believed that cancer is caused when an outside substance—a carcinogen—enters the body and influences the cancer genes. But if you understand the white blood cells' dominance over the autonomic nervous system, as we've studied, you'll conclude that the cause of cancer is, without doubt, within our own body. In other words, our way of living—our lifestyle—causes cancer.

If cancer is caused by something that enters the body from outside, without our recognition, the only way we can prevent it is by not taking in harmful things. If the real cause is our negative way of living or worries, though, we know how to deal with it. In fact, we often hear testimonials from people who've recovered from cancer by using alternative medicines, overcoming their fear of cancer, improving their diet, or laughing frequently. I can't help but investigate these phenomena from the viewpoint of a researcher. What is the mechanism that causes cancer to naturally shrink and disappear when worry is eliminated? What's really happening in our body in terms of immunology? I've conducted research to uncover this, and I decided to publish this book in order to share the results.

CANCER CAN'T BE HEALED WITH THREE MAJOR TREATMENTS

If you understand that cancer occurs as a result of a suppressed immune system, you begin to question the usefulness of today's three most popular treatments for cancer—the so-called "three major treatments": surgery, chemotherapy, and radiation.

According to today's standard practice, it's best to find cancer as soon as possible, take it out surgically, and continue with chemotherapy to supposedly fight and suppress the cancer. When an advanced cancer is found that can't be easily treated through surgery, standard protocol is to proceed immediately with chemotherapy to poison the cells, and radiation to shrink them. This reliance on the three major treatments pervades the entire field of cancer treatment.

These three treatments have something in common. They're all methods to physically shrink cancer. Surgery eliminates cancer, and, if successful, can cause cancer to become smaller or disappear. But by destroying tissue, surgery shocks the physical body and suppresses immune system functioning. In other words, surgery causes immunosuppression throughout the body.

The other two methods, chemotherapy and radiation, cause an even stronger immunosuppression response. In fact, they shrink cancer cells by harshly suppressing immunity, which I'll discuss in more detail in chapter 2. But these three treatments are successful at shrinking cancer only temporarily. Once the treatment is over, the number of lymphocytes available to protect the body is drastically decreased due to suppression of the immune system. In other words, the treatment ends when there is no energy left for the immune system to fight. When stress causes the cancer to return with full force, the body no longer has the power to fight, and therefore nothing can be done to prevent the cancer from growing.

Some people believe that radiation therapy won't damage the body because the radiation is only directed at the cancer cells. In reality though, even if it's directed at a limited area, the immune system of the whole body is weakened, and thus suppressed. When any part of our body's system is damaged, our body-wide sympathetic nervous system is under pressure to restore the damaged area. This intense activation of the sympathetic nervous system results, in turn, in further suppression of the immune system. This doesn't just happen from radiation—it's the same mechanism that suppresses immunity in the event of a severe burn or serious injury from an accident.

As we discussed, the three major cancer treatments are not appropriate cures for the core problem of cancer because they all suppress immune power—our natural physical ability to reverse cancer. It's not unusual for people to become so thin after major cancer surgery that they look like a different person, or to become so exhausted after going through chemotherapy that they can't live a normal life, or to become so tired after radiation therapy that they can't do anything. This tells us how much damage these treatments inflict on our body.

In recent years, some doctors and patients have begun to recognize the paradox of these three major treatments and the problems with modern medicine. At the same time, an increasing number of patients are looking for doctors with whom they feel comfortable and from whom they're willing to receive treatment. And an increasing number of doctors are actively practicing alternative or complementary medicine along with traditional and approved standards of practice. I suspect that it's time to begin reflecting on the thoughtless three treatments that regulate cancer treatment today.

BOOSTING IMMUNE POWER LEADS TO NATURAL REMISSION OF CANCER

Since the 1990s, I, along with my fellow clinical doctors such as Dr. Minoru Fukuda, have practiced treatments based on the principle of the white blood cells' influence over the autonomic nervous system, and I have witnessed many cases of the natural remission of cancer. As I observed other doctors' practices, I realized that both doctors and patients need to dedicate themselves to boosting patients' immune systems by stimulating the parasympathetic nervous system whenever one of the three "standard and traditional" treatments are used. Patients need to acknowledge and understand that the cure of the core problem occurs only when they are willing to change the stressful and complicated lifestyle that caused their cancer to begin with. And it is imperative that doctors are willing and able to support them. My colleagues have all learned to ask their patients what's causing them stress or what problems they have in their lives, and to advise them accordingly. If patients are unwilling to totally change their way of life, they won't be able to eliminate the conditions that have suppressed their immune systems to the point of causing cancer. If doctors truly want to reduce or eliminate patients' pain and help them recover from illness, they will naturally want to administer treatment with an attitude that supports their patients in making the simple—or complex—internal and lifestyle changes that will sustain their health after treatment. Encouraging patients to rediscover and strengthen their will to live is an essential part of the recovery process. I always hope that patients will receive treatment with a focused will to change and improve their lives.

In chapter 2, I expand upon the following four principles, which cancer patients must understand in order to change their cancer-causing lifestyles. First, change a lifestyle that includes too much stress. Second, eliminate the fear of cancer, because cancer can be healed if you boost your immune power, as shown in the examples in chapter 2. Third, refuse or suspend treatments that exhaust your physical body and immune system. And last, actively pursue treatments that increase your immune power. If you dedicate yourself to treatments using these guidelines, your cancer will begin to disappear.

WHY BOOSTING IMMUNE POWER HEALS CANCER

An increasing number of doctors, myself and my colleagues included, have begun to practice alternative or complementary medicine to boost their patients' immunity. These mechanisms are supported by the science of immunology. I will explain this thoroughly in this text.

Alternative medicine approaches treatment very differently from modern medicine. It's important to understand the theory that supports the success of these treatments, as I explore in depth in chapter 6. According to this theory, the white blood cells are the regulating influence on the autonomic nervous system. If you don't understand this theory, you'll gauge your progress solely by what has happened to you in the past—which may have no relationship to your present experience—and may wind up accepting treatment blindly. That's why, despite many cases of cancer remission, modern medicine still fails to understand this process, and only shrugs its shoulders. I decided to write this book in order to address this dilemma.

I believe that if doctors and patients understand the interaction between the autonomic nervous system and the immune system, they won't employ treatments that damage the body in an effort to return it to health. They'll choose more effective healing processes that lead patients to a smooth recovery. An increasing number of people have cured their cancers by applying alternative or complementary medicine because they had doubts about modern medicine. Some have even recovered from cancers that were much progressed. In spite of an increasing number of these examples, however, there has so far been no medical or immunological explanation that was recognizable enough to convince both the public and their doctors of the effectiveness of these alternative treatments. And while traditional folk medicines such as propolis, meshima kelp, agaricus, and brown rice claim to boost immune power, there has been no strong underlying theory to support the idea that boosting the immune system helps cure cancer. Traditional folk practices do not set out a scientific rationale or clarify the mechanisms of how these traditional foods boost immune power. In this book, I'd like to explore and discuss these matters holistically.

Of course, it's not always possible to "refuse" contemporary medical approaches to cancer treatment. Chapter 2 includes guidelines on how to use modern medicine effectively in ways that minimize damage.

I believe that, as a result of the many cases reporting the effectiveness of folk or alternative medicine to treat cancer, diseases caused by suppressed immune system, and allergies, a revolutionary change in the modern medical approach to treatment is being developed even now. I hope that if I organize my immunological theory clearly, and let people know of it, I can support this new process of medical treatment for difficult diseases for the benefit of both doctors and patients.

CANCER DOESN'T NEED TO BE FRIGHTENING

People are usually very afraid of cancer. They seem to think it's incurable once you have it. However, according to the experience of my fellow doctors, a high percentage of patients can achieve remission as long as they have some immune power left—in other words, as long as the body is not severely exhausted. As long as you have immune power, there's no need to fear. To give you a simple example: if you're able to eat normal meals and lead a normal life at home, the probability of progressive cancer going into remission is 60 to 70 percent. This means that the majority of patients will recover. Eating normal meals and living a normal life at home may mean a number of things: changing your diet; actively practicing something to enhance blood circulation, such as bathing; and spending your days in good spirits and laughter, doing things you enjoy. The more you engage in a healthy lifestyle, the higher the probability of remission. Cancer is caused by a depressed immune system that results from a distorted lifestyle. To put it more simply, it's an illness caused by bad habits. That's why reorganizing your life, including the emotional and mental aspects, brings about healing.

The question then arises, is there any hope for a patient whose body has been exhausted beyond a certain point? Of course, there is. For example, if your cancer has spread too much and your will for recovery is weak, it can be very difficult to achieve total remission. But if you change your way of life or increase your will to live, the cancer's progress will slow down. Even if the cancer doesn't disappear completely, it's possible for even seriously affected individuals to have better quality of life. Some are even able to return to a life that's almost normal. Many worst-case cancer patients have survived years longer than their modern medical prognosis had suggested, once they engaged in immunotherapy.

It's my hope that patients can overcome their fear of cancer, because doing so will enhance the effect of their treatments. What do you think happens to the human body when we're afraid? We get tense, we stiffen up, and our blood circulation slows down. In other words, fear creates additional tension in the sympathetic nervous system. This increased tension further decreases the ability of the immune system to function. So, fear increases your chances of becoming ill, and even worsens your illness.

As stated previously, cancer is caused by a distorted lifestyle and bad habits. So, by changing your stress patterns, you can get rid of cancer. As much as 60 to 70 percent of progressive (metastasized) cancers will go into remission. I hope you'll take this fact to heart. If you're scared because you have cancer or worried that your cancer will return, your fear will help bring it back. It's fear that creates a physical condition that's ripe for cancer. The first step toward the prevention or remission of cancer is eliminating fear.

MODERN MEDICINE ITSELF CAUSES CANCER PAIN

One reason people fear cancer is that they have the image of cancer patients suffering in pain—losing their energy after going through hours of exhausting surgery; surviving only by intravenous drip, unable to eat, losing hair and weight due to the side effects of chemotherapy or radiation therapy; spending days in bed or in a wheelchair, eyes blank from the morphine used to control pain. It's natural for the average person to fear cancer after witnessing their family or friends going through these scenes, or after seeing images like these in the media.

But if you think carefully you'll realize that this suffering is not caused by the cancer itself. It's caused by medications or operations that suppress the body's healing power and its ability to recover from illness. Your body needs its own vital energy to recover. Blocking this energy, or letting energy-suppressing medications drain it away, is the true cause of suffering and pain. The conflict between your body's natural healing process and modern energy-suppressing treatments is a tragedy, because a tremendously increased bloodstream could cause pain. But tremendous pain and suffering are not likely to occur if treatments support your body's energy and immune system.

In fact, patients currently receiving immunotherapy treatments from my colleagues don't suffer a terrible draining of energy from these treatments. They have more energy, less pain, and feel better as they heal. Doctors who practice adoptive lymphocyte therapy, another method to boost immune power, also report that their patients don't experience the terrible pain and energy depletion suffered by other patients who go through chemotherapy, radiation therapy, or surgery. Of course, patients may experience temporary fever, discomfort, or some pain during recovery and remission even when using immune therapies. But this pain or fatigue shouldn't last forever. After all, most pain that cancer patients experience is a product of modern medicine.

The pain and fever experienced during cancer recovery are healing reactions as the body tries to regain adequate circulation in the bloodstream. That's why, when you take strong medication to suppress an immune response, you experience a very powerful reaction when the course of medication is finished. On top of this, modern cancer treatments often administer narcotics such as morphine to patients suffering unbearable pain, after having to tally damaged their immune system via chemotherapy. But these narcotics severely suppress the immune system, creating even more tension in the sympathetic nervous system. And once the course of narcotics is finished, the pain that's been suppressed comes back in full force. In the meantime, the ongoing suppression continues to deplete the immune system's ability to function.

Because medication completely tenses the sympathetic nervous system, it also drastically depletes your stores of vital energy. As you know, drug addicts are as thin as old people. The same is true of terminal cancer patients who are on narcotics. If you think about how these patients look, it's easy to understand that narcotics suppress immune power.

MODERN MEDICAL TREATMENT DEPENDS COMPLETELY ON MEDICATION

When we're sick, various symptoms tell us that our immune system is active and working on our behalf. These symptoms include fever, pain, diarrhea, nausea, and coughs. While these symptoms can be quite troublesome, their purpose is to get rid of the waste products that have built up inside you. The goal of doctors is to reduce discomfort while the body undergoes its healing process. Over the past few decades, modern medical pharmacology has progressed to the point that it can mask these healing symptoms with relative efficiency.

But in the course of research with my colleagues, I began to understand that these painful symptoms are necessary for healing to occur. As part of the natural process of recovery from illness, living creatures experience harsh symptoms of release, and begin to heal afterwards. Modern medicine has focused solely on eliminating symptoms, not on actually getting to the core reasons that symptoms exist in the first place and dealing with those reasons. This inappropriate focus has led us blindly in a direction that's diametrically opposed to healing. We've begun to see that this "approved medical process" often subjects patients to even more severe pain.

When you experience pain, fever, reddish swelling, or rashes, your body is basically "on fire" because your blood flow is increasing rapidly. This sudden increase in blood circulation helps your body flush out the waste that's generated as your immune system successfully fights invaders. But this process is often quite uncomfortable.

For example, when you have fever, you feel exhausted. When the fever worsens, you may feel so sick that you have to lie down. It's important to understand that both the fever and the exhaustion are part of a natural healing reaction, in which your body is trying to send increased blood and lymph to the affected tissue in order to remove waste so that newly energized cells in that area can heal. When you have fever or pain, it means you're beginning to heal. Conversely, if you don't have some kind of fever, healing isn't going to take place. Once you understand this, you'll realize that it's not necessarily good for your body to take medicine to suppress fever and fatigue. This is the underlying reason that allopathic treatments don't bring true healing.

POWERFUL MODERN DRUGS COMPLICATE DISEASE

In the past, when medicinal formulations weren't as powerful as they are today, the negative influence of allopathy (chemical pharmaceuticals) was not as strong. Back then, allopathic medicines could reduce symptoms by only 20 to 30 percent. So, patients' struggles, and discomforts were eased, but the body's natural healing reaction still had a 70 to 80 percent activity rate. While it might have taken longer for a patient to heal, the level of medical allopathic components was acceptable.

But as medical science advanced and pharmacology compounding greatly "improved," extremely powerful medicines began to be produced. These powerful medicines, including anti-inflammatories, pain killers, steroids, and immunosuppressant, completely suppress all symptoms, as well as the body's natural healing processes. Administering these medicines, which are very effective at suppressing pain, stops the body's healing reactions immediately. Because their discomfort is temporarily gone, patients think they're "recovered," and tell their doctors that the treatment is going well. But if such strong allopathic medication is continued, there's a very real danger that the body will be unable to repair itself at all. Ironically, in some cases the disease actually becomes more difficult to cure. This is clear proof that allopathic medicine can't bring about true healing.

ALLOPATHY CAN'T HEAL CHRONIC DISEASE

In some cases, allopathy can be effective. For example, in acute diseases for which powerful allopathic medication is administered for just a short period of time, we've come to expect that the "disease" will be "cured" because the medicine and the symptoms balance each other out in the short term. But when it comes to chronic disease, I believe that allopathy is exceedingly dangerous. Forcefully suppressing the body's mild healing symptoms over the long term can completely stop the work of healing. The real problem that medical science faces today is not acute disease, but chronic disease. Chronic diseases are becoming harder to cure and more intractable.

To understand why medical treatment based on allopathy has flourished, we need to take a look at the historical development of Western medicine. Throughout history, "taking something" to alleviate symptoms of dis-ease and illness has been grounded in the knowledge of plants and their various effects. With the advent of printing, more careful documentation and cross-referencing of applications and results became possible, leading to a desire to further improve the process of delivering health care. As modern chemical industrial practices became more precise, research was conducted into why certain plants and substances affected health. When chemists thought they understood what was happening, they devised ways to re-create what nature was doing. Experiments and tests seemed to indicate that man could create things better than nature could. Medication played an important role at the onset of Western medical practice, and as a result, the medical system made great effort to provide precise dosages of specific chemicals and to control access to and distribution of those chemicals.

One of Western medicine's first successes was the development of anesthesia, which enabled patients to undergo surgery without being knocked out by alcohol or remaining conscious, held down while the doctor chopped off whatever needed removing—and experiencing the full agony of such pain. This was an enormous advancement. Next we developed an awareness of the importance of sterile technique, which greatly reduced the danger of infectious disease. Antibiotics were the next step, and the combination of these two advancements brought about enormous improvements in the technical fields of surgery and emergency medical science. Western medicine and its accompanying pharmacological products have made tremendous contributions to the treatment of acute conditions and injuries.

But Western medicine, which functions so brilliantly in emergencies and critical situations, fails us when it comes to treating chronic or ongoing symptoms and conditions. Most modern medical treatments of collagen disorders, cancer, allergy, Parkinson's, and other diseases are accompanied by side effects that cause organ damage such as ulcerative colitis and has not helped. The number of patients with these kinds of chronic diseases is only increasing. As I witness this, I can't help questioning what it is that modern medical treatments are trying to achieve. Continuing my research, which began by questioning whether Western medicine can really heal disease, I started to realize that uncomfortable symptoms are actually part of the healing process. I began to understand the need to encourage this kind of reaction to a certain point.

IMPORTANCE OF HOLISTIC MEDICINE IN UNDERSTANDING WHOLE BODY SYSTEM

I'm not alone in questioning modern medicine this way. In recent years, the idea of holistic medical treatment, holistic medical science, and the importance of approaching the total body-mind-spirit system has become more accepted. This may be due to the increasing failures of modern medicine.

In the past decade or so, medical science's progress has been primarily analytical, focused on unveiling aspects of molecules and genes. But in truth, this hasn't brought us any closer to curing the fundamental problems of disease. To be honest, the only progress that's been made has had little practical effect on medical treatment.

Because of this, many of us have begun to consider the importance of holistic medicine, or Total Body Treatment. The question then becomes, how can we achieve this type of medical treatment? I feel that neither we in the medical field nor our patients really know the answer. It's often said that doctors need to improve their bedside manner, but even if doctors are nicer to patients or try harder to see things from their viewpoint, if they're continuing to practice the same allopathic treatments, the fundamental problem of modern medicine will remain. True holistic medical treatment can't be achieved in this manner.

UNDERSTANDING THREE INNER BODY SYSTEMS THAT CULTIVATE LIFE FORCE AND BALANCE PHYSICAL CONDITION

So, what's needed in order to achieve whole body healing, so that doctors can practice with confidence for their patients' good?

I believe that, in order to practice holistic medicine, one needs to understand the wholeness of the human body system and its function in a holistic way. The human body contains many systems, some of which affect the functioning of the entire body. A few of these, which I discuss in future chapters, include the autonomic nervous system, the white blood cell system, and the metabolic system. Understanding these systems can help us comprehend the mechanism of body and disease.

The metabolic system, for example, transforms resources into energy and stores that energy for later use. No other system in the body is more important in keeping us alive. We take in and use energy, storing the excess to use as needed. All the activities of our body, including our cells, rely on this energy system. Since all of our activities are associated with this system, all of our diseases are, without exception, associated with it as well. If we approach health with this point of view, we begin to understand why excessive burning or accumulation of energy can fail our body's activities and begin to realize how this can be connected to different diseases. If you understand the energy system, you will not fail to understand what happens inside the human body.

RELATIONSHIP BETWEEN AUTONOMIC NERVOUS SYSTEM AND ORGANIC ACTIVITY

The autonomic nervous system is highly important as well. It consists of the sympathetic and parasympathetic nervous systems and is closely related to the energy system: The sympathetic nervous system deals with creating tension and stimulation in the body, and the parasympathetic nervous system controls relaxation functions. The balance between these opposites initiates action in us; therefore, no disease in our body occurs independently of the autonomic nervous system. I believe that this system embraces every single disease. Thus, when you look at white blood cells, which are controlled by the autonomic nervous system, you can see how diseases occur and heal. Basically, white blood cells take the form of macrophages.

Granulocytes evolved from macrophages to manage bacteria, as did the lymphocytes that administer the immune system. These white cells are controlled by the autonomic nerves; therefore, an imbalance in the autonomic sympathetic and parasympathetic nervous systems influences the occurrence and healing of disease, including infectious diseases. For example, if you strain yourself or experience too much stress, the sympathetic nervous system will become agitated and produce too many granulocytes, causing disease that damages tissues. On the other hand, if you're too relaxed, the parasympathetic nervous system will dominate, and an increased number of lymphocytes will cause allergic disease. This provides a comprehensible solution to the mystery of all disease. If you pay attention to the autonomic nervous system, you will thoroughly understand the mechanism of disease.

Therefore, I think a truly appropriate approach to holistic medical treatment is to pay attention to the total body system. Of course, it's also important for doctors to improve their bedside manner; however, this can be interpreted in different ways and depends entirely too much on an individual's personal attributes and effort. More important, I believe that if doctors apply their knowledge as specialists and approach the proposed system objectively as a means to understand the mechanism of disease, they will find methods to deal with and ways to treat imbalances of the autonomic nervous system. And ultimately, this will lead to appropriate medical treatments.

A NEW MEDICAL TREATMENT BASED ON THE ENERGY SYSTEM

The issue of physical energy has not been given its due consideration by medical practitioners. The human body gains energy when we consume food (nutritive energy) and transforms it by combining (burning) it with the oxygen that we inhale. Experts from various fields have recently begun to discuss the importance of food and breathing, because these processes ultimately relate to the transformation and consumption of energy itself.

It's a pity, though, that those experts who believe in the importance of food discuss only food, while those who stress the importance of breathing understand only breathing. The body can only produce energy by using both together. We have to have both: food and breath. We can't live without either one, or too much of either creates excess energy, causing the body to fail. This energy system supports the activities of all living creatures, including humans, while functioning holistically within a system of mutual and total balance. So, having a good understanding of the body's blueprint at the molecular or genetic level doesn't mean that we can totally eliminate illness. Genes or cell structures made of genes can't function on their own. They can be active only when there's life energy.

Dr. Katsunari Nishihara, a former instructor at Tokyo University and the current director of the Nishihara Research Institute in Roppongi, Tokyo, has been conducting a progressive study applying the body's energy system to medical science and treatments. Dr. Nishihara's work includes studies of gravity, animal evolution, and the relationship between breathing and immunity problems. I believe that when researchers like Dr. Nishihara are evaluated appropriately, true medical science will at last be achieved.

FOOD AND BREATH: THE SOURCES OF VITAL ENERGY

We can move the body's energy systems with food and breath. So, it's important to consume nutritious food, and to digest and eliminate it appropriately. It's not good to eat too much or too little, nor for food to stagnate in the digestive system (constipation) or be eliminated too soon (diarrhea). As we know, there are many essential bacteria in the intestines that help food ferment during digestion. It's critical that bacteria are present at all layers. Antibiotics destroy these bacteria, which is why long-term antibiotics are so damaging to our body. Taking antibiotics casually is a mistake.

Since energy is utilized more easily when it's first burned or transformed, when you're deprived of heat you waste energy. In other words, if your body is cold, you need a certain amount of energy to warm it. Wearing something that makes your body cold, staying too long in a cold environment such as an air-conditioned room, or making your intestines cold by drinking too many cold drinks all cause you to lose energy. If you're already in a weakened state, this can lead to illnesses.

AIR CONDITIONERS AND REFRIGERATORS INCREASE ILLNESS

One type of modern convenience that seemingly makes our lives more comfortable has in reality caused an increase in serious illness: refrigeration and air conditioning. Humans are warm-blooded mammals, which normally require an inner-body temperature of 98.6°F (37 to 38°C). But increasingly, external factors are cooling our bodies below this temperature. When the environment becomes cooler, the body uses much more energy to keep its temperature stable. Our civilization has created this condition. We can therefore say that one of the fundamental causes of modern chronic disease is our civilization itself. One particular instance of this is that children today prefer cold drinks, consuming much more cold juice and milk than in the past. This inner coolness deprives them of energy and strength by cooling their throat and digestive systems. It's very dangerous to eat ice cream in winter, for example.

Many female office workers also suffer because of air conditioning. Office temperatures are set to the comfort of men, who have, on average,

15 percent more hemoglobin than women, and thus run at a statistically higher body temperature. Women, with their lower body temperatures, are then exposed to these low air-conditioned temperatures at their offices. Once they're free from these cold environments, their bodies try to warm up. Their blood vessels loosen up, and the flow of blood increases. If the change is drastic, discomfort can occur. The result could be an unexplained stomachache, which leads to a hospital visit and treatment by narcotic painkillers, because the true cause of the pain is unknown. Unfortunately, this kind of medicine itself cools the body. The patient has stepped into a world of cold from which there's no way out.

Many people know, from experience or intuitively, that cold is a woman's enemy. But patients are taking the wrong medicines because they don't understand the mechanism by which cold causes disease. They may believe that they're managing pain, but instead the cold begins to destroy their energy system, causing a variety of diseases. I suspect that many cancers of the female organs are triggered by continued cold. Diseases such as dysmenorrhea, endometriosis, hysteromyoma, salpingitis, and oophoritis are thought to be caused by being cold or by taking narcotic painkillers long term. It's therefore even more important to understand the concept of energy.

As I mentioned earlier, this energy system is related to the autonomic nervous system, which commands cells throughout the body to use energy efficiently. The autonomic nervous system can tell us about our body and its condition as a whole.

AUTONOMIC NERVOUS SYSTEM UNITES ALL CELLS

Autonomic nerves unite all our body's cells. All living creatures evolved from a monad—a single cell that managed all functions on its own, including eating, digestion, the gathering of energy, elimination of waste, and destruction of foreign objects. But as cells evolved, each one began to take on a different role, tailored to just one part of the organism's functioning. As we now know, genes can be turned on and off, causing cells to focus on just a small part of their full genetic abilities. In fact, most of our genes are turned off. Only a few are turned on—those that target the particular functions needed by skin cells, intestinal cells, nerve cells, and so on. The autonomic nervous system commands these specialized cells to start or stop working.

But some cells remained able to do all things. The white blood cells still retain the characteristics of the monad they once were. In short, most of their genes are still "on," and they still contain the ability to carry out all the various functions of a cell, just as monadic amoeba does. White cells have forms similar to amoeba, with the same ability to eat targeted objects, digest, and decompose. With this ability, they serve as our body's defensive cells. They're able to fight against and destroy outside intruders, and eliminate harmful abnormal cells produced in our body. In sum, white blood cells are our body's defensive system.

As we've observed, in order to understand holistically what goes on in the body—in other words, illness or health—we need to know the mechanism of the energy system, autonomic nervous system, and white blood cell system, and their relationship to each other. If you understand only one of these systems, you can't understand the physical condition of the body in its totality. It's important to understand the balance of these three systems and their mutual influences.

MODERN MEDICINE IS DROWNING IN ANALYSIS

Medicine and science focus primarily on analytical research. The most advanced medical studies are of genomes and molecules. I think that researchers are devoted to this study in the hope that if they continue to focus on small matters, the whole picture will someday be revealed. The reality is, however, that the more researchers remain focused in this way, the more specific their research needs to be—and as a result, they will never grasp the whole picture. I think it's impossible that looking at details will bring us back to the starting point. In my opinion, this is a serious blind spot in modern science.

Scientific progress, including medicine, has always sought something imperceptible. Over time, the focus has shifted from tissues to cells, from cells to molecules, from molecules to atoms and electrons, and finally to the elementary energy particles that form atoms. But this is far from grasping the whole picture—an event that has never actually occurred. This type of research lets us see different worlds, but not matter in its entirety.

In reality, studies of components always end as just studies of components. I'm not saying that studies of components are meaningless. They're important on their own because, as this research has progressed, it has revealed bacteria, viruses, molecules, and genes, and has helped me construct my own immunological research with scientific theories based on experiments and data.

The problem is that the scientific community has been very partial to analytical research. In my opinion, 50 percent of medical research should be devoted to analytical research of components. The other 50 percent should be research into understanding the human body and illness holistically, by thoroughly observing the whole system.

MODERN MEDICINE HAS KNOWLEDGE BUT NOT WISDOM

I hope that the doctors who actually administer medical treatments are able to understand "dis-ease" from a holistic point of view as well. Medical education today can be problematic. Studying medicine takes a huge amount of time, and a successful practitioner must have tremendous knowledge. Our future doctors are eagerly engaged in trying to learn proven facts and knowledge. But this situation discourages them from questioning and trying to solve problems on their own. In other words, too much knowledge and education are their obstacle. They seem to lose their ability to look at mysteries, ask intelligent questions, integrate exploration and answers, and solve these mysteries on their own.

This non-questioning attitude shows up when these doctors actually enter the field of medicine and begin working with patients. Their view of patients is based on knowledge from textbooks alone. They're satisfied to imitate more experienced doctors, or to do what they've been told to do in terms of treatment. It's not unusual for doctors to administer treatments thoughtlessly, believing that what some accomplished researcher or famous professor does must be the most advanced technique. I'm not saying all doctors are like this, but it seems that fewer doctors really try to understand for themselves the condition of diseases or what's causing their patient's illness. This tendency can be seen not just in medicine, but in many fields of modern society as well, such as economics and education. It's a pity that, all too often, people have factual knowledge but no practical, useful, and applicable wisdom.

OPEN-MINDED APPROACH TO MYSTERY OF PARKINSON'S DISEASE

To fully understand the condition of a patient's illness, one needs to be flexible and wise. That's not easy. But at the same time, it's interesting for researchers. It's good for both patients and doctors when doctors increase their knowledge and ability as they observe patients' conditions, work on the mystery of disease, and attempt to heal their patients.

Recently, I've been studying Parkinson's disease. Patients suffering from Parkinson's disease have stiff muscles. The most obvious symptoms are stiffness and shakes. Current medical practice prescribes a medication that's a precursor to dopamine, which activates and tenses the sympathetic nerves. This treatment was discovered when researchers studying the brain of one Parkinson's patient found that the patient's substantia niagra cells (the part of the brain that produces dopamine) were much damaged. A dopamine precursor was suggested to cure this damage. The idea spread rapidly, and it has since become common sense to treat Parkinson's disease with dopamine precursor. In fact, those researchers won a Nobel Prize.

However, dopamine is a neurotransmitter that causes tension in the sympathetic nerves. When its precursor is given, the patients' body becomes even stiffer than before, to the point where he or she is hardly able to move. As I observed my Parkinson's patients, I began questioning this treatment. I wondered if they were really being cured.

In fact, the number of Parkinson's disease patients has increased drastically in recent years, though no one knows the reason. As I studied patients' symptoms with a seed of doubt in my mind, I began to think that this phenomenon could be due to the very seriously stressed or highly tensed sympathetic nerves that cause Parkinson's disease.

Parkinson's patients usually suffer from insomnia. Many also have a serious problem with constipation. These symptoms clearly indicate that the sympathetic nerves are tense. When you look at the autonomic nervous system, it's clear that Parkinson's patients are suffering from severe stress of the sympathetic nerves, regardless of the cause.

This made me question even more whether dispensing a dopamine precursor could heal the disease when at the same time it caused increased stress on the sympathetic nerves. Moreover, dopamine precursor doesn't work in the brain alone. Because it's dispensed orally, it spreads throughout the body, causing more tension everywhere. In fact, patients become unable to speak or walk after dopamine treatment.

As I continued to think, I started to realize that, rather than using dopamine precursors, we should relax patients by improving blood circulation to the whole body, thereby giving the muscles throughout the system a fuller flow of blood. It's widely known that patients who suffer from Parkinson's disease are usually very hard working. Because hard-working people have a hard life and are constantly tense, they tend to fall into a state of what I call "sympathicotonia" (excess tension in the sympathetic nervous system). Considering this, I think that managing stress in the sympathetic nerves and the poor circulation caused by this tension will result in a true cure.

My fellow researcher Dr. Minoru Fukuda made a very

interesting statement based on his observation of Parkinson's patients. When a patient suffers from Parkinson's disease, their body shakes involuntarily. Older people are the same. Observing this, Dr. Fukuda once said, "Ah, stiff muscles severely lack blood circulation. I wonder if that's why the body shakes, to send more blood to the area. It's almost as if their body is massaging itself. That may be what the tremor is about: shaking the body."

If you observe the illness carefully and think for yourself like Dr. Fukuda, you will naturally come up with the keys to a cure, enabling you to find the right direction for treatment. What would a patient need if they stopped taking dopamine precursor for Parkinson's disease? Looking at the situation practically, one can see that they need hot baths or exercise to increase blood circulation, and brown rice and other fiber-rich foods, such as vegetables and mushrooms. You may think it's impossible to cure a difficult disease like Parkinson's with such a simple method. But we've had many patients who were disabled as a result of medication begin to walk and speak again in just a week or so.

STRIVING FOR MEDICAL CARE WITH WISDOM, NOT JUST KNOWLEDGE

This type of thinking can be applied to the treatment of not just Parkinson's disease, but any disease. Today's medical treatment is heavily dependent on medication. If you have a stomachache or headache they'll give you a painkiller, and if you have cancer they'll give you an anti- cancer drug. Many people today say immunity is critical in curing cancer. But if they get cancer, they too will take anti-cancer drugs that severely suppress immunity. Patients need to recognize these contradictions in themselves.

This discernment comes not from knowledge, but rather from correcting your way of living and becoming more aware of your own senses. I believe that we need to break free from the bondage of fractured knowledge and reawaken our natural animal ability to sense danger.

The type of medical science I've developed is based on dissociating from "medical knowledge" and going back to the fundamentals in order to understand the activities and reactions that occur in our body. In the past hundred years, since the beginning of the 1900s, modern medical science has accumulated tremendous knowledge. This knowledge has been very important and valuable, but at the same time it has created numerous problems as patients have been left stranded. Therefore, my practice—and this book—focuses on the fact that we need to get out from under this mountain of knowledge and return to the fundamentals, as we think about how we as organisms react to stimulus, failure, and treatment.

THE IMPORTANCE OF MIND

One factor I believe should be more highly respected in medical research and treatment is the mind. I believe that the mind has a great influence both on how patients become ill and how doctors cure them. Over the course of my many years' involvement in medicine, I've come to understand this.

Let's take a look at how patients' minds create problems. Human behavior is determined by our thoughts. If someone becomes ill by working too hard or leading a life that's too easy, the cause of the illness is directly connected to the state of mind that allowed them to behave that way. In other words, one becomes healthy by having the right attitude and leading a life that reflects it. After all, if the mind is damaged, the body is affected accordingly.

LIVING ACCORDING TO NATURE: OUR TRUE STATE

I believe that all creatures live most harmoniously when they live by the law of nature and think in accord with nature. Humans are very advanced creatures. We've experienced many changes during our long period of evolution, and as a result we've gained various abilities that make us strong. We're able to adapt to a certain level of environmental change. But if we live an extreme lifestyle that's beyond our ability to adapt, our physical system becomes damaged and we become ill.

One day when I was talking with the biologist Dr. Emiko Furuta, Director of the Comparative Immunology Research Institute in Japan, I realized that living organisms contain a function whereby damaged cells exclude themselves or die out on their own. We humans have changed throughout our history as vertebrates, mammals, primates, and primitives. In the process of evolution, we've expanded our ability to adapt to our environment. But there have always been things we can't adapt to, that damage our body and cause illness and decline. When this happens, our body has the ability to let damaged cells kill themselves. This phenomenon, known as apoptosis, is the process by which cells commit suicide.

Macrophages are the type of white blood cells that control immunity. They are, in fact, osteoclasts. Osteoclasts feed on and manage the metabolism of bones. Through my research, I began to understand that macrophages not only eat bones but kill themselves by eating their own cells. Macrophages are known to scavenge red blood cells that have finished their tasks, but this isn't their only function.

When we fail to adapt to our environment or situation, we become haggard. I think this shows that the living organic system in which macrophages eat to destroy themselves has failed to adapt.

Animal bodies, including human bodies, tend to go back to their fundamental state in emergencies. We consist of many specialized cells working together to create a whole, with specific genes activated. When we face an unusual emergency situation, this specialization stops, other cells are eaten by macrophages, and as a result only macrophages remain. Living organisms appear to have a tendency to end their own life this way, even though this may seem like a failure in a highly evolved being. According to Dr. Furuta, this happens to any animal less evolved than humans in a harsh environment.

It's fundamental to the life of an organism that even our cells are programmed to destroy themselves when they're not in accord with nature. I believe that macrophages and immunity control this programming. If that's so, then the immune system is related to both the maintenance and termination of life. If you follow the law of nature and boost your immunity, your health will be enhanced and you will be free from illness, because the immune system is closely related to life itself. In other words, immunity may be what we call the "life force."

Chapter 1
The Real Cause of Disease

There are a great variety of diseases in the world. Despite the great advancements of modern medical science, the cause of many diseases, such as ulcerative colitis and Crohn's disease, is still unknown. We don't yet know the cause of familiar diseases such as alveolar pyorrhea and hemorrhoids, though we can explain the symptoms. Neither do we know exactly what causes difficult diseases such as collagen disease and cancer. Since we don't know the cause, the treatment is usually allopathic—in other words, pharmacological. If there's pain, we dispense painkillers. If there's fever, we dispense antifebriles. If there's diarrhea, we dispense binding medication. If there's cough, we dispense cough drops. And so on.

I will discuss this in greater detail in chapter 5, but if you understand the fact that white blood cells dominate the autonomic nerves, you will understand the cause of most disease. In particular, once you understand how granulocytes, one of two elements in white blood cells, become overactive, you will solve the mystery of most mucosal and tissue problems.

Modern medical science puts a very low value on granulocytes. At most, they're used in blood tests to determine contagious diseases. Eighty percent of granulocytes have characteristics called neutrophils (we sometimes call these granulocyte neutrophil). In a patient with appendicitis (inflammation of the appendix), if we suspect that infection is being caused by some kind of bacteria, we check the white blood cells. If there are too many neutrophil or granulocytes in the white blood cells, we conclude that the appendix is infected.

Granulocytes are considered beneficial because they eat harmful objects that enter our body. If an increase of neutrophil or granulocytes is observed, the patient is diagnosed with an infectious condition and, as a result, prescribed antibiotics to control bacteria. If an inflammation causes pain, an anti-inflammatory painkiller is prescribed. Since infectious diseases usually cause fever, an antifebrile is also prescribed. In fact, antifebrile and anti-inflammatory painkillers have the same ingredients. But these methods focus on allopathy, not on the function of the granulocytes themselves, which are only measured for testing.

AN INCREASE IN GRANULOCYTES FROM STRESS CAUSES DISEASE

Granulocytes increase when the sympathetic nerves are dominant. When they increase too much, they fight with normal bacteria, characteristically causing a purulent inflammation. If they migrate to where there are no bacteria, their unregulated activity destroys tissue with active oxygen. In short, granulocytes cause suppuration only when there are bacteria, and cause inflammation by destroying tissue when there are no bacteria. If you understand this mechanism, you will begin to see into the mysteries of various diseases. Diseases such as alveolar pyorrhea, stomach or duodenum ulcers, ulcerative colitis, Crohn's disease, and hemorrhoids are all inflammations caused by damaged mucosa. Acute pancreatitis, acute nephritis, and cataplectic deafness are commonly known to occur when a patient has strained himself or become overly stressed. These diseases happen when the sympathetic nerves become too dominant because of stress, which causes granulocytes to overproduce and begin attacking surrounding tissues. People have been taken to the hospital with acute pancreatitis due to lack of sleep after two consecutive all-night mahjong games. Others contract the disease after having too much alcohol. Acute nephritis patients are usually very stressed out. I often hear of people suddenly becoming deaf when they have domestic problems such as marital discord and divorce. As a result of cases such as these, people are beginning to realize that stress can cause disease. But since they don't know the specific mechanism of how stress causes disease, they can't solve the fundamental problem. If you know that extremely stressed sympathetic nerves result in increased granulocytes, which in turn damage tissue, you understand the problem. On top of this, extremely stressed sympathetic nerves cause increased tension, shrinking the blood vessels and blocking and reducing the bloodstream, thus damaging tissue even more.

DRAMATIC INCREASE IN GRANULOCYTES DAMAGES MUCOSA

Granulocytes are short-lived cells that survive for only a day or two. Normally, they're produced in the bone marrow, sent out into the bloodstream, and die in mucosa. When granulocytes following this course become too active, they damage mucosa in different parts of body. For example, if they increase too much, granulocytes can travel out to the epithelium of the skin. When you lack sleep or work late into the night, you may notice red rashes when you shave in the morning. This is caused by an increase in granulocytes. Women may notice this rash when they put on make-up in the morning after staying up late or not sleeping at all. Randomly scattered spots indicate just a mild inflammation of the epithelium, but if the stress lasts long enough, the granulocytes will continue to increase, as will the number of spots. The surface of the skin is strong enough that it's rarely damaged, but the subcutaneous tissue and sweat glands underneath the skin are sensitive and damage easily. Young people can have serious acne all over their face. This is not just due to their youth. A serious problem with acne indicates that they're worried about something, because the sympathetic nervous system is extremely dominant. An unhealthy diet can cause this sort of stress as well, though even then, worry is probably the source of their bad diet. People with worries usually have greatly increased granulocytes.

It's important to understand that a tension mechanism exists that increases granulocytes to the point where the stress can damage tissue. This has nothing to do with an increase in granulocytes due to bacteria. Determining the validity of this principle underlies the entire basis of my immunology position. In order to observe whether granulocytes increase in an organism under stress, we experimented by observing a rat that had been placed between wire netting. Although the rat was not infected with bacteria, the granulocytes in both its blood and tissue drastically increased, eventually reaching and damaging its mucosa. This experiment clearly shows how stress causes ulcers.

NEWBORNS WITH INCREASED GRANULOCYTES SUPPORT THE STRESS THEORY

When I realized that stress causes granulocytes to increase, I instantly thought about the phenomenon of newborn babies with excessive amounts of granulocytes. An adult has on average about 5,000 to 6,000 white blood cells in one microliter of blood. This number rarely exceeds 10,000. But newborns usually have in the neighborhood of 15,000 white cells, primarily neutrophils, a type of granulocyte. This granulocytosis of newborns is discussed in nearly every pediatric text. While this phenomenon is described as a fact, no literature examines why the number of neutrophils is so high. But as I conducted my experiment with the rat, the idea came to me that granulocytosis in newborns must be caused by stress as well.

The question then becomes, what's causing stress in newborns? Most people assume that this stress is caused by their trip through the narrow birth canal. But I don't think so. What's the biggest change for a newborn when it first comes out of the mother's womb? Taking oxygen and air into their lungs for the first time. A fetus is connected to its mother's womb by an umbilical cord that circulates all the oxygen-rich blood it needs. It receives its oxygen from its mother. When it gives its first cry, it uses its lungs to breathe oxygen for the first time, and the density of oxygen it takes in increases drastically. This sudden onrush of oxygen increases an infant's metabolism and causes stress. All babies cry right after they're born, and none without difficulty. Their facial expressions look like they're dying from pain. Their faces are red with congestion (in fact, we call babies "little red ones" in Japan). As I pictured this, I began to think that infants' granulocytes increase due to the stress of taking in essential oxygen all by themselves.

I was excited to discover something so significant and told my co-researcher Dr. Fukuda all about my theory right away. By the next day, I had become calmer and began experimenting in order to confirm my idea. First, I examined blood from a fetus and from newborn animals. I discovered that the amount of granulocytes was normal before birth. Since I needed to experiment with humans, I asked a pediatrician at the university to test the blood of a newborn and the blood in the umbilical cord. By pinching the cord right after delivery, the doctor was able to carefully remove the cord blood before it was affected by lung breathing. I later learned that blood circulation between a newborn and its mother stops immediately once the baby begins to breathe with its lungs, because its abdominal muscles automatically close the umbilical cord. So, lung breathing doesn't affect cord blood. But to be safe, we compared blood taken from the cord to blood from a newborn that had already started to breathe with its lungs.

To my surprise, the results were obvious. The total number of white blood cells increased to 15,000 immediately after delivery. Moreover, the number of cells increased rapidly minute by minute. Within an hour, granulocytosis was completely manifest. In short, when babies cry after delivery, in an excited state with freshly inhaled oxygen, the number of white blood cells, or granulocytes, increases rapidly. By the time they stop crying, the change has already occurred. When I saw the results of this experiment, I was deeply moved. I had already been very excited before the test, but this confirmed my theory."

This helps us understand some of the phenomena that newborns go through. For example, it's well known that newborns can't drink milk right away. As a result, they lose weight and grow wrinkled for a day or two. But why? A newborn baby becomes excited and tense after inhaling oxygen, which increases granulocytes. Their sympathetic nervous systems are obviously extremely tense. On the other hand, the digestive system is controlled by the parasympathetic nervous system. When an infant's sympathetic nervous systems are tense, it can't drink milk on the first day. During the next few days, as the tension begins to decrease, infants start drinking milk and become plumper and less wrinkled.

I was even more surprised to realize that granulocytes increase not only in peripheral blood, but in the liver as well. The liver also shows an increase in GOT and GPT, which indicate hepatopathy. In the womb, the fetus produces blood in its liver, but when the new mechanism of hemopoiesis is complete, this ability vanishes right away. Once a baby is born, this mechanism is transferred to the bone marrow deep inside the body. In the process, the red blood cells containing fetal hemoglobin produced in the liver are destroyed. This causes jaundice in newborn babies, usually about a week after birth. Why does it take such a long time? When we have a bruise from internal bleeding, it doesn't turn yellow right away. It becomes purple first, and then turns yellow in a week or so. It's the same with a baby's liver. Jaundice shows up after about a week as a result of the large number of destroyed red blood cells in the baby's liver. We now understand how jaundice occurs in newborns.

ALL DISEASES ARE CAUSED BY TENSION IN THE SYMPATHETIC NERVES

When I learned the truth of granulocytosis, it became clear that sympathicotonia causes granulocytes to increase, resulting in damaged tissue. This helped me see the hidden causes of various diseases. It became clear to me how we tense our sympathetic nerves by straining ourselves or worrying too much, and how this causes illness. Once I understood that stress and sympathicotonia are the basis of jaundice in newborn babies, I realized that stress causes many other diseases that damage tissue. For example, people who work hard get pyorrhea or stomach ulcers from worrying, and young people suffer duodenal ulcers due to stress from work. Even children studying for exams suffer from ulcerative colitis due to stress. These are all examples of tissue damaged from stress. Another example is middle-aged men who have too much alcohol or work too hard and end up with hemorrhoids. Our mucosa is very sensitive and prone to damage from stress. Stress can also cause acute pancreatitis, acute nephritis, or temporary deafness. With this understanding, I began to learn how to heal disease based on the core problem. I don't think it's necessary to deal with symptoms, because that doesn't really solve the fundamental problem. If you manage your stress, on the other hand, your disease will begin to heal.

Even collagen disease, which is particularly difficult to understand and treat, can be explained with this theory. Collagen diseases include rheumatoid arthritis, systemic lupus erythematosus (SLE), Hashimoto's thyroiditis, hyperthyroidism, Sjogren's syndrome, peliosis, and auto- immune hepatitis. They display a variety of symptoms, but all are caused when immunity becomes low due to stress, allowing an internal virus to become active and damage tissue. When tissue is damaged, blood flows into the affected area to fix the problem. This increased blood flow causes inflammation, which makes people feel sick. If you talk to a collagen disease patient, you'll discover that they're under stress. Attacks are triggered by cold symptoms, usually fever—in short, an extreme decline in immunity due to stress.

Once I understood how mucosa and tissue can be damaged, and how this causes collagen disease, I began to see the solution to other diseases as well—even the mechanism that causes cancer. I'll discuss cancer and collagen disease in more detail later, but here's a brief explanation. When someone is under constant stress and when that stress becomes a chronic stimulus to the body, the regenerating epithelium or secreting glands usually become damaged. The epithelium and glands regenerate constantly. When they're damaged, they regenerate even faster. We often hear of "cancer genes," but there are actually no special genes that produce cancer. What we call cancer genes are merely the proliferation genes that normal cells use to propagate. When some type of encumbrance is applied to these cells, they can become continuous proliferators, or cancerous. These genes don't cause any harm when cells regenerate at a normal pace. But when stress causes tissue to regenerate too frequently, there's too much burden on the genes. When cells are damaged during regeneration, active oxygen causes genetic disorders, and the gene loses its ability to adjust. That's how cancers are produced.

Until recently, it was believed that substances that cause genetic disorders came from outside the body. We thought that cancers were caused by external substances such as food additives, cigarettes, UV light, and exhaust. In reality, however, we ourselves create cancer through stress, which causes tissue to regenerate excessively and increases granulocytes, which produce active oxygen. Once we began to understand this mechanism, our group of doctors, including Dr. Fukuda, talked with and examined our cancer patients to see if they were under stress. We discovered that all, without exception, had severe stress: a man who worked too hard, a woman with serious worries, a young woman severely chilled by air conditioning, and so forth.

We realized that if you don't manage your stress, you can't solve your fundamental problem. By understanding the basic mechanism of diseases, you learn how to treat them. On the other hand, if you ignore the fundamental problem, you can only deal with symptoms.

DISEASES CAUSED BY THE FAILURE OF THE NEW IMMUNE SYSTEM

I've explained how disease is caused by a failure in the body due to the excessive reaction of granulocytes to stress, and how this increase in granulocytes damages tissue. The fundamental problem of these diseases is that they create tension in the sympathetic nerves; as a result, the thymus is likely to shrink, which causes granulocytes to increase. In other words, diseases occur when the "old immune system" (a concept I'll explain further in chapter 5) is active. But are any diseases caused by a failure of an evolved immune system? The answer is yes—allergic diseases. Children tend to have more allergies because they have more lymphocytes. When these children grow up, they're likely to have allergies as adults as well.

People say their body is allergic, but that's not a full explanation of the problem. We need to consider the reason they have so many lymphocytes. As I'll explain in chapter 5, lymphocytes are influenced by the parasympathetic nervous system. When the parasympathetic nervous system is dominant, the constitution of lymphocytes is high. When the parasympathetic nervous system is excessively dominant, lymphocytes increase too much and cause allergic problems. To solve the problem of allergies, we need to consider carefully why this is so.

Why does the parasympathetic nervous system become too dominant? In short, it happens when we're too relaxed. In the case of children, they're often overprotected. In the case of adults, they eat too much and lack exercise. Many of us have learned to deal with stress by eating too much. Eating is the easiest and fastest way to make the parasympathetic nervous system dominant. When you eat, you relax, but you don't solve the fundamental problem of stress.

Allergies occur when immunity against an outside antigen becomes too strong because an excess of lymphocytes are targeted to that particular behavior. Allergies may manifest as atopic dermatitis, bronchial asthma, pollinizes, and other diseases. The catarrhal problems that often accompany viral infections also stem from overreacting lymphocytes. When children have a high fever due to a cold, a very serious situation can develop. As they grow older, their fevers aren't as high anymore because the amount of lymphocytes has changed. Lymphocytes fight viruses, but when there are too many, they can become overly aggressive and cause too strong a reaction. This worsens the inflammation and can cause an abnormally high fever. Because of this, children who tend to have high fevers when they have a cold are sometimes called thymicolymphatic.

TOO MANY LYMPHOCYTES AND SEVERE COLD SYMPTOMS

When we think of viral diseases, the first thing that comes to mind is the common cold. Because colds are very common, people seem to think they're easy to prevent. But being immune to a cold is a very delicate and difficult matter, because the key is the increase and decrease of lymphocytes. In some cases, too few lymphocytes are available to prevent viruses from causing serious cold symptoms. Conversely, too many lymphocytes can react with viruses too quickly and cause serious symptoms. It's therefore very difficult to give advice to someone with a cold, because there can be two totally different causes.

When someone has too many lymphocytes, they tend to overreact to other things besides colds, including bug bites, lacquer poisoning, urtication, and so forth. They also overreact to medicines that cause anaphylaxis, including aspirin and antibiotics such as penicillin. But people with excessive lymphocytes tend to overreact to many types of outside stimuli, so we can't solve the problem by concluding that it's solely one of allergic reaction.

Many more people suffer from allergies today than thirty or forty years ago. This shows how much our way of life has changed. Before and just after the World Wars, people were under greater physical strain than they are today, because there were few modern conveniences to ease their harsh lifestyle. As a result, the sympathetic nerves tended to be more dominant. People were also starving back then. I therefore suspect that people generally had more granulocytes. In contrast, our lifestyle today is much easier and there's less physical activity—but we grow up spoiled, with far too much to eat from the time we're young. This makes our parasympathetic nervous system more dominant and increases lymphocytes. There are children suffering from allergies who eat cake every day for dessert. As our way of life has changed, the diseases we suffer from have changed as well.

DISEASES CAUSED BY THE LACK OF LYMPHOCYTES OR GRANULOCYTES

I've briefly discussed diseases caused by an excess of lymphocytes and granulocytes, but I should also mention that other diseases are caused by their lack.

Diseases caused by a lack of granulocytes are very unusual, because granulocytes are unlikely to decrease unless one has a congenital condition. But one symptom of decreased granulocytes can occur as a result of medical treatment. When hepatitis patients receive interferon treatments, their granulocytes decrease drastically. Interferon, a type of cytokine, causes apoptosis, or cellular suicide; as a result, granulocytes start to die off. Granulocytes are often seen as something negative because they produce active oxygen. But in actuality, our body becomes more active and excited when oxygen increases. That's why, when a patient goes through interferon treatments and their granulocytes decrease, they become less lively and are likely to be depressed. It's commonly known that hepatitis type C patients who receive interferon treatments can become severely depressed and commit suicide.

When we lack granulocytes, we can't manage bacteria or produce active oxygen, and as a result we're unable to be active. I've seen advertisements for health products recently that claim to reduce active oxygen because it's harmful to our body. But if we reduce it too much, we'11ack energy. When we're too relaxed, we have no life force. Granulocytes are probably lacking when we feel that way. And when we can't manage bacteria, we don't have enough energy. That's because we lack granulocytes.

On the other hand, there's a condition called immunodeficiency, in which lymphocytes decrease. When granulocytes increase due to stress, lymphocytes decrease accordingly. This is a common phenomenon. Most diseases occur when lymphocytes are low. Based on my observations, about 80 percent of diseases occur when lymphocytes are low as a result of increasing granulocytes. So only 20 to 30 percent of diseases are caused by excess lymphocytes and a lifestyle that's too relaxed. Most diseases are caused by too many granulocytes and too few lymphocytes.

TOO MUCH RELAXATION IS ALSO HARMFUL TO OUR BODY

So, to increase lymphocytes, is it enough to make the parasympathetic nervous system dominant? I'm afraid it's not that simple. The parasympathetic nervous system relaxes us, but too much relaxation causes discomfort. When tissue is damaged by stress or injury, the parasympathetic nervous system repairs it. The parasympathetic nervous system is stimulated by chemicals such as acetylcholine, prostaglandin, histamine, serotonin, and leukotrienes. These parasympathetic nerve stimuli widen blood vessels and cause red blood cells to swell or rupture, often accompanied by the discomfort of pain or fever. Chemicals that stimulate the sympathetic nerves, on the other hand, such as adrenalin, noradrenalin, and dopamine, excite us and make us more active. When this happens continually, the result is a numbing of perception.

The parasympathetic nervous system makes us relaxed and more sensitive to pain when it's moderately active, but causes fever, more pain, and inflammation when it's too active. An active parasympathetic nervous system causes blood vessels to widen and blood flow to increase. But if the blood vessels widen too much, the blood pressure can become too low, leading to anaphylactic shock. When lymphocytes are too high, allergies can result, also leading to shock if the increase is extreme.

In contrast, the sympathetic nerves cause excitement by narrowing the blood vessels, eventually increasing blood pressure and pulse. This also can cause blood flow to stop in extreme cases. So, an excessively active sympathetic or parasympathetic nervous system can result in poor blood circulation by narrowing or widening the blood vessels.

ANTIPHLOGISTICS AND ANTIPYRETICS PREVENT HEALING

As we've observed, the parasympathetic nervous system is mysterious. It's supposed to help us feel comfortable, but it can cause discomfort when it's too dominant. When it's moderately active, it relaxes us and helps us store energy. However, blood flow sometimes needs to increase to enable tissue to repair as part of the healing process. So, we must sometimes bear a certain amount of discomfort in order to heal.

But in treating this discomfort, modern medicine stops the healing properties of the parasympathetic nervous system. This is a big problem—it prevents us from healing the underlying disease. Modern medical practitioners routinely prescribe medicines such as antiphlogistics to reduce swollen tissue, and antipyretics to cool down a fever. While these medications do take care of the symptoms, they also stop the body's natural healing activity and processes, which are ultimately needed to repair damaged tissue. So, the medications don't really heal disease—they treat it the wrong way. Unfortunately, modern medicine lacks studies focused on treating disease with an understanding of this fundamental problem. Almost no one had done this sort of work until we began our research. Western medicine wrongly believes that stopping inflammation heals disease. This misunderstanding has led them in the wrong direction.

This problem was less serious in the past, when medicines were weaker and less effective, easing symptoms only slightly. In those days, medications didn't have the power to stop all healing activity. They were intended to ease pain so that patients could heal slowly. That's why they were actually more effective in healing disease.

Today, medicines have become so strong that they can stop inflammation completely. Of course, this stops healing activity as well, and as a result we're unable to achieve total healing. This is a very serious problem, particularly with medicines such as antiphlogistics and steroids. Anti-inflammatories and steroids both stop inflammation, and therefore create the same problem. When medicines are used to relieve symptoms, patients may feel better. But the treatment is merely stopping the body's healing reaction and preventing the fundamental problem from being healed. As a result, diseases become chronic. So, medicines that relieve symptoms aren't necessarily good. It's easy to make this mistake, so I'd like you to understand it well.

I'm not totally rejecting anti-inflammatories and antipyretics. I don't think it's a bad idea to use medication to lessen 20 or 30 percent of a patient's symptoms. But if you don't understand the concept that these medicines don't really heal anything, you're likely to use them until the symptoms are completely gone, thereby worsening the fundamental problem. This is a serious concern, in my mind.

THE DANGER OF ALLOPATHIC TREATMENTS THAT PREVENT BLOOD CIRCULATION

Anti-inflammatories can be used as a poultice to cool down the body. How does it work? Basically, it stops blood flow. Steroids are even more effective at cooling the body. People who take steroids every day often complain that their body is so cold they have to wear a sweater even during the summer. They say that their body feels like a refrigerator. That's how much the flow of blood is slowed to cool the body.

If you slow down blood flow, symptoms of inflammation also slow down or stop. That's how anti-inflammatories work. This is very different than curing inflammation by treating disease. I'd like you to really understand this. Modern medicine always uses medication. Medication is used entirely too readily when symptoms don't appear to improve or disappear. I appreciate when my patients use their own discernment to decide whether medication is truly helping them heal or worsening the overall situation by merely treating superficial symptoms.

When the parasympathetic nervous system becomes more active in the course of healing, there's some discomfort. This completely natural phenomenon is rarely acknowledged in modern medical science. That's why we've gone in the direction of treating patients in ways that aren't in their long-term best interest. Fortunately, some patients seem to know that something's wrong, either intuitively or from experience. These are the patients who avoid modern medicine. Many patients with chronic back pain, for example, begin going to chiropractors or massage therapists because orthopedists are not really helping.

Unfortunately, though, many patients who choose massage therapy continue to use external painkillers, because they don't really understand the problem that painkillers and anti-inflammatories create. Combining the two really does not help treatment. I recommend staying away from painkillers, in favor of massage, acupuncture, or moxa alone. These treatments stimulate the parasympathetic nervous system, improve blood circulation, and arouse the body's healing capabilities. If you include painkillers or anti-inflammatories in this regimen, the medications will suppress the body's healing ability and negate the benefits of the physical treatment, ruining the effect.

The fact that even patients who choose alternative treatments cannot or will not stop using medication shows just how programmed people have become when it comes to modern medicine, and how much they expect of and rely on pharmaceuticals. It's time that we, as modern medical doctors, focus on treating the fundamental problem, not the problematic symptoms, in order to meet patients' expectations that they will be well after treatment. I'm not at all denying or criticizing the value of some aspects of modern medical treatment. But I very much wish that medical professionals would improve their treatments and regain the credibility that has been lost.

Chapter 2
Cancer Is Nothing to Fear

Cancer remains a serious problem for those who suffer from it, despite modern medical advancements. Cancer has been the top cause of death in Japan since 1981, when it overtook cerebrovascular incidents. Because 30 percent of deaths are now caused by cancer, many people consider it an incurable and frightening disease.

When someone has cancer, it seems—from the point of view of modern medical treatment—that there's no way out. But from an immunological point of view, cancer is actually very curable. If you understand immunology, there's no longer any need to fear cancer.

Cancer occurs when the immune system is extremely suppressed. Stress severely suppresses immunity because the sympathetic nervous system is under constant tension. Tension inhibits the formation and activity of granulocytes and lymphocytes. A lack of granulocytes and lymphocytes causes all sorts of problems. If you learn to manage the stress that has created this increased tension in the sympathetic nervous system, thereby strengthening and activating the parasympathetic nervous system and bringing about a better balance, the immune system will be healed. In this chapter, I will discuss in detail the mechanism that causes cancer and how to treat it.

EXTREME STRESS CAUSES CANCER

Until we reported the results of our study, it was believed that cancer was caused by external carcinogens. For a long time, it's been thought that cancer resulted from a genetic disorder that was stimulated by external substances such as food additives, ultraviolet rays, exhaust fumes, burnt proteins such as those found in grilled fish, and so on. But no matter how much I investigated my patients' backgrounds; I couldn't validate this theory. Their lifestyles simply did not include too much UV or burnt fish. The majority of them had an average diet and an average living environment.

In the course of our in-depth investigations, we discovered that most cancer patients had suppressed immune systems and very low lymphocyte levels. As discussed in the previous chapter, when lymphocytes are low it's an indication that the sympathetic nervous system is tense. This led me to suspect that stress from overwork or worry was the cause. To back up my theory, I interviewed several patients. Most reported leading a very stressful life. About eight out of ten reported extreme stress, such as having to work late every day, problems adapting to a new job, returning to work after retirement, or serious trouble brought about by a misunderstanding. One patient was very busy handling a job and housework, another was sad because his child was ill, and a third had a bad relationship with her husband.

Along with these patients suffering from emotional stress were patients whose sympathetic nervous systems were tense as a side effect of medication. One patient took painkillers constantly to ease the pain of dysmenorrhea caused by drafts from an air-conditioned office that kept her body extremely cold. As I observed and analyzed my patients' backgrounds, including their various symptoms and diseases, I came to understand that tension in the sympathetic nervous system is what triggers cancer.

THE REAL MECHANISM OF CARCINOGENESIS

How is sympathicotonia (overstimulation of the sympathetic nervous system) related to carcinogenesis (the development of cancer cells)? Let's take a moment to discuss and better understand the mechanism of carcinogenesis. When the sympathetic nervous system is moderately stimulated, the pulse is faster and blood circulation is better. But if sympathicotonia continues, the flow of blood through the circulatory system is reduced. When blood flow slows down, granulocytes automatically increase. These increased granulocytes destroy red blood cells, one by one. That's why cancer patients are usually pale and gaunt.

The areas of the body in which the "mother" cancer cells can grow include the epithelium (outer surface) of organs made of ectoderm—such as skin and nerves—and the epithelium of organs made of endoblast—such as the digestive system and liver—as well as the glandular system that surrounds epithelium. Skin cells, intestinal epithelium, and gland cells reproduce quickly. Cells that reproduce frequently have active cell division, resulting in an increased number of dividing errors and lots of waste matter. Epithelium cells and the glandular system usually contain bacteria, which attract granulocytes, so they're more likely to be exposed to the active oxygen that granulocytes produce. This active oxygen damages productive genes and causes cancer.

The study of genes has progressed dramatically in the last fifteen years or so. We've learned that cancer genes are composed of substances formed when normal genes split and reproduce. When tension in the sympathetic nervous system stimulates the multiplication of reproductive epithelium, granulocytes rush in and damage the area through active oxygen generation, transforming the DNA of productive genes into genes with instructions to produce cancer cells. This is the mechanism of carcinogenesis. There's no such thing as a gene that begins as a "negative" gene.

Immunodeficiency can also be a factor in cancer. Immunodeficiency can be innate or acquired, but either way, if it continues for more than several years, the outcome almost without exception is cancer. Why? I'll discuss the details more thoroughly in chapter 5, but in short, when our body is working normally, our stable, balanced immune system constantly watches for abnormalities. When one is found, the immune system uses lymphocytes to destroy the abnormal cells—such as cancer cells—as soon as they appear. This internal protection system is always there. But when immunodeficiency (an overly tense sympathetic nervous system) continues for too long, the resulting long-term lack of lymphocytes becomes a problem. When the number of granulocytes increases due to stress or other factors, cancers begin to grow in the epithelium cells and spread to other areas.

Until now, the cause of cancer has been considered unknown. Many people think it's caused by a physical abnormality in the genes or external carcinogens that stimulate the body for a long time. But because neither of these theories really explains the true mechanism of cancer, we have no fundamental treatment method for it. As a result, we've only come up with harmful treatments to deal with cancer. We kept it too simple: we decided that the best way to treat cancer is to shrink or remove it.

Many people believe that the easiest way to remove cancer is through surgery. The next most likely treatment involves chemicals, such as chemotherapy; the third treatment involves radiation. These are considered the three major treatments, and they do help shrink cancer. But does shrinking cancer really lead to true healing? Since the core problem, an unbalanced autonomic nervous system, hasn't been healed, the true cause of cancer continues to exist. That's why cancers often flare up again after the initial remission. Until the fundamental cause is removed, other treatments only work temporarily.

This too I will explain in more detail in future chapters. Here, I merely wish to reiterate that the serious problem these three treatments share is that they all totally suppress the immune system. They stop our critical immune capability, which protects our body and helps us heal. Because this immune imbalance continues after treatment—at an even stronger level than before—even if cancer is removed or shrunk temporarily, we will lose the ability to fight back when it returns.

CANCER GOES INTO REMISSION WHEN IMMUNITY IS BOOSTED

Our immune system watches for abnormal activity, protects our body, and helps us heal. That's why we can fight and win against cancer by enhancing the power of the immune system. It's critical that you understand this at this point. We can then return to the fundamental question: how to help your immune system work at its full capacity, and how to eliminate cancer-causing factors from your life. By reevaluating our lifestyle, we can stop working too hard and stop being worried. This is the basis for the true healing of cancer.

CANCER CELLS ARE NOT NECESSARILY STRONG

Most people seem to believe that cancer cells are so strong they won't disappear once they're produced. But cancer cells are actually not so strong.

When we experiment on rats, we have to inject them with a million cancer cells to cause them to develop malignant cancer. If we inject only 10,000 or 100,000 cancer cells, the cells will all be destroyed by lymphocytes. But if we expose rats to radiation and thereby reduce their lymphocytes, they develop cancer when injected with only 1,000 cancer cells. That's how vulnerable cancers are to lymphocytes. So, if you have a lifestyle that maintains a high number of lymphocytes, you're less likely to get cancer.

It's said that about a million cancer cells are produced in our body every day. But thanks to hard-working lymphocytes, we don't "get cancer." One million cancer cells are about the size of a single sesame seed. There are about sixty trillion cells in our body, and cancer cells the size of a sesame seed are produced and destroyed every day. If our lymphocytes are working actively, cancer won't develop.

My colleagues have witnessed the healing of cancer when immunity is activated. If you change your lifestyle by including treatments that stimulate the parasympathetic nervous system, the number of lymphocytes in your body will increase in a few months. Cancer patients are usually in a state of low immunity, with very low lymphocyte counts—in general, 30 percent of an average person's count. Studying the data of our patients, we realized that cancers naturally go into remission when the number of lymphocytes becomes greater than 30 percent of the average. So, it's very important to help the body increase the number of lymphocytes to 30 percent or higher. While this may seem a small percentage, I'd like you to look at the actual number of lymphocytes. We know that natural remission occurs when there are about 1,800 lymphocytes in one microliter of blood. If a patient is thin, the count could be as low as 1,500 or so. To increase the number of lymphocytes, it's important that we reevaluate our lifestyle and its patterns.

THE FOUR TOP RULES FOR HEALING CANCER

The most important way to increase lymphocytes is to improve patients' attitudes. Cancers naturally regress when attitude improves, so patients should not allow themselves to feel desperate. People are usually shocked when they're first told they have cancer. They seem to think they're never going to be well again. I often hear of people who are so worried when a test finds something suspicious that they can't think of anything else or fall asleep for a month. This kind of emotional stress worsens the sympathicotonia (stress of the sympathetic nervous system) and reduces lymphocyte production. Naturally, the body's strength declines as a result, and the possibility of cancer growth increases.

My colleagues and I suggest four rules for cancer patients who wish to heal:

1. Reevaluate your lifestyle patterns.
2. Eliminate your fear of cancer.
3. Don't blindly agree to any treatment that suppresses immunity, and if you've already begun such treatment, stop immediately
4. Stimulate the parasympathetic nervous system. If you act on these four rules, the number and percentage of lymphocytes in your system will increase, and cancer cells will naturally begin to regress.

I've already discussed the first rule (lifestyle) and the second (fear). I'd now like to discuss rule number three (treatments that suppress the immune system) and four (treatments that support the immune system) in greater detail.

First, rule number four: stimulate the parasympathetic nervous system. The parasympathetic nervous system is easily activated when you stimulate your intestines by eating. As I discussed previously, digestive system functioning is ruled by the parasympathetic nervous system. Therefore, the easiest way to stimulate the parasympathetic nervous system is to stimulate the intestines by eating something healthy, such as vegetables, mushrooms, and well-cooked brown rice.

I recommend brown rice in particular for a reason. Brown rice is highly nutritious. It contains protein, fat, vitamin B, and minerals, as well as carbohydrates. Nothing is better for increasing lymphocytes than eating brown rice. If you continue to eat brown rice for a week or so, you'll begin to feel warm. You may find that you have more dreams, as well, because more blood is reaching your brain. Fiber and vitamins from vegetables and §-g1ucans from mushrooms reduce abnormal fermentation within the intestines and improve constipation. Vegetables provide abundant vitamins and minerals, which you can enhance by taking supplementary vitamin C, A, and niacin. It's important for cancer patients to get as much nutrition as possible by eating normally, or as close to normally as possible.

The parasympathetic nervous system is also related to blood circulation. You can stimulate the parasympathetic nervous system through activities that enhance blood circulation. I recommend light exercise, hot baths, and walking as much as you can. Blood circulates better when you move your body. If you want to heal disease, get a little exercise every day. Even if you're old, I recommend brief exercise that moves your whole body. Even rocking in a rocking chair can be a gentle but powerful energy boost for your system.

HEALING CANCER WITH LAUGHTER

Lightening up your attitude is another important way to activate your parasympathetic nervous system. I strongly recommend that you laugh often. When your face is serious, your sympathetic nervous system is likely to be tense. I understand that when people are sick they feel depressed and upset, but I'd like you to summon your courage and live life with a smile in order to promote healing. Even laughing at trivial matters can help you feel happier. Laughter activates the parasympathetic nervous system. So, laugh out loud! Most cancer patients seem to have serious faces and rarely laugh. Their sympathetic nervous systems are tense. So, when I see my patients smiling during their course of treatment, I feel happy. I suggest that you look in a mirror and force yourself to smile when you feel depressed. Eventually, you'll feel like laughing. This will open the door to healing.

> *Whenever I feel afraid, I hold my head erect*
> *And whistle a happy tune so no one will suspect I'm afraid.*
> *While shivering in my shoes, I strike a careless pose*
> *And whistle a happy tune, and no one ever knows I'm afraid.*
> *The result of this deception is very strange to tell*
> *For when I fool the people I fear I fool myself as well!*
> *I whistle a happy tune and every single time*
> *The happiness in the tune convinces me that I'm not afraid.*
> *Make believe you're brave and the trick will take you far.*
> *You may be as brave as you make believe you are.*
>
> — *"I Whistle a Happy Tune," from The King and I,*
> *by Richard Rodgers and Oscar Hammerstein II*

Laughing supports healing—not only of cancer, but of various other diseases as well. One famous example is American journalist Norman Cousins, who fell ill with systemic collagen disease. His entire body was in pain from an inflammation that made him feel that he was on fire. His doctor gave up on him, telling him that his disease would never go into remission. But Cousins didn't give up. He studied medical books and articles, and after much consideration he stopped taking steroids and started watching funny movies and reading humorous books in order to make himself laugh. As a result, he boosted his body's own healing ability, enabling him to overcome the effects of the steroids. He eventually overcame collagen disease as well. By increasing his body's own immunity, he managed to bring about a total remission from collagen disease—normally considered a very difficult thing to do.

Cousins later became a medical critic and eventually a medical philosopher. There's much to learn from his books, such as Anatomy of an Illness as Perceived by the Patient. The treatments for collagen disease and cancer are very similar. Both diseases occur because of suppressed immunity. I recommend that cancer patients study and learn from Cousins' example.

ARGUMENTS OVER THE THREE MAJOR CANCER TREATMENTS

I'd next like to discuss rule number three: don't blindly agree to any treatment that suppresses immunity, and if you've already begun such treatment, stop immediately. Unfortunately, each of the three major cancer treatments—surgery, chemotherapy, and radiation—suppresses immunity. While they shouldn't be totally rejected, these treatments do contradict the true healing of disease from an immunological perspective.

CONCERNING SURGERY

Surgery itself drastically suppresses immunity. When we're injured or burned from something outside of the body, our body increases its rate of activity. This phenomenon shows that our parasympathetic nervous system, which supports relaxation, kicks into hyperactivity when tissue is damaged. This is often experienced as shock. Our cells are normally coated with two layers of fat. When cells are damaged by an injury or burn, these protective fat layers pop and inner substances flow out. These substances are very strong oxides that stimulate the sympathetic nervous system and increase tension in the body. This, of course, occurs during any surgical procedure. In surgery, tissue is damaged with a scalpel, greatly stimulating the sympathetic nervous system and increasing the growth of granulocytes. If a patient already suffers from an increased granulocyte count, which can damage tissue and contribute to the development of cancer in the first place, this surgical side effect is far from helpful. In fact, many cancers have been known to metastasize throughout the body following surgery. I therefore think it's better to avoid surgery if possible.

That being said, it's not necessarily a bad choice to have simple surgery if the cancer is at an early stage and easily removable. The problem is that cancer itself has a tendency to stimulate the sympathetic nervous system. In other words, cancer keeps the sympathetic nervous system tense. So, while it can be helpful to remove cancerous tissue in order to stop its short-term growth, it's important that patients not deceive themselves into thinking that the cancer is completely healed as a result.

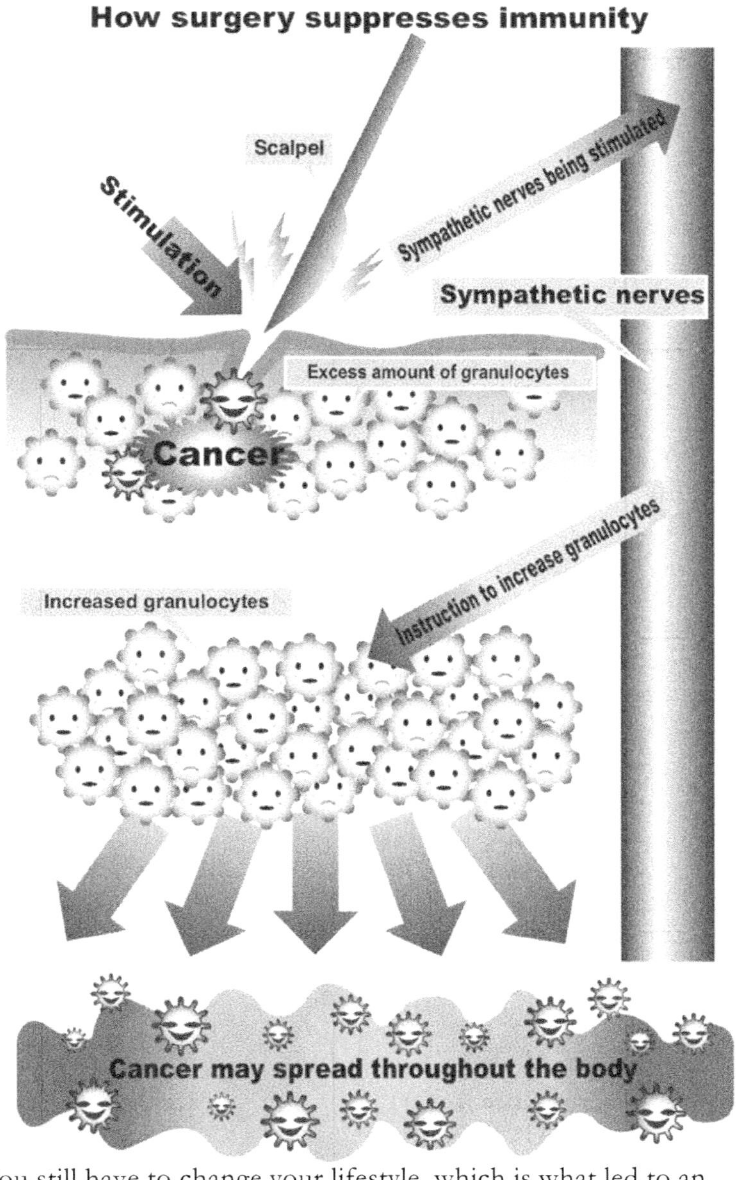

You still have to change your lifestyle, which is what led to an overly tense sympathetic nervous system and caused your cancer to begin with. Follow the four rules listed above. Otherwise, it's very possible that you will find cancer growing in other parts of your body.

While the practice has become less common than it used to be, I don't recommend removing lymph nodes either. This was supposedly done to prevent cancer from spreading. But the lymph nodes are where cancer-fighting lymphocytes are produced. If you remove them, your body's immunity will be even more suppressed. Many people have had their lymph nodes removed only to find that their condition did not really improve. In fact, in many cases, it grew worse. Fortunately, more doctors are now aware of this situation.

Considering all these side effects, it's best to avoid surgery whenever possible. Simple surgery is fine, but it's important to keep surgical invasion to a minimum. The most important thing is to improve your life according to the four rules, and not believe that surgery is going to heal you completely.

TESTIMONIAL 2

The Effects of Anti-Cancer Drugs: Countering Side Effects of Chemotherapy with Immunotherapy

"Four summers ago, following a pregnancy test, I was diagnosed with a hydatidiform mole (a diagnosis resulting from a test that shows a high level of ß—hCG). It's very possible that this will eventually cause choriocarcinoma, a kind of cancer that's known to be very difficult to heal. When you have a hydatidiform mole, the abnormal villi that grow in the uterus have to be completely removed, so I had three surgeries. I was later told that the condition had recurred because the doctor didn't treat me properly after the surgeries, mistaking me as a miscarriage patient.

"The doctor said he thought it was cancer and that the only way to heal it would be with anti-cancer drugs. I was afraid of cancer, so I accepted his opinion. I started taking chemotherapy pills, which made me so tired and nauseated that I couldn't even get out of bed. The doctor then changed my treatment to a chemotherapy infusion, which is a little milder than the pills, but I still suffered after-effects, and I lost a lot of weight. One of the most significant after-effects was losing bunches of hair, which fell just by touching it. I cried. My skin color turned dark, as well, especially around my eyes, and the joints of my fingers were like those of a corpse.

"Despite all my suffering, the effects of the treatment weren't helping. A friend of mine who was very concerned about my situation told me about Dr. Minoru Fukuda and his acupuncture treatment, which she'd seen in a magazine. The magazine said that Dr. Fukuda healed breast cancer with massage, needles, and lasers, not drugs. It was hard to believe, but I started massaging my nails the way Dr. Fukuda instructed. It doesn't require any tools, and all you have to do is massage the side of your nails. I practiced this three times a day for about a month and, to my surprise, I began to feel better. The terrible nausea wasn't as bad anymore. This gave me a hope of remission. I called Dr. Fukuda's clinic and was told that I should stop taking the anticancer medication and come see him immediately.

"Two days after my call, I received my first acupuncture treatment from Dr. Fukuda. He listened to my story and told me that I would be fine. He started by putting needles in my head, shoulders, and the tips of my feet and fingers. At the same time, he treated my emotional problems. He told me that I was too serious and should relax and be more easygoing. I began to realize how stress had caused my illness.

"The effect of this treatment showed up the very next day. When you take anti-cancer drugs, your urine smells like chemicals. The first urine the morning after my first treatment with Dr. Fukuda smelled even stronger—as if all the chemicals in my body were being flushed out. After this, I stopped feeling nauseated for the first time in ages. I received his treatment once a week, and it was obvious that my body was becoming healthier. I had more appetite and gained some weight. I felt much more energetic and I was able to walk the twenty-five minutes from the Nigata station to Dr. Fukuda's clinic. My body was warmer, and I didn't have to go to the bathroom as often. About a month later, my hair started to grow back. The darkness in my skin disappeared and my skin looked brighter.

"Despite this visible improvement, my lymphocyte count was not increasing very much. When I began treatment, my count was about 1,000 per microliter. I was told that long-term treatment would probably be necessary to increase this to a normal level. Even as I improved, when I strained myself physically or mentally, the number dropped immediately. This nearly instantaneous reaction made me even more aware that stress does in fact affect my white blood cells.

"Although my lymphocyte count didn't increase very much, there were many signs of remission in my body. My blood became thinner and I stopped having pain during menstruation. I felt like I was reborn. I totally retained my health, and now I'm even healthier than I was before I became ill."

Chemotherapy is widely practiced today. In the beginning, anti- cancer drugs were shown to be very effective in treating leukemia. As a result, these drugs gained a good reputation, and people got the wrong impression about them. Patients become gaunt when they undergo chemotherapy. Their immune systems are seriously suppressed. While their cancer may shrink, they can be left with post-treatment infections and no power to fight back.

It's obvious that anti-cancer drugs put an enormous strain on patients' bodies. But why do patients become so gaunt? Because anti- cancer drugs prevent the division and reproduction of cells. As I explained previously, cancers often get started in the reproductive system. Cancers themselves have no cell growth inhibitors. So, once they start dividing and reproducing, they keep right on going. Anti-cancer drugs prevent cells from reproducing, but the effect is not limited to cancer cells. They interfere with cell reproduction all over the body, including the organs. When you use anti-cancer drugs, your skin becomes damaged, your hair falls out, and you stop producing saliva. Anti-cancer drugs also damage the intestinal epithelium cells and cause diarrhea. Diarrhea occurs when anti-cancer drugs interfere with the ongoing division of cells in areas where cell division is going on. Since there's not much cellular division going on in the brain or in most nerves, these areas aren't very affected. Hemocytes, including lymphocytes, are reproductive cells, and therefore, very much influenced by anti-cancer drugs. The presence of cancer is a clear indication of both a low lymphocyte count and a high granulocyte count. Both of these indicate that the sympathetic nervous system is under serious stress. When you begin a course of anti-cancer drugs, the sympathetic nervous system becomes even more stressed, creating more tension and further reducing the number of lymphocytes (and increasing granulocytes). That's why I consider anti-cancer drugs to be so harmful.

WHY ANTI-CANCER DRUGS (CHEMOTHERAPY) CAN'T HEAL CANCER

Some of you may think drugs are good because they shrink cancer. And in fact, they do. But you need to think about the mechanism that makes this happen.

When you take anti-cancer drugs, you prevent the normal cycle of cell reproduction—a necessary component in the process of repairing and replacing old or damaged cells. True, they stop cancers from growing. But the stronger the drugs, the more they suppress your body's essential cellular maintenance. When normal cell maintenance stops, cancer cells naturally shrink because they can't reproduce. If anti-cancer drugs only affected out-of-control cancer cell reproduction, there would be no problem. But anti-cancer drugs don't just attack cancer cells. They control your body's natural metabolic and biological activity, which in addition to suppressing cancer completely deprives you of your energy and healing ability.

Is it possible to prevent cancer cells from growing by applying anti-cancer drugs directly to cancerous areas? In fact, there is one drug like this. If you inject it into an artery and aim it at a cancerous growth, it will shrink the cancer and won't greatly decrease the number of lymphocytes. But the final result won't be satisfactory. Why? Because patients don't learn to manage and change the lifestyle that caused the cancer in the first place. When there's no lifestyle change, cancer often comes back in different parts of the body because there's no improvement in the fundamental problem.

It's the same with surgery. You can't solve the problem by just removing or shrinking cancer. It's only worth going through painful surgery or chemotherapy if you manage to enhance your lifestyle with immunotherapy or something similar afterwards. Many patients have total remission of their cancer thanks to immunotherapy or related treatments after surgery.

With this in mind, it's best not to use anti-cancer drugs unless there are high expectations for a good result. There are in fact some cases in which anti-cancer drugs can be effective. Leukemia is one example. If the cancer is expected to heal, you can probably use drugs. In the case of Lance Armstrong, a seven-time champion of the Tour de France, who overcame cancer with surgery and harsh chemotherapy, I think his success was greatly due to his own extraordinary physical ability, youth, and passionate desire to recover. It seems that the younger the patient, the more effective the chemotherapy.

But there's a strong tendency today to use anti-cancer drugs routinely on larger cancers or ones that have progressed to different parts of the body, where there's no real expectation of remission. Again, these drugs suppress immunity, making the patient gaunt and further reducing their chance to heal the fundamental problem behind their cancer. It's important to understand these facts about anti-cancer drugs.

IRESSA: AN EXAMPLE OF A PROBLEMATIC ANTI-CANCER DRUG

Iressa (the brand name of the generic drug gefitinib), a lung cancer drug, has caused many casualties since December 2002, and it symbolizes the problem of anti-cancer drugs.

Iressa was approved exceptionally quickly because it was a "dream drug"—supposedly strongly effective at shrinking cancer without the side effects that are so common with most anti-cancer drugs, which severely reduce white blood cell counts. Because it came in the form of a convenient oral medication, many patients had high expectation of a positive outcome. However, within six months of its going on the market, in July 2002, there were more than 120 casualties. Most patients who died from Iressa suffered from a side effect known as interstitial pneumonia, an inflammation of the lung tissue between air vesicles. The symptoms are very painful: patients can't breathe, and cough incessantly.

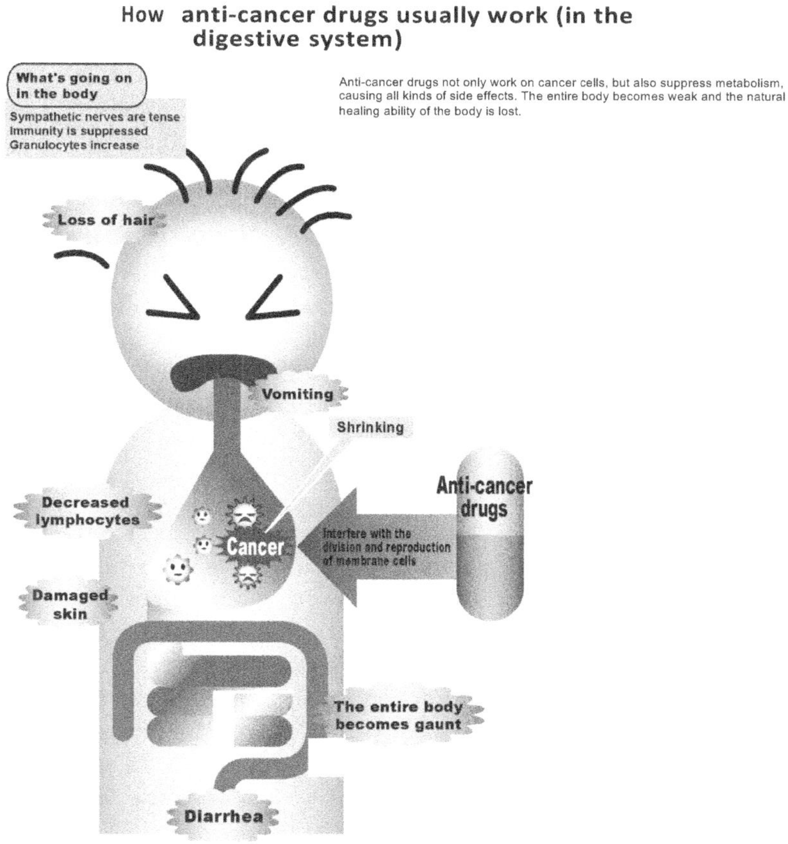

How Anti-Cancer Drugs Usually Work (In the Digestive System)

Anti-cancer drugs not only work on cancer cells, but also suppress metabolism, causing all kinds of side effects. The entire body becomes weak and the natural healing ability of the body is lost.

Iressa was approved by Japan's Ministry of Health, Labor, and Welfare before it was offered in any other country. Because the ministry had been criticized for taking too long to approve medical substances, it approved Iressa very quickly. As reported by the media, the ministry's problems seem similar to ones that some American pharmaceutical companies face—in this case, not reporting or only partially reporting adverse side effects prior to granting approval. The media also revealed that Iressa has been taken by patients for intestinal cancer, breast cancer, bladder cancer, and pancreatic cancer even though it's supposed to be solely for lung cancer patients who've been on other anti-cancer drugs, who can't have surgery, or who've had a recurrence of cancer. In some cases, doctors found themselves unable to reject their patients' urgent requests.

These problems, however, seem very superficial to me. What must be understood here is that shrinking cancer isn't the same as healing cancer. Iressa aims to shrink cancer, but that doesn't necessarily mean it's going to heal it. Along with preventing cancer cells from growing, it can also prevent healthy cells from replacing themselves to keep the rest of you healthy.

As I discussed previously, cancers are products of weakened immunity due to tension in the sympathetic nervous system, which causes an increase in granulocytes and excessive damage to tissue. Even if you're lucky enough to have your cancer removed without any side effects, if you don't improve the state of your sympathetic nervous system—which caused the cancer in the first place—there's a great possibility of recurrence.

Iressa is a new type of anti-cancer drug that works solely on the protein molecules that help cancer grow. It's been said that because Iressa focuses only on the protein molecules produced by cancer cells, it doesn't attack other tissues. In reality, however, Iressa has caused many, many side effects in just a short time. Of course, there are some patients whose cancers have shrunk with Iressa and have experienced almost no side effects. But I believe it's important to look at what these patients will experience over the next few years. In one case, a patient whose cancer was gone after taking Iressa died just a few weeks after happily leaving the hospital. I suspect that, for this type of disease to occur, their lymphocyte level must have dropped to below 10 percent. Patients who experienced good results with Iressa may have succeeded in shrinking their cancers, but I wonder if they've regained their normal healthy life. We can't ignore the fact that, in a large proportion of cases, patients died soon after leaving the hospital, relieved that their cancer had shrunk. We need to investigate this thoroughly.

I feel pity when I hear of these incidents involving Iressa.

Most people seem to believe that lung cancer is so malicious that it can never be healed. This impression probably stems from the fact that lungs are very difficult to operate on, because the tissue is made up of very small branches. Yet from an immunological perspective, lung cancer is in fact the easiest cancer to treat. Even taking a deep breath and stretching your chest can improve your condition. I encourage cancer patients, rather than giving up right away, to investigate immunotherapy that deals with improving one's way of life as a whole.

As I've discussed, recent problems with Iressa are indicative of issues with anti-cancer drugs in general. I hope this information will have an impact on the future medical treatment of cancer. It may encourage people to stay away from anti-cancer drugs completely.

TESTIMONIAL 3

66-Year-Old With Stomach Cancer, Given Three Months To Live, Extends His Life for Six High-Quality Months Through Immunotherapy (Written by His Wife)

"In the early summer of 2002, my husband began losing weight. I was concerned to see this, given that there had been no significant change in his life following retirement from the job he'd had for many years, and given that his lifestyle was relaxed. In the middle of June, I finally took him to a nearby hospital because he had lost several pounds in a month. The doctor suggested an examination right away, and my husband was given a test. The results came back a week later. He was suffering from stomach cancer.

"I nearly fainted. The doctor said that having surgery would be very difficult because of the amount of water in my husband's stomach, and he said that my husband had only three months to live. I couldn't believe what was happening. My husband had lived a healthy life until a few months ago. Even I knew that stomach cancer was a frightening type of cancer that's usually very malicious and quick to spread. I couldn't tell my husband about his problem, so without letting him know, I studied books and information about cancer so that I could help. The doctor recommended anti-cancer drugs since surgery wasn't an option, but I refused them. I knew that anti-cancer drugs are very damaging to the patient, and that there was little hope of recovery from stomach cancer anyway. The doctor didn't push it after that because he knew that my husband was only going to survive for a short while.

"I wanted to try anything we could. While reading a book about autoimmune therapy, I became convinced that there was a possibility he could recover, and I determined to try it. So, one month after my husband was diagnosed with stomach cancer, we visited the Tajima Clinic in Kyushu, which practices immunotherapy.

"My husband seemed to know that he had some serious problem, but until this point he hadn't been told that he had cancer. He first realized this fact as Dr. Keisuke Tajima explained his immunotherapy. Accepting the fact that he had cancer, he decided to try out the therapy.

"From then on we visited the clinic once a week for treatment, which quickly changed his body. Three days after the first visit, the skin of his torso, which had been as pale as cement, regained color and looked like normal skin. His urine also increased. At the same time, the coldness he had been feeling started to disappear, and was gone within two weeks.

"After a few weeks, he began going out, rather than staying home all the time because of fatigue. He went out for a walk to practice his hobby, pachinko. In spite of the initial prediction that he would die in three months, three months later he was still alive, leading a life close to that of normal people. He was even eating normal meals, rather than those of sick people. If he had used anti-cancer drugs, things would have had been different. I was willing to let him do what he wanted.

"In November, he didn't go out much to do pachinko because it was petting cold. Instead he spent more time at home watching TV. In order to help his immunity grow, I prepared three meals a day, choosing favorite foods that were easy to digest and good for the body. By the end of November, the water in his abdomen decreased and his urine increased, eliminating the swelling in his legs.

"However, his condition didn't improve any further. In the middle of December, when the cold was severe, he had to lie in bed all the time because his legs were so weak. Still, he didn't feel any pain, and was just relaxing at home watching TV. Since he couldn't visit the clinic anymore, the doctor came to visit him for immunotherapy once a week.

"The last time he was treated was December 26, and he passed away three days later, in the early morning of December 29. The night before, he was watching TV after an evening meal of rice porridge. He usually went to sleep before midnight, but that night he told me he couldn't fall asleep. He took some sleeping pills, which had been prescribed for an occasion like this, and fell asleep for a while. But he woke up around 2:00 a.m. and, out of the blue, told me to pay the hospital. I had a feeling that he was giving me his last request. Around 3:00 a.m. he was hungry, so I fed him with an anpan, his favorite pastry, but he couldn't eat. But he tried to lick it to taste it. Then around 3:30 a.m. he said, "Everything is complete now," which were his last words. Around 6:00 a.m. he passed away as if he was sleeping, without saying anything or struggling.

"Even though immunotherapy couldn't give him a full recovery, I'm very grateful for it. I understand that he couldn't attain full remission because his cancer was stronger than his life force, not because the therapy wasn't effective.

"When he was diagnosed with cancer, it was already too late. If he had gone through modern treatments such as anti-cancer drugs, he would have been in a hospital bed, leading the life of a sick person for the rest of his life. Instead, he was able to live three extra months and have a normal life at home, even after the death sentence. I'm sure he was very happy with that. Thanks to immunotherapy, he had his last moment without any regret, which his last words clearly show."

HISTORICAL BACKGROUND OF PROLIFERATION OF ANTI-CANCER DRUGS

People tend to use anti-cancer drugs without questioning them—a situation attributable to conditions in Japan when the drugs first became available. Anti-cancer drugs first became common just after the World Wars. Before, during, and after the war, the Japanese people were very poor and undernourished, and were forced to do hard physical labor. Their way of life caused tension in the sympathetic nervous system, accelerating the growth and aggravation of cancers. Stomach cancers, for example, became aggravated so quickly that patients died almost instantly after being diagnosed. This gave people the impression that cancers grow fast, and treatment developed that enabled patients to act quickly upon being diagnosed. It was believed that cancers needed to be beaten as soon as possible.

Compare this to the way we live today. We're freer from hard physical labor than in the past. We don't suffer from hunger. We don't have to be cold, thanks to modern heating systems. These factors make the parasympathetic nervous system more active. There should therefore be more lymphocytes in our systems, making it harder for cancers to grow. But because of our old belief that cancers grow fast, we eagerly use anti- cancer drugs. There are of course some fast-growing cancers, and we do need to use discernment in treating these. But I've rarely met anyone who had a total remission of cancer using drugs. It's time we reevaluated our tendency to use drugs blindly for all cancers.

ABOUT RADIATION THERAPY

Radiotherapy, like anti-cancer drugs, suppresses immunity. It's said that radiation is very accurate and able to attack cancer cells precisely. In cancers of the lung and esophagus, for example, radiation is applied directly to the site of the cancer. But even when limited areas are irradiated, immunity all over the body is suppressed. Many patients say they feel tired after radiation therapy. It's because their immunity is suppressed and their whole body is inactive.

In the case of lung or esophageal cancer, the bone marrow where blood is produced is not actually irradiated. Rather, a small portion of tissue located apart from the bone marrow is irradiated. But still, the whole body's immunity is suppressed. This mystery can be solved from the point of view of immunology. Just as surgery leaves wounds or a scar, radiation damages tissue, causing the inner substance of cells to flow out and creating tension in the sympathetic nervous system. When you irradiate tissue, you destroy not just cancer cells but the healthy cells that surround the cancer. This stimulation tenses the sympathetic nervous system and produces granulocytes. Moreover, damage to bone marrow cells and the immune system also restrain the production of lymphocytes. Radiation itself causes cancer. It is therefore not an ideal treatment method.

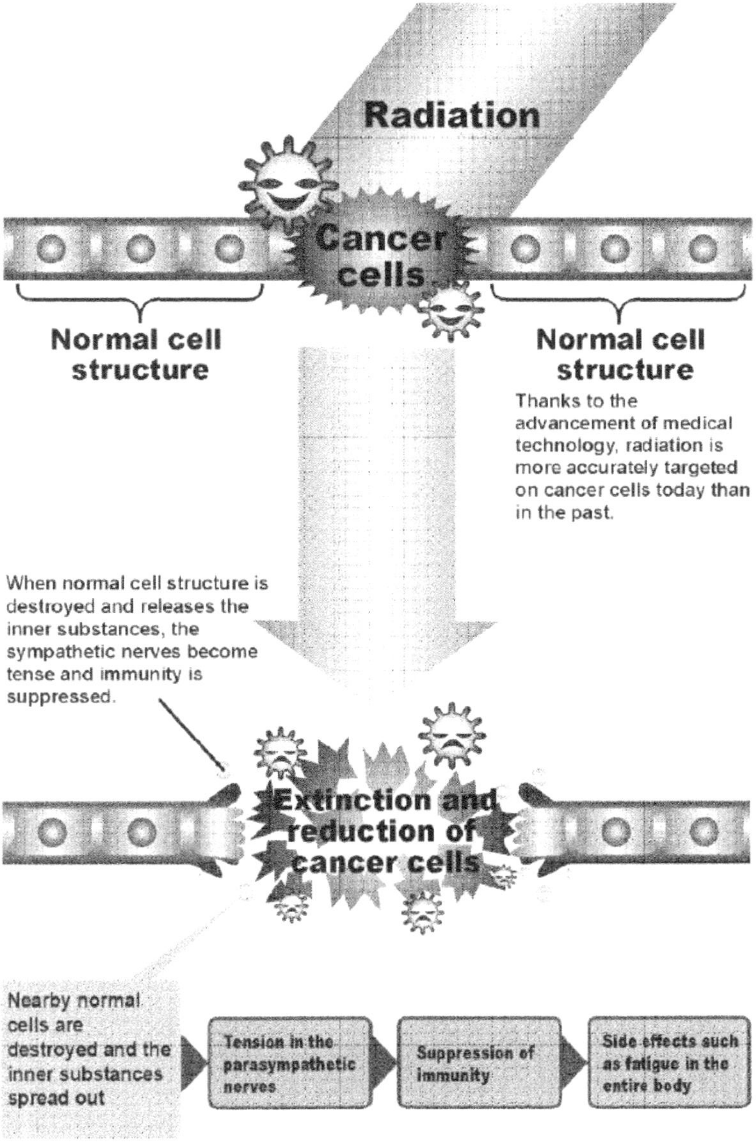

THE NATURAL REMISSION OF CANCER AFTER FEVER AND PAIN

If you follow the four rules, your cancer will stop growing. And when lymphocytes increase to a certain level, cancer cells will naturally recede. My colleagues and I have seen this healing phenomenon daily with our own eyes. During their treatment, about one third of our patients experience symptoms similar to those found in autoimmune diseases, such as fever or aching joints, which increase activity in the parasympathetic nervous system. After experiencing these symptoms, patients' cancers start to recede naturally. Why do these uncomfortable symptoms occur? The primary types of cells that attack cancer cells are NK cells, extrathymic T cells, cytotoxic T cells, and B cells. Fever, pain, and discomfort occur when these white blood cells attack cancer because of the body's inflammatory reaction. Diarrhea may also occur. If you have lung cancer, you may cough. If you have cancer of the large intestine, you may produce bloody stools. If you have bladder cancer, your urine may be bloody. These are signs of healing.

I'll explain this mechanism in more detail. The parasympathetic nervous system is linked to relaxation, but when it's activated too quickly it produces substances such as prostaglandin, acetylcholine, histamine, serotonin, and leukotrienes. These can cause fever and pain and produce uncomfortable symptoms. Patients and doctors who lack a good understanding of immunity may try to stop this process because they don't realize that these symptoms occur naturally as part of the healing process. Doctors may prescribe painkillers, anti-inflammatories, antipyretics, and especially steroids. These medications stop the pain and fever, so the patient seems better. But stopping these symptoms actually prevents the healing process from occurring and is therefore the total opposite of healing cancer fundamentally.

When the healing reaction that leads to cancer remission begins, symptoms can be so severe that patients may have to stay in bed for a week or so. But afterwards, the number of lymphocytes will begin to increase, and the cancer will begin to recede. I hope that cancer patients who are considering trying to heal through immunotherapy will remember this reaction. You have to be careful: if you don't understand how this process works, your concern might lead you to consult a doctor who will prescribe medicine that stops the healing process altogether.

This healing reaction was known in the past as the paraneoplastic syndrome, and it always occurs during a course of healing in cancer patients. But this fact has been forgotten, because these types of reaction haven't been seen since the spread of anti-cancer drugs after the World Wars. Because they're caused when the immune system puts up a fight, they won't occur if immunity is suppressed with anti-cancer drugs. The most commonly known paraneoplastic syndrome is malignant melanoma, which occurs when melanoma naturally recedes. It begins with fever and joint pain, followed by the appearance of albino-like spots, and finally the remission of malignant melanoma. This happens when autoreactive T cells or extrathymic T cells in conjunction with the autoimmune system attack malignant melanoma cancer cells and normal melanocytes at the same time. Malignant melanoma is well known because their location on the surface of skin makes them easy to spot.

Although this process has become less widespread, my colleagues and I have witnessed it when we administer treatments that activate immunity. Sometimes fever and pain are accompanied by neurological symptoms such as numbness. This is because cancer occurs in the epithelium, where there are many nerves. When cancers are attacked, the nerves are immediately stimulated, affecting peripheral nerves and causing numbness and pains. This is called a paraneoplastic neurological syndrome, and it's important to remember.

Young doctors today do not even seem to be aware of this healing reaction. They've never witnessed it because they only practice treatments that suppress the immune system, such as anti-cancer drugs and radiation. But after fifty years, this phenomenon has come back. So, if you have uncomfortable symptoms during immunotherapy treatment, consider them to be potential healing reactions and don't try to make them stop right away. Think of the symptoms as healing reactions and you can overcome them with patience, leading to the natural remission of cancer.

WHY FAR-INFARED ONNETSU THERAPY IS EFFECTIVE FOR CANCER

Far infrared therapy is closely related to the paraneoplastic syndrome. Its effectiveness is often attributed to the fact that cancer cells don't tolerate heat. While that's true, it's more important to understand that when you have fever, your lymphocytes are fighting. When you have a cold, for example, you have a fever because your lymphocytes are fighting the virus. So, it's not that cancer cells are intolerant of heat, but that in this heated state lymphocytes can be more active. I think that far infrared therapy could become popular in the future, so it's worth giving it a try.

Once you're aware that lymphocyte activities are supported by fever, you won't feel that you need to cool a fever down whenever it occurs. You may want to cool down because your body feels dull and heavy. But when you have a fever, healing reactions such as the paraneoplastic syndrome are activated. Far infrared therapy promotes the process of fever, lymphocyte activation, and healing.

Unfortunately, when cancer patients have a fever, modern treatments cool it down right away. Many patients are not able to have a fever at all because of anti-cancer drugs and other treatments. Considering this, I believe that far infrared therapy is not far off course.

TYPES OF TEMPERAMENTS THAT INCREASE YOUR SUSCEPTIBILITY TO CANCER

Observing the experiences of my fellow doctors has led me to believe that there are certain personalities and states of mind that make it easier for cancers to develop. Most of these patients work too hard, worry over small matters and strain themselves until their sympathetic nervous system is tense. Many people believe that cancer is caused by genetic or inherited factors. Of course, I believe that some genes may be connected to cancer. But someone's personality is not determined or controlled by a single gene or a few genes. It may be molded by a number of genes that become connected in complicated ways. I think it's very unusual for one specific gene to be related to cancer.

COMMON DRUGS THAT INCREASE CANCER RISK

I have discussed the fact that anti-inflammatories and painkillers cause tension in the sympathetic nervous system. Taking such medicines for a short period of time to manage temporary pain is not a problem, but when they're consumed for a long period of time they can decrease your immunity to cancer. For example, middle-aged people with knee or back pain are more likely to be prescribed painkillers, which they may take for years. This can cause cancer. Painkillers are also used in poultices, which suffocate blood circulation and create tension in the sympathetic nervous system. Symptoms that occur when taking painkillers, such as fast pulse and gauntness, are the result of tension in the sympathetic nervous system.

Anti-anxiety drugs and sleeping pills slowly tense the sympathetic nervous system. In some cases, these types of drugs need to be taken for long periods of time—but you should understand the possible danger. A tense sympathetic nervous system will cause you to lose weight and increase your risk of cancer.

METASTASIS IS A SIGN THAT CANCER IS HEALING

The four rules I discussed previously are worth practicing once cancer has spread to another part of the body. We should first correct our misconception that metastasis is a sign that cancer is worsening. When cancer moves, it's a sign of healing. So especially when cancer metastasizes, I'd like you to have hope and follow the four rules.

Thanks to the research of Dr. Minoru Fukuda, we have confirmed that cancer tends to move when the number of lymphocytes increases. The cancer spreads in order to survive when it's attacked by lymphocytes.

Our group has experienced many cases in which cancers naturally recede after spreading. Metastasis is not scary—it's a sign of healing.

When metastasis occurs, people feel desperate because of this old belief that metastasis is a sign of worsening cancer. That's when sympathicotonia occurs and aggravates the cancer. As a result, people waste this opportunity and cause their cancer to increase. When cancer spreads, check your lymphocyte count. If the number has increased, it means you're fighting the cancer with your body's healing power. It's also important to understand that when your immunity is boosted and you're fighting the cancer, tumor markers temporarily increase. If you know this, you won't get stressed out about the increase and decrease of the number of tumor markers. I'd like you to practice the four rules with hope and confidence.

CANCER IN THE ELDERLY SHOULD BE HEALED SLOWLY

It's commonly known that old people's cancers grow slowly, regardless of type. It's not unusual for their cancers to take the form of a chronic disease, and they often die of old age with the cancer, without needing to treat it. Why? Cancer cells are reproductive. Old people's cells reproduce very slowly in general, and their cancers reproduce more slowly accordingly. I will discuss this in more detail in chapter 5, but in short, old people's immunity is different than that of younger people. It's a type called "old immunity"—a state in which there are more lymphocytes watching for abnormal events in the body and making it harder for cancers to grow. So, if you're diagnosed with cancer when you're old, don't undergo treatments that harm your body. Instead, enhance your parasympathetic nervous system and blood circulation by taking a bath or going for a walk, which will cause your aging lymphocytes to be more active, prevent cancer from growing, and in some lucky cases heal cancer. It's dangerous to put yourself into a situation that weakens your immunity and deprives you of physical strength. Therefore, I can't recommend the use of anti-cancer drugs or surgery, which severely damage the body. When you have cancer in your seventies, eighties, or nineties, you should avoid these exhausting treatments and enjoy a lifestyle that causes cancer to recede gradually.

THE PARADOX OF CANCER SCREENING

Cancer screening is not a bad way to find cancers at an early stage. But we must also consider the disadvantage of taking these tests, given that most of us fear this disease so much. Cancer screening can cause unnecessary fear. It's usually done to determine whether further examination is necessary, so even something. small may be considered suspicious. In other words, anything can be unnecessarily taken seriously. Screenings usually detect ten to twenty times more cancers than actually exist, causing people to undergo more testing to sort out the actual cancers. Only one out of twenty or forty people with suspicious test results actually has cancer.

It's more likely that, if they find something suspicious on your test, you'll undergo a lot of stress even though you don't actually have cancer. You might feel depressed if you're told that there's a possibility you have cancer and you need further examination. I know this from my own experience. The shock I felt was tremendous. I was so disturbed; I couldn't eat at all. On top of this, three or four weeks can go by between the result of the screening and the follow-up examination. During that period, all you can do is worry about your future and your family's future. This is tremendously stressful. It's serious enough to cause sympathicotonia, which itself can cause cancer. And in the end, most of those who are screened don't have cancer, so they go through this risk unnecessarily.

In fact, we could estimate that more people who undergo cancer screenings develop cancer due to stress. If cancer screenings are beneficial in detecting and reducing cancer, areas that practice these screenings should have a lower rate of cancer patients. But this isn't the case. Many reports indicate that groups doing cancer screenings have more cancer patients than other groups that are not doing screenings, though these results haven't been published.

When you think about it, cancer screenings contradict the second rule—that we shouldn't fear cancer. Today, many people fear the image and idea of cancer. So, cancer screenings that keep people in a state of worry could be a risk factor in causing cancer. Of course, if the thought of having cancer doesn't scare you, you won't have a problem with being screened. But not many of us are like this.

EARLY DISCOVERY AND TREATMENT FOCUSING ON LYMPHOCYTES

Cancer screenings are contradictory because they cause unnecessary stress to people who don't need to go through it. But, in fact, it is better to discover and treat cancer as soon as possible. When cancers grow, the number of granulocytes and lymphocytes decrease, and the treatment will be difficult and long. If you're suspicious about something, it's probably better to be examined for it.

If you're diagnosed with cancer, keep an eye on your lymphocyte count. In the early stages of cancer, lymphocytes don't decrease much, but they start decreasing drastically as cancer develops. We can gauge the likelihood of healing by watching the increase and decrease of lymphocytes, so it's an important factor to understand.

Doctors who utilize radiation treatment and anti-cancer drugs usually don't pay much attention to lymphocytes. They may be afraid to see their patient's immunity dropping drastically. I suspect they'd feel guilty if they saw how their treatments are suppressing their patients' immunity.

Most patients who come to us after having gone through treatments with anti-cancer drugs are not aware of how much the treatments damaged their lymphocytes. If I ask them if they've received data on their lymphocytes from their doctors, they usually haven't. We need to improve this. When you're dealing with cancer, you should keep tabs on your lymphocyte count.

ADOPTIVE LYMPHOCYTE THERAPY FOR INTELLECTUALS

Adoptive lymphocyte therapy is a treatment used to increase cancer- fighting lymphocytes. You can't use other people's lymphocytes, because your body would reject them, so your own lymphocytes are grown in a test tube and reintroduced into your body. This method seems to work well if the anti-cancer drugs and radiation that damage lymphocytes have been suspended. However, when it's practiced in a hospital along with anti-cancer drugs, it's not as effective. This is because lymphocytes grown in a test tube are so weak that they can be easily damaged by anti-cancer drugs. So, your immunity will be better and stronger if you activate lymphocytes in your body, rather than growing them in a test tube.

Because the idea of growing your lymphocytes in a test tube and reintroducing them into your body seems quite logical, intellectual patients seem to do better with this method. But what affects the results more than anything else is the hope that you experience during the two weeks while you wait for the lymphocytes to grow. This positive feeling may actually activate immunity.

CHANGING YOUR CANCER-CAUSING LIFESTYLE

When I interview my colleagues' patients, I discover that most of them have had a lifestyle that interferes with their bloodstream. One patient had headaches from working late every night, for which he regularly took medication. He continued this for about twenty years, until he discovered that he had a brain tumor. Many lung or breast cancer patients have had a lot to worry about in their chest. A high-level businessman who constantly eats gourmet food without exercising will have more fat around the belly and end up with prostate or bladder cancer. Some ovarian or uterine cancer patients report that they have been regularly taking painkillers for stomachache.

Metaphors sometimes make a lot of sense. When someone stores sad feelings in their chest, the blood circulation in that area becomes blocked. As a result, blood rushes into the area to manage the blockage, causing pain. If you constantly take painkillers to deal with the pain, you fall into a cycle of cancer. Moreover, when people are worried, they tend to droop, and their breath becomes shallow. Drooping puts pressure on the thorax and creates bad blood circulation, and shallow breathing causes bad blood circulation around the lungs. Damage begins in an area of weakness. This causes granulocytes to overproduce, eventually leading to cancer.

But there's something you can do to prevent this process, even if it's already begun. You can enhance blood circulation in the blocked areas. If you have lung cancer, breathe deeply with your chest stretched out. This helps you take in a lot of oxygen and forces blood to circulate. If you have a brain tumor, exercise your neck. Even though you can't really exercise your head, moving your neck automatically increases blood circulation in your brain and your whole head. I also recommend exercising your mouth. If you discover cancer, exercise to force more blood circulation in the area.

TOO MANY LYMPHOCYTES CAN ALSO CAUSE CANCER

I've primarily discussed the mechanism of cancer caused by overly active granulocytes. About 70 percent of cancer patients fall into the category of having too many granulocytes and too few lymphocytes. But 20 to 30 percent of patients' cancers are due to too many lymphocytes. Why? When you have too many lymphocytes, the parasympathetic nervous system is dominant. It's like being overweight due to lack of exercise. Acetylcholine or prostaglandin, which are used by the parasympathetic nervous system to become active, widen blood vessels. Therefore, when you're too relaxed and the blood vessels open too wide, the resulting blood circulation problems can cause cancer. In some cases, blood doesn't circulate well because the vessels are too wide. These cases tend to be accompanied by swelling.

Based on my colleagues' experiences, cancer patients with excessive lymphocytes can heal easily. Since they have so many lymphocytes to begin with, they have the ability to fight cancer and heal quickly if they reduce the number of lymphocytes to a normal level through acupuncture or herbal medicine. Even in these cases, however, patients need to change their lifestyle. If your life is too laid back, you can develop cancer. You need to have a more active lifestyle to keep cancer from coming back.

THE EFFECT OF ONE MIRACULOUS CANCER DRUG THAT HAS DISAPPEARED

Advertisements and articles about alternative medicines for cancer appear in the newspaper every day. I suspect that this is because more and more people are becoming dissatisfied with the results of Western medicine. I believe that patients' positive attitudes and trust in alternative medicines are helping them recover their immunity. Most alternative medicines that are currently receiving attention activate immunity—that's what makes them effective. It's been said for a long time that radium hot springs are helpful. I think this is because cells are destroyed by very small amounts of radiation, which stimulates and enhances metabolism and leads to healing. Considering this, I think radiation treatment can produce results if used in a small amount, just enough to activate immunity.

In fact, several drugs came out about twenty years ago that are totally different from anti-cancer drugs—a type of medicine grouped as biological response modifiers. BCG vaccine or Maruyama vaccine can be categorized this way. Renchinan and OK432 were also approved for treatment of cancer. The medication OK432 is made up of streptococcal bacteria, which produce erysipelas, and Renchinan is an ingredient from reishi. All of these substances have a history of shrinking cancer, but most of them disappeared from the medical field because they weren't effective. But I think the problem was that they were being used on patients together with anti-cancer drugs. That's why they didn't produce positive data. If they had been used separate from anti-cancer drugs, the results could have been successful. These medicines were so popular that they earned about five to ten billion yen a year, but they've since disappeared, which is a pity.

Recently, agaricus, meshima seaweed, monkey-feet mushroom, and propolis have become common. Patients who've been healed by these substances may have given up on their anti-cancer drugs because their cancer was too far along, or the drugs were too much for their body. Agaricus, and monkey-feet mushroom are mushrooms, so too large a dose can cause diarrhea. (Since they're not easy to digest, they stimulate the digestive system and cause peristaltic movements, which in excess can cause diarrhea.) Diarrhea is a sign of extreme functioning in the digestive system and means that the number of lymphocytes has increased tremendously.

It appears that if you take it upon yourself to practice alternative medicine, believing that it's going to heal you, it can enhance your immunity. As long as you don't use it together with anti-cancer drugs, you may have good results.

SOME WARNINGS CONCERNING CANCER TREATMENTS

At this point, I'd like to introduce some stories from my colleagues who instruct their patients to follow the four rules. We often discuss these cases during our study group with Dr. Minoru Fukuda; Dr. Nobuaki Kawada; Dr. Keisuke Tajima from Nagasaki, who just recently joined us; and Dr. Akihiko Ikeda from Uji, Kyoto. We all practice autonomic nerve immunotherapy to stimulate the parasympathetic nervous system.

First and most important is your willingness to work with the four rules. If you're too dependent on doctors, you won't experience the full effect.

Second, it's important not to be examined for cancer too frequently. It takes at least one to two months for your immunocompetence to increase enough to produce healing. It takes even longer for cancer to begin to recede. So, you won't see a satisfactory result if you're examined during the first three or four months. In the beginning, you should simply focus on the treatment.

You need to be especially careful in your judgment, because tumor markers have a unique way of moving. In fact, an increase in a tumor marker is not necessarily a sign that cancer is growing. When you follow the four rules and increase your immunity, cancer begins to be destroyed, and as a result the tumor marker level goes up. If you follow the four rules sincerely, you don't need to worry about tumor markers.

Neither should you worry about x-rays, CT scans, or MRIs. When your immunity improves, the center of the cancer will probably begin to die, even if the cancer appears bigger. You don't need to worry about metastases either. Sometimes cancers vanish after they move. We've experienced this many times.

More important than test results are whether or not your subjective symptoms have improved. Important signs of healing are that you're able to eat, that your body isn't cold anymore, that there's color in your face, that you don't get tired so easily, that you don't have constipation anymore, and so forth. If you've stopped taking anti-cancer drugs or radiation treatment, it's especially important that you try to feel these subjective symptoms on your own. Even if you don't see an improvement in test results, your outcome will be good as long as your subjective symptoms continue to improve.

Chapter 3
Healing Dermatitis Without Medication

The most common allergies among children are atopic dermatitis and bronchial asthma. Both have become serious problems in the past twenty years or so. According to the National Seiiku Medical Center Research Institute, 90 percent of young people born in the 1970s are likely to be allergic to ticks and cedar pollen. Only 40 to 50 percent of those born in the 1950s and 60s have those allergies, so it's obvious that the number of allergic individuals is increasing.

According to the Japanese Ministry of Health, Labor, and Welfare, there were 399,000 atopic dermatitis patients in 1999. Of those suffering from allergies, 15 to 20 percent were infants, 6 to 10 percent were schoolchildren, and 2 to 4 percent were youth. Moreover, an increasing number of patients have allergic symptoms serious enough to hinder their normal lives.

Despite this explosion of allergy patients, the fundamental nature of allergies is said to remain unknown. How and why allergies occur remains unclear, nor do we really know how to deal with them. This seems strange, considering how advanced modern medicine has become.

One possible explanation is that allergic diseases, including atopic dermatitis, are caused by an overly active parasympathetic nervous system. I will discuss this further in chapter 5, but recall my basic theory of immunology, in which a dominant sympathetic nervous system leads to an increase in granulocytes, while a dominant parasympathetic nervous system leads to an increase in lymphocytes. While my observations in the previous chapter show that cancer is caused by an extremely suppressed immune system, atopic dermatitis seems to be caused by the opposite situation—extreme overactivity and overabundance in the immune system. In the case of atopic dermatitis, granulocytes decrease, and lymphocytes increase. In other words, atopic dermatitis has been observed against the background of a continuously overactive parasympathetic nervous system.

Considering the recent drastic increase in allergy patients, there must be important factors besides genetic ones affecting children. I believe that the way children live today causes the parasympathetic nervous system to be dominant, resulting in excessive lymphocyte production. Today, with greater household affluence and a resulting abundance and improved living conditions, children are well taken care of. When the Japanese were a poor society, children were usually actively involved in the important physical work of doing chores and helping on the farm. Today, children are rarely required to do physical labor; indeed, child labor laws actually prohibit children from doing "labor"—at least for pay. Moreover, with this greater affluence parents are better able to take good care of their children. They're also increasingly protective, because with the increase in economic wealth there's been a corresponding decrease in the number of children per family. Children are much more protected than in the past, beginning in infancy. When babies cry, their sympathetic nervous systems become tense. In the past, parents didn't rush to comfort their babies when they cried. Modern parents, on the other hand, seem driven to comfort their babies as soon as crying starts. When babies are picked up and held, they become comforted; when comforted, they become relaxed. Because babies are held and comforted more, they're more relaxed and have less opportunity to cry. So, the parasympathetic nervous system is programmed to be more dominant from infancy.

Diet too has become much richer in the past several decades due to a better economy. This increased nutritional abundance also causes the parasympathetic nervous system to dominate. On top of this, children in urban areas don't (or aren't allowed to) play outside, and so don't have sufficient opportunities for outdoor physical activity to activate the sympathetic nervous system and balance this relaxation. In the past, children worked in the field, did physical chores around the house, or played outside until dusk, but this is no longer the case. Today, because children stay home reading comics or playing videogames, they're not aided by changes of activity and changes in their level of stress and tension, which strengthen both the sympathetic and parasympathetic nervous systems. Playing outside also gives children the benefits of exposure to sunlight. Ultraviolet rays help activate the sympathetic nervous system. Indeed, our bodies require ultraviolet rays for optimal health. When you play outdoors and receive the sun's ultraviolet rays, your body gets tired. You sleep well at night because you've received energy from the sun, and you've spent your energies in ways that have strengthened you. This kind 3f beneficial tension is not present in the lifestyle of today's children.

Oddly, drinking too much of any kind of carbonated beverage also causes the parasympathetic nervous system to be more dominant. Carbon dioxide (CO2), such as in car exhaust, relaxes our body. So, do carbonated drinks, because of their CO2 content. If the only oxygen available is from carbon dioxide, we'll die. For example, if you work in a crowded room that has no ventilation, you'll soon feel sleepy, because as the oxygen level goes down due to people's breathing, the level of carbon dioxide goes up. The same thing happens when you use a fireplace in a room with no ventilation. And when we want to relax, one of our first responses is to each for a carbonated drink such as soda or beer.

When carbon dioxide is absorbed by our body and dissolves into our body fluid, it combines with the available oxygen and becomes carbonic acid. I'll explain this in more detail in chapter 5, but in summary, when you consume oxygen, your body becomes more active—a process that is call "oxygen stress." Conversely, when oxygen is removed from your body, you feel relaxed. If you live in a place where there's a lot of carbon dioxide, oxygen is regularly removed from your body, and you feel more relaxed. This happens because the parasympathetic nervous system becomes dominant. Our big cities contain a ridiculously large number of cars. If you live in an environment such as this, your parasympathetic nervous system will naturally become more dominant because of the higher ratio of carbon dioxide compared to that in suburban and rural areas.

In conclusion, I believe that these multiple factors affect our children's parasympathetic nervous systems, resulting in widespread allergy problems. Again, the fundamental cause is our living environment. In a case such as this, one suddenly realizes the need to find a healing approach different from the allopathic treatments used for treating cancer. Too frequently, the misapplication of allopathic treatments produces negative results.

Allergic symptoms are created when the body attempts to

eliminate antigens, or foreign objects. Atopic dermatitis, for example, is a reaction that creates greater blood circulation in an area in order to dilute the concentration of antigens that have entered or accumulated there. Bronchial asthma is a reaction that rapidly closes the trachea and causes strong exhalations in an attempt to keep antigens from entering. In other words, both symptoms—swelling and breathing difficulties—are uncomfortable, but when we look at them from a wider perspective, we see that they're the body's natural healing responses to invasion by antigens. If you suppress these natural reactions allopathically, the fundamental problem won't be solved. Allopathy won't lead to true healing.

So, what will lead to true healing? First and most important is to correct the excessive dominance of the parasympathetic nervous system. In other words, we must change our children's lifestyle into one that activates the sympathetic nervous system.

To begin with, nursery schools, kindergartens, and elementary schools should all provide more opportunities for children to be physically active outdoors. Children should play in the schoolyard or fields, using their bodies and absorbing ultraviolet rays. Of course, they don't need to be so tanned that they win the world sun-tanning contest! It's important, especially in the southern hemisphere, to be careful with ultraviolet rays so that children don't later develop skin cancer. But it's also important to allow a moderate amount of ultraviolet light to stimulate the sympathetic nervous system.

In fact, children with excessive lymphocytes tend to be pale. When you're pale, you're likely to be sensitive to stimulation. Children who are so sensitive that they swell up from just one bug bite are usually very pale. Tanned children don't experience such an intense effect from bug bites. Skin pallor and lymphocyte count seem to be closely related. When children are somewhat tan, they tend to have more granulocytes. This is because active oxygen in the granulocytes causes additional pigmentation of the skin. When you exercise and have a lifestyle in which you absorb ultraviolet rays, granulocytes increase, thus preventing lymphocytes from being produced in excess. That's how you become physically stronger, so that you don't overreact to certain stimuli.

In human infants, we notice a drastic increase in granulocytes during the four to five days following birth. This is due to the initial lung stress caused by the process of learning to breathe oxygen. In general, children live in a physical state that supports a higher level of active lymphocytes as they develop their ability to handle the stress and tension of life, at least until they're about four years old. During these years, they receive the largest amount of parental attention and comforting as they interact with their environment. You may think this would cause children to become too relaxed, but the physical stress created by growing so fast between the ages of one and four tends to balance things out. The ratio of lymphocytes and granulocytes is very close to being perfectly balanced between ages four and fifteen. When lymphocytes are 50 percent or greater, they're considered predominant. Between the ages of fifteen and twenty, this situation generally reverses, and granulocytes stabilize at about 60 percent, with lymphocytes settling at about 35 percent—a typical healthy ratio for adults. So, having more lymphocytes until the age of fifteen or so is not necessarily a bad thing, depending on the lifestyle factors that produce those levels. If children have too many lymphocytes because of overprotective parents, lack of physical activity, excessive consumption of carbonated beverages, eating too much of the wrong kinds of foods, being overweight, and so forth, these factors, along with a variety of emotional stresses, can cause allergies.

TESTIMONIAL 4

Five-Year-Old Overcomes Atopic Dermatitis With Alternative Treatment

"My daughter developed atopic dermatitis (eczema) when she was only three months old. It began when the skin around her mouth started to fester. I consulted a pediatrician and was told that this was a typical eczema common in babies. But the symptoms became more serious and, when she was about five months old, clear fluids came from the area when she scratched. I took her to a polyclinic, where she was diagnosed with atopic dermatitis and prescribed a steroid ointment to apply morning and night. This managed the inflammation right away.

"But I began to be very afraid of the steroids after an incident that happened when I took my daughter with me to a department store one day. It was so warm inside that I was perspiring, and my daughter was blushing pink as well. But the skin around her mouth was totally pale. That's exactly where I applied the steroid ointment every day. She looked like a wax doll that had no blood. Since then, I've resisted using the steroids and have avoided them as much as possible. I found a non- steroid cream to use, and when my daughter turned two I began giving her herbal medicines. I only applied the steroids when her condition was really bad.

"When my daughter turned four and started swimming in the pool at her kindergarten, her symptoms became more serious. They spread throughout her body and didn't improve at all, even when she stopped swimming and began using the steroid ointment again. She was so itchy that she couldn't sleep at night, and she was very tired during the day as a result. She totally lost her childlike characteristics.

"One day, I learned about Dr. Minoru Fukuda's treatment method in an article in a health magazine. The fact that he didn't use any medication appealed to me. I visited him with my daughter, wondering if a four-year-old could receive acupuncture treatments.

"Dr. Fukuda applied needles to her toes, fingers, and head and, massaging her feet, said, 'It must be hard having such cold feet. They'll be warm soon.' Her blood was not circulating well because of the side effects of the steroids. At the first treatment, she cried because of her fear of needles and pain, but she quickly learned that it took away the itching, and she became more willing to be treated. We continued to visit the clinic twice a week.

"During the first two weeks of the treatment, she experienced some painful reactions from steroid elimination. Her whole body swelled up and festered, and yellow fluid came out through her skin. Once the fluid stopped coming out, all the skin on her body began to come off. I couldn't help feeling sorry for her.

"But once this healing response was over, my daughter retained her childlike ways. First, her appetite increased. Then she suddenly began wanting to play with her friends again. As she continued the treatment, her physical strength and immunity improved, and she stopped petting sick. She used to suffer repeated bouts of pneumonia and bronchitis, but this year she lasted the whole winter without catching even one cold. According to Dr. Fukuda, at the time she began her treatments her lymphocyte count was very low for a child her ape, but the number increased with the treatments, which in turn increased her own natural immunity.

"Her atopic dermatitis is still not completely healed. She sometimes has an attack of itches in the middle of the night. But it's not as bad as it used to be, and yellow fluid no longer comes out through her skin, although if she scratches, a tiny amount of blood may come out. And her body is no longer cold. Her feet and hands used to be so cold for someone her ape, and she had trouble falling asleep. She doesn't have this problem anymore.

"She may have problems again in the future, but we'll never use steroids again. She's retained her childhood. I'll never let go of the happiness that we pot from alternative treatment."

HARMFUL MODERN SUBSTANCES CAUSE ALLERGIES

Allergic reactions generally occur as a side effect when we fight harmful substances that enter our body. So, an infant's atopic dermatitis may be caused by the elimination of chlorine, food chemicals, and minute particles of gas exhaust. For example, bath water can cause serious problems if it contains too much chlorine. Strong chlorine added to swimming pools in order to kill germs can cause serious allergies as well, as can agricultural chemicals clinging to vegetables and fruits.

On top of this, carbon dioxide deprives us of oxygen and activates the parasympathetic nervous system, which causes a relaxation response. Other substances deprive us of oxygen as well. Metals combine with oxygen—iron, for example, which creates the process of rusting. So, any metal can cause some kind of allergy. Aluminum poisoning, lead poisoning, and mercury poisoning are all examples of allergic symptoms.

One of the most common ways that metal touches the human body directly is through fillings in teeth. The amalgam used in fillings often contains up to 50 percent mercury, which slowly dissolves, leaching into the blood, nerve, and cellular systems and quite often causing an allergic reaction in someone who already has an excess lymphocytes. That's why modern dentists increasingly try to avoid the usage of amalgam. Dentists also use various kinds of metallic substances for crowns, which, depending on the substance, can also cause allergic reactions. Fortunately, many dentists today are aware of the problem of metal-reactive allergies. You should consult your dentist to make sure that you don't have an allergic reaction to your fillings. If you do have a reaction, you should change dental materials immediately.

THE PROBLEM OF "SICK BUILDING" SYNDROME

The way children live today activates the parasympathetic nervous system and causes allergies. But other stimuli cause an even greater number of allergy problems. Our modern living environment provides a rich environment for allergies. Modern houses are usually very airtight, meaning that they don't ventilate, or "breathe," causing carbon dioxide to accumulate. Common allergens, dusts, and molds can easily build up as a result. In addition, wall-to-wall carpeting produces and stores more dust than traditional tatami mats do. Because of this airtight architecture, toxic substances in building materials and furnishings increase and become more pervasive. This causes what's become known as "sick building" syndrome. Substances such as organic solvents from cleaning products and fumes from burning candles accumulate and remain in our rooms, increasing the number of potentially harmful allergens—and the resulting allergic responses—especially if ventilation is poor. Organic solvents used to bond building materials are volatile, containing gas-like chemicals that continuously "out-gas" into the environment, filling the air. Because these solvents are organic, they have what's chemically described as a "benzene ring." In other words, when these chemicals are inhaled, they deprive the body of its internal oxygen. When the body wisely tries to get rid of these chemical particulates, they come out as allergic reactions while the body struggles to adapt. Therefore, when you build a house, you should try to avoid using these toxic substances. When organic solvents were first introduced, we were happy to smell the fragrance of a new house—but today we can't be so naive.

ALLOPATHY CAUSES PERSISTENT ATOPIC

DERMATITIS

People today are prone to allergic reactions because of complicated factors such as lifestyle as well as antigens and toxins in the environment, which encourage lymphocytes to be predominant. You can't get better through allopathic treatments if you don't also correct these fundamental and environmental problems. Allergic reactions are the result of the body's necessary process of eliminating harmful substances. Allopathic medicines chemically prevent these wise and natural reactions and responses. When the medicine runs out, the toxins that have built up can explode and severely worsen the symptoms. If these symptoms become severe as to be unbearable, patients can fall into the trap of applying allopathic treatments to stop them over and over again. We need to stop this. It's quite important to understand the fundamental cause.

I'm not saying that allopathic treatments are always bad. But I think you need to understand that there's a danger in being committed to allopathy alone. If your current course of treatment isn't working, you need to rethink what you're doing and look into the possibility of changing direction. Allopathy is not likely to cause addiction if used for just a short period of time, but neither will it heal the disease if used for years. You should keep this in mind.

Many mothers are distressed when their children have atopic dermatitis. While this is understandable, it's not always necessary. Having atopic dermatitis means you have excessive lymphocytes. If you have lots of lymphocytes, you tend to live longer. It's long been known that people who are often sick as children tend to live longer. So, if your children have atopic dermatitis due to excessive lymphocytes, you can look forward to their longevity. If they exercise and correct their excess lymphocytes, their predisposition will no longer be a curse. This very struggle tends to strengthen the body's ability to deal with the stress of living and may contribute to a longer life.

STEROIDS DON'T HEAL ATOPIC DERMATITIS

Various allopathic treatments are used today for atopic dermatitis, including antihistamines, antiserotonins, antileukotrienes, anti-inflammatories, steroid hormones, and so forth. But being allopathic, these don't solve the fundamental problem of atopic dermatitis. Steroids, for example, remain as oxidized fat stored in your tissue. Since steroids are dioxides, meaning they contain two active oxygen components, they bind with granulocytes and cause inflammation. Steroids can be used for short periods of time, but if used for longer periods such as six months or a year, the inflammation caused by these dioxide substances can become a chronic problem. Should you need to increase the amount of steroids to stop inflammation, you wind up trapped in a bad cycle. So, if steroids don't improve the problem after a few months, you need to stop using them.

Unfortunately, people tend to use allopathic treatment to manage problems temporarily because changing their lifestyle patterns and habits is difficult and challenging and takes a lot of time. That's why it's very important that patients are smart enough to know if their allopathic treatment is really helping them heal or just temporarily suppressing symptoms.

If you don't know this, you can't protect yourself. Patients of atopic dermatitis are becoming younger and younger. Many infants suffer chronic atopic dermatitis because of chlorine in the water. As they attempt to eliminate the chlorine that clings to their body, they become red and swollen. Once you know this, you'll realize that you need to rinse your baby's body with chlorine-free water, at least at the end of their bath. If you do this every time, their symptoms will calm down.

But instead, medicine is used to manage the redness and swelling, and parents and caretakers continue to unknowingly wash their babies in chlorinated water. This doesn't take care of the problem. Patients need to question why and try to understand the true cause of the problem. Otherwise they won't change their environment or the inappropriate treatments. There's no point blaming the doctors, whose schools and courses of study have taught them to rely on allopathy. You must take matters into your own hands and learn what kind of treatments are offered, what's available, and personally pay attention to what your body is saying and notice what results you're having. In some cases, patients have been so unthinkingly dependent on their doctor's wisdom for five or ten years that their problems have become incurable.

TESTIMONIAL 5

Recovery fom Persistent Atopic Dermatitis

and Steroid Addiction (Male, 25 Years Old)

"I was diagnosed with atopic dermatitis in the second grade. My entire body itched, so my mother took me to a hospital where I was given an ointment. In the beginning, this medicine worked so well that the itching disappeared instantly, and my skin became smooth. The doctor told me that I should apply the ointment only when the itching was persistent. But the itching pot so bad that I couldn't study or sleep. By the time I entered middle school, I was applying the medicine a few times a week.

"When I was in high school, the atopic dermatitis, which had previously been only below my neck, started to spread all over my face, and the itching was unbearable. If I didn't use the medicine, the itching would turn into pain, and if I scratched, clear fluid would come out—and it only pot worse. But if I used the medicine, I didn't have this problem, so I kept putting the medicine on every day.

"I had no idea that I was using steroids. I knew that steroids caused side effects, but my doctor didn't tell me that the ointment I was using contained steroids, so I kept using it regularly. When I moved away to college, I used it every day, and always got more medicine when I came home during breaks.

"In the summer of 1995, I prepared to go to college in the United States. I left with half a year's worth of medicine, enough to last until my return at Christmas break. But I ran out of medicine in November, and the suppressed symptoms exploded. My skin got dry and cracked open, and pus-like fluid came out. The itching and pain were indescribable. My face was especially bad. It was so swollen that I couldn't move my eyelids or lips. After a few days, I was hardly able to breathe, so I pretty much stayed in bed except for going to classes. I thought I should do something, so I went to the school nurse.

"I didn't know it back then, but I later found out that this torturous pain and itching were a rebound reaction that happens when steroids run out. The American doctor wanted to prescribe a steroid, but I refused, not knowing that the medication I was using was itself a steroid. So, I was instead prescribed a non-steroid medication.

"My rebound experience was worse than you can imagine. The non-steroid medication didn't work at all, so I took an internal steroid for just three days. My skin recovered and the itching went away like magic. I thought it was almost scary that this medicine worked so well. "Then I received a package of my usual medicine from Japan. I was excited to get this 'non-steroid' ointment, and I put it on my skin, but it didn't work as well as before. I was very worried. I questioned whether my predisposition had changed after taking the internal steroid medication, or whether this ointment was in fact steroid as well. With these questions I returned to Japan for Christmas break.

"When I went back to my family doctor, I asked him what the ingredients of the medication were, and he told me they were steroids. I was surprised and wished I could stop taking it, but I needed to keep using it to stop the itching so I could concentrate on my studies. My skin was healthy as long as I applied the ointment. But I always looked tanned, even though I wasn't.

"My mother was shocked that I was experiencing such a strong rebound reaction to the steroids. When she read an article in the newspaper about Dr. Minoru Fukuda's treatment for atopic dermatitis, she immediately took me to his clinic.

"Dr. Fukuda scolded me for having used steroids, but at the same time I felt his compassion to help me heal. He began by putting needles on the sides of my fingernails, toenails, crown, pharynx, and forehead. Usually, this treatment would make people bleed, but I didn't bleed. He said that meant that my body was not doing too well. I wasn't really sure that such a simple treatment could heal my problem. To my surprise, however, I had no itching or rebound even without using steroids during the two weeks I received this treatment.

"A little while after my return to the United States, the itching started again. Dr. Fukuda had given me an ointment with an active carbon, telling me I should never use steroids again. I did use a little steroid when things were very bad. But I didn't have to increase the amount of steroid as long as I used the ointment with active carbon.

"As soon as I got back to Japan in May for summer break, I went to see Dr. Fukuda. When he checked my lymphocyte level, which was as low as 6 percent, he found out that I was using steroids. He forcefully explained that if I kept using steroids there would be no turning back, and that I should stop immediately. I understood that my body was indeed in a dangerous situation.

"A few days later, the rebound began. The skin of my entire

body was swollen, dry, and cracked, and a liquid came out that smelled really terrible. I was extremely itchy and painful, and I couldn't even open my eyes. I was so exhausted that I had to stay in bed every day, but the fluid coming out from my skin ran through my underwear and pajamas and seeped into my bed, leaving a bad stench. Dr. Fukuda told me that the steroids that had built up in my body were being eliminated and that I would feel better when they were gone completely. I visited the clinic every day. The swelling went away, and I could open my eyes for a few hours after he put in some needles.

"After two weeks of this very bad rebound, I could finally get out of bed. I started to go out for a walk for twenty or thirty minutes a day.

"After four weeks, I had to go back to the States. Dr. Fukuda told me that I should never use steroids again. There was much compassion in his words, and I felt that he really wanted me to recover from steroids. My skin was better, and I could open my eyes and mouth, but I wasn't completely healed yet. I applied a little bit of steroid ointment to avoid panicking while on the airplane, but that was the last time I ever used steroids.

"In the States, I had to recover from steroids all alone. Dr. Fukuda advised me to exercise, and I went for walks between classes. I began little by little, because my skin was as stiff as a wooden board and my body couldn't move freely. It helped to warm up my body and perspire, which moistened my skin for a few hours. Dr. Fukuda told me that when you exercise, your blood circulation is more active, which helps you eliminate steroids and increases lymphocytes. I trusted his advice, so I kept walking a few hours every day. I increased my speed a little bit each day.

"I also drank a lot of water to support steroid elimination—about six to eight liters of bottled water a day. I was careful about my diet as well. For the first month, I totally avoided greasy food, spicy food, meat, and processed food. I made salads with organic vegetables.

"In two months or so, it was obvious that I was recovering. There was less pus-like liquid, and I didn't itch as much. I was able to sleep longer. My skin was still dry, but it began to regain and retain moisture and the swelling had gone down. After a month or so, my normal white skin came back. I didn't realize until then how easily I used to get tired. I was now doing so well that I didn't feel tired even when I had to study for a long time.

"I had another rebound reaction in November. But this time no fluid came out and the itching was below my skin. For some reason, I became anxious when I had sudden itching at night, but it was much less severe than the rebounds I had experienced previously. This continued for about a month.

"After five months, I went back to Japan. I went to see Dr. Fukuda right away and shared my experience of rebound with him. He congratulated me for overcoming such a bad steroid addiction. My mother was in tears with happiness to see my white skin.

"I haven't experienced any rebound since then, but Dr. Fukuda told me that it's not quite over yet. But I'm confident that I can overcome another episode. When I was dependent on steroids, I used to panic that I would run out of medication, and I couldn't live a normal life. I was living a life of boredom. The struggles of rebound are, for sure, beyond imagining. But I'm certain that I can recover completely one day if I have willpower, enhance the strength of my parasympathetic nervous system, and commit myself to a treatment process that increases my lymphocytes. It's very hard, but it's been well worth overcoming the hell-like struggle in order to regain a healthy normal life."

STEROIDS ARE CAUSING AN INCREASE IN ADULT ATOPIC DERMATITIS

Children in undeveloped countries tend to take on adult characteristics sooner due to a reversal in the natural predominance of granulocytes and lymphocytes. The reason is that these children are more stressed by heavy labor and harsh cold or hot weather conditions than children in developed countries. In addition, children in undeveloped countries often have insufficient food, naturally leading to the predominance of the sympathetic nervous system. As a result, they produce more granulocytes, and have fewer allergies. In the past, Japanese children were like that too. There were very few children with allergies compared to today. But today, our lifestyle has become more abundant, and therefore the nature of white blood cells has become unbalanced between granulocytes and lymphocytes. Children in affluent countries like Japan, the United States, and Europe generally have more lymphocytes until they're fifteen to twenty years old).

As white blood cells grow into their adult forms, allergies naturally tend to recede. In the past, people generally healed from allergies naturally and effortlessly. If you give children steroids to treat atopic dermatitis over a long period of time, however, it's not likely that they'll be able to heal naturally. Using steroids deprives their bodies of that opportunity. Steroids have cholesterol structures. They're difficult to eliminate because they become oxidized fat, which is stored in tissue, and it takes a lot of effort to get them out. When applied externally, steroids remain on the skin, causing inflammation through the oxidization of cholesterol, which may develop into festering sores. When that happens, allopathic doctors usually use even stronger steroids to suppress the inflammation. This can easily turn into steroid addiction. Even if people want to quit, they often can't bear the rebound effect and fall back into a cycle of addiction. Therefore, you have to be very cautious when using steroids. As I mentioned previously, if you've used steroids for a long time, you may experience rebound to some extent. But if you don't quit, your situation will become more dangerous.

It may be easier to understand this problem if I discuss it in the context of drug use among athletes. At one time, many athletes used steroids to enhance their muscles, but a number of them started having physical problems as a result. In socialist countries such as the former East Germany and Soviet Union especially, athletes eagerly used steroids to build muscle. This severely damaged their health. When you take in substances that have a cholesterol structure, such as male hormones, female hormones, steroid hormones, or vitamin D, your metabolism is enhanced. Your muscles become stronger, your saccharometabolism becomes higher, and you become more active and energetic as a result. If you take these substances for too long, however, the cholesterol builds up and causes arterial sclerosis. In other words, it accelerates your aging process. Florence Griffith-Joyner, a former Olympic athlete, is believed by some to have died from this. It's dangerous to dispense a substance with a cholesterol structure that has more than physiological density. Even strong athletes can suffer damage. This chemical substance is now prohibited in the field of athletics. When you use common sense, you can see that steroids are not something to be taken thoughtlessly.

Steroids can be produced naturally in the human body. They don't cause any harm as long as their presence is natural. But that doesn't mean you can take in as much of the substance as you want. Anything can cause problems when there's too much of it.

SIDE EFFECTS FROM STEROIDS CAN HARM MENTAL ACTIVITY

The side effects of steroid use can take a long time to appear. I think that's one reason that doctors who treat patients with atopic dermatitis or bronchitis aren't very aware of them. This is especially true in the case of external medications and inhalers, which aren't as strong as internal medications, and so can delay recognition and understanding of the problem even more. This may be why people neglect the side effects of steroids. But I'm not alone in warning the public about the danger of steroids. I'd like to introduce content from the Website of the Japan Ophthalmological Society as an example.

First, an article entitled "Correct Treatments by a Professional Ophthalmologist" states, "Steroids are commonly used to treat allergic problems such as atopic dermatitis, but since they have various side effects, they are applied only for a short period of time, and only when the symptoms of conjunctiva allergy get worse." I agree with this opinion. I've complied the following information about steroid side effects from their Web site.

SERIOUS SIDE EFFECTS OF STEROIDS

Steroids, which are highly effective for allergies and atopic dermatitis, are commonly prescribed, especially by dermatologists. However, you need to be aware of and cautious about the following serious side effects:

1. **Cataracts:** It's believed that steroids were once administered systemically to treat allergies and atopic dermatitis. It's now theorized that this usage clouded the lenses of the eyes, which can worsen cataracts.
2. **Glaucoma:** Steroids may increase ocular tension, which can narrow sight by putting pressure on the optic nerves. This condition is called glaucoma and can result in blindness if appropriate treatment is not administered.

Suppression of growth: When steroids are administered systemically to children, they can suppress growth, a condition called apophysis, which can interfere with their entire physical development.

Other side effects: Steroids can lower immunity and, as a result, make you an easy target for viruses and bacteria. You may catch a cold more easily or take a long time to heal. Used externally, not for ophthalmologic purposes, steroids can cause problems with dermatitis.

These are serious side effects. But there's another side effect that shouldn't be neglected—steroid mental disorder. Taken externally, internally, or through inhalation, steroids can destroy the rhythm of daily life, causing you to get sleepy during the day and wakeful at night. As a result, you will feel stressed out and anxious, and your healthy life will disappear.

ALLERGIC PROBLEMS SHOULD BE DEALT WITH BY SOCIETY AS A WHOLE

The number of allergy patients hasn't stopped growing. In fact, I believe this number will keep increasing if society as a whole remains the way it is. There are many problems that society needs to deal with, including the widespread presence of agricultural chemicals, building materials and their adhesives, and exhaust fumes of all kinds. Until recently, people blamed the factories and chemical companies but now that we understand that carbon dioxide is produced though the consumption of gasoline, we need to change the fundamental way our society uses energy. This is not an easy task. Thermal power generation produces much of our carbon dioxide. We need to consider other sources of energy, such as water, nuclear power, wind, or solar power, which don't produce as much carbon dioxide.

I traveled to Russia recently to treat children with bronchial asthma at a clinic in the countryside. Allergic symptoms such as atopic dermatitis and bronchial asthma are often healed when patients spend time in a clinic away from the city. But the Japanese have not yet come to this realization. Allopathic treatments are practiced without changing the patient's environment or lifestyle, and as a result people struggle even more. This isn't very smart. In Japan, people rarely travel for healing anymore, unlike in Russia. If you have atopic dermatitis or bronchial asthma, you need to avoid polluted air and go to a clean place where the treatment can be more effective. But the reality is that people try to heal everything with medicine. What is practiced in Japan is only superficial suppression, not authentic healing.

It's sad that many Japanese patients choose treatments that depend solely on medications that cause more damage. I was really impressed by the Russians. They have clinics all over to treat allergic diseases. They're treating the problem while they're surrounded by nature, exercising, and leading physically and emotionally healthy lives. In Russia, people commit to traveling to special locations for treatments that enable them to get better, even though life there is less socially stable following the break-up of the Soviet Union. Yet we Japanese don't make this simple commitment, even though we're both more stable and more affluent. We need to be more committed to solving our fundamental problems by going to places with clean air, avoiding exhaust fumes, and building strong healthy bodies with lower lymphocyte levels. We can do this, even if only during summer vacation. We rarely hear of such treatments in Japan. We're too quick to use medicine in our futile search for instant and superficial results, which I find very strange.

Chapter 4 How to Heal Chronic Disease

THE REAL PROPERTIES OF COLLAGEN DISEASE AND OTHER DIFFICULT DISEASES

It's well known that collagen disease is a difficult disease (categorized medically as "persistent") that takes a long time to treat. It's sometimes called autoimmune disease. The symptoms vary, and there are about fifty different types. There are collagen diseases of the whole body, or of certain parts of body, such as specific organs or tissues. Some of these include chronic rheumatism of the joints, SLE (systemic lupus erythematosus), Hashimoto's disease, sclarea, dermatomyositis, Sjögren's syndrome, hyperthyroidism, and autoimmune hepatitis.

But in fact, our understanding of collagen disease has been completely wrong. It's believed that collagen disease results when an overactive immune system attacks itself. We've therefore developed treatments that suppress immunity through immunosuppressant or steroids. But when I conducted research on collagen disease as an autoimmune disease, I realized that collagen diseases are caused by suppressed immunity. Our concept of the disease has been completely backward.

In collagen diseases, the body produces autoantibodies. These were the keys to solving the mystery. Autoantibodies always appear naturally in the process of aging, not just as a result of disease. This happens when

the thymus shrinks and the power of the "new immune system," (which I'll explain in chapter 5) is reduced. Autoantibodies may also appear in the later stages of pregnancy. When you're pregnant, your thyroid—the central control for your child's new immune system—shrinks, and granulocytes and the old immune system become more active. When you're exposed to severe stress, as well, steroids are naturally secreted and your thyroid shrinks. When the stress becomes so strong that it damages tissues, autoantibodies appear. Autoantibodies also appear when someone suffers from chronic GVH disease, which often occurs after bone marrow transplants. In this case, the thyroid once again shrinks and the "old immune system" (again, see chapter 5 for a more thorough explanation) becomes more dominant, resulting in an increased number of granulocytes. In sum, autoimmune diseases are caused when T cells and B cells develop due to a shrinking thyroid, causing the old, hidden immune system to become prominent and produce autoantibodies, and causing autoantibody T cells to appear, causing disease. We can't label anything as absolutely good or bad. The symptoms of collagen disease are harsh and difficult for patients, as I will discuss, but at the same time it's possible that these symptoms are part of a positive reaction to correct abnormalities in the body and restore balance.

SEVERE STRESS CAUSES COLLAGEN DISEASE

Whenever I interviewed patients about how they came to have collagen disease, they told me about episodes of stress or viral infection. Many patients contracted collagen disease after having a terrible cold. In other words, the disease seems to be triggered when tissue has been severely damaged, or immunity has been suppressed.

It all has to do with the "old immune system" and the "new immune system," which I'll explain in more detail in chapter 5. In short, I believe that an increase in autoantibodies—one of the symptoms of collagen disease—happens when the new immune system, which reacts to antibodies from outside, is extremely suppressed. In a recent article in the academic journal Immunology Today, a researcher explained his theory that autoantibodies appear as part of a healing reaction in order to eliminate abnormal tissue. I agree. I think that organic activities that happen in the human body won't cause damage, no matter how uncomfortable they may be. Organic activities within our body are always healing powers. In other words, they occur to prolong our life. Sometimes we experience uncomfortable reactions in the process of eliminating damaged tissue or tissue that has become harmful. I've observed many phenomena like this in the course of my research into organic activities. When the body is finished repairing a damaged area, the "old" immune system, which dealt with the damage, calms down, and the "new" immune system takes over, preparing to deal with any abnormal objects or viruses from outside. Therefore, when autoantibodies are present, they can be thought to be part of an immune reaction whose purpose is to watch for suspicious objects.

In inflammations such as chilblains, sunburn, and common burns, blood flow is increased and rushes to the affected area. During an inflammation emergency in which cells are damaged, the thymus shrinks and suppresses the "new" immune system, and the "old" immune system is activated to eliminate and repair the damaged tissue. We believe that the same thing happens in the case of collagen disease, based on the fact that autoantibodies appear. When collagen disease shifts, it usually begins with poor blood circulation, increased granulocytes, and tissue damage as a result of severe viral infection or stress. Then the "old" immune system increases blood flow in order to repair tissue, which causes reactions such as fever. This is a healing reaction. I therefore think the most important factor in treatment is to allow the inflammation to run its course throughout the body and wait for the tissue to recover. When my colleagues treat their collagen disease patients by stimulating the parasympathetic nervous system, these patients begin to heal. It may be painful at the beginning because of the initial inflammation, but in most cases the pain lasts only a week or so, and the patient recovers in about a month. Even patients who've suffered for years can heal surprisingly quickly and easily.

But collagen disease has been regarded as over-augmented immunity, so by suppressing immunity, the medical field has been administering the wrong treatment. When you suppress immunity, the "new" immune system is suppressed, and the "old" immune system remains active.

This causes T cells produced outside the thymus (extrathymic T cells and autoantibody-producing B-1 cells) to attack tissue, and as a result the inflammation won't stop. When immunosuppressant or steroids are applied, they temporarily stop the inflammation, so they appear to work—but that's not what happens.

Why did the treatment for collagen disease go in this wrong direction? I believe it's because of the trend of the times. Collagen disease, like cancer, used to be a fast-growing disease that worsened easily. Like cancer, it's caused by the kinds of stress that suppress immunity. In the past, people lived in ways that contributed to collagen disease: they were malnourished and had to do hard physical labor, so their sympathetic nervous systems were constantly tense. But in modern, affluent Japan, we can relax as much as we want. Collagen disease should therefore be easier to heal now than in the past.

LONG-TERM USE OF STEROIDS MAKES COLLAGEN DISEASE INCURABLE

But, in fact, like chemotherapy or anti-cancer drugs in cancer treatment, steroids made collagen disease more difficult and complicated to heal. Steroids were discovered more than fifty years ago. Since that time, a huge amount of synthetic steroids have been produced. As I stated earlier, steroids were given to collagen disease patients to suppress immunity and stop inflammation because of the misconception that the inflammation present in collagen disease is caused by an overactive immune system, rather than a suppressed one. As a result, this disease has become almost incurable.

In the 1950s and 60s, when steroids first came into use, it was an unwritten law that they shouldn't be used for long periods of time and that patients should stop using them as soon as possible. Dr. Edward Calvin Kendall, a co-recipient of the 1950 Nobel Prize for his research on steroids, has advised that doctors who prescribe steroids be responsible for stopping their usage because of their addictive properties. I learned this in medical school. As a clinical doctor, if I prescribed steroids, I always had patients stop the treatment before they left the hospital.

But over time, the misconceptions surrounding collagen disease have remained, and the dangers of steroid use have become less recognized. The long-term use of steroids makes it much harder for patients to stop. If patients stop taking steroids in order to begin healing naturally, they experience severe rebound, with fever and inflammation. True healing can't be achieved without overcoming this reaction, and yet people revert too easily to steroid use because the withdrawal symptoms are so difficult. On top of this, doctors are less reluctant to use steroids than they were in the past; some young doctors continue to use steroids for maintenance even after inflammation is gone.

Doctors who blindly believe in steroids also tend to believe that collagen disease patients are constant complainers about their disease. They think it's fine for patients to have mild symptoms, as long as those symptoms aren't too intense and there's no severe inflammation, because they believe that collagen disease is chronic. But when I consider the function of the immune system and the number of lymphocytes and granulocytes, I think most symptoms result from the steroids themselves.

Patients who use steroids complain that they're cold even in the summer, and they shiver in air-conditioned rooms. This phenomenon proves the fundamental harm caused by steroids. As I discussed previously, substances like steroids that have cholesterol-like structures stick to tissue and turn into oxidized fat. This causes granulocytes to rush in and the sympathetic nervous system to tense up. Tension in the sympathetic nervous system narrows blood vessels and makes you feel cold, because there's not enough blood circulation.

OTHER DISEASES CAUSED BY STEROIDS

From the moment steroids are prescribed, collagen disease patients are drowned in medicines. Their blood pressure rises because their sympathetic nervous system is tense, so they have to be treated for hypertension. Increased sympathetic nerve tension also quickens their pulse, which creates additional worries, and they begin taking an antianxiety agent. This, as a result, speeds up their saccharometabolism, causing diabetes and forcing them to take more medications. And since poor blood circulation leads to joint damage, with ensuing back and knee pain, they start taking painkillers. In this way, patients who use steroids to maintain their health end up with more problems as a result of the endless cycle of allopathic treatments. Yet, many doctors don't realize that steroids are a fundamental cause of all these problems.

Again, I'd like to emphasize that collagen disease occurs when immunity is suppressed—not when it's overactive. Stopping inflammation prevents healing because inflammation is a natural biological reaction to invasion, caused when blood flow is increased in order to support tissue repair. If you don't know this and you're just eager to stop the inflammation, you won't ever be able to get truly well. This contradiction is a fact of life for those taking collagen disease treatments.

RELIEF FROM STRESS IS KEY TO HEALING

As I've stated previously, many people experience some kind of severe stress prior to the onset of the set of symptoms we call collagen disease. Viral infection is also likely to occur when a patient's immune system has been lowered through stress. The symptoms of collagen disease result from extremely suppressed immunity. Patients need to examine their lives to see if they're under stress in any way, and if they are, they need to take a break from their stress. In my discussion of cancer in chapter 2, I mentioned, as an example of how changing one's lifestyle can activate immunity and bring about healing, the American doctor Norman Cousins, who healed himself from serious collagen disease through the power of laughter. His life was very difficult before he contracted collagen disease. It's obvious that this stress caused his disease.

Collagen disease is accompanied by very uncomfortable symptoms, but if you resort to taking steroids, you'll be in trouble. It's natural to feel cold and depressed when you have collagen disease. But if you're too serious and live your life in sadness every day because of this difficult disease, the tension in your sympathetic nervous system will increase and worsen the situation. It's critical that you turn your perspective 180 degrees and create a stress-free lifestyle, in order to heal your disease with laughter, like Dr. Cousins.

TESTIMONIAL 6

Eliminating Pain of Rheumatism Through Parasympathetic Nerve Stimulation Treatment *(Female, 70 Years Old)*

"I've been suffering from rheumatism for 30 years, since I was about 40 years old. My family owns a farm. I was always busy as a housewife managing the house and farm, working literally from morning till night. About the time I turned 40, I felt a difference in my body. But I couldn't tell anyone that I wanted to go to the hospital, and I let it be for several years.

"When I was 48 years old, I felt acute pain in my knees and couldn't do farm work anymore, so I finally went to hospital. A blood test showed I had rheumatism. Once they removed the water from my knees, the pain disappeared. Since I didn't have any other obvious symptoms and because I was so busy, I stopped visiting the doctor and instead used anti-inflammatory medication from the pharmacy to manage the pain. I was fine for a year or so, with no dramatic change in my symptoms. But my stomach became damaged as a side effect of the medication, and I began vomiting whatever I ate. Then, when I caught a severe cold, I began having serious rheumatic symptoms, and I had no choice but to go to the hospital right away.

"The joints all over my body were swollen, and I couldn't even walk or sit. The doctor wanted to prescribe a medication for rheumatism, but I didn't want to take it anymore because of the side effects. I begged the doctor and was allowed to go to an acupuncturist's clinic while still remaining in the hospital. In about three months, this reduced the swelling in my joints and enabled me to walk, but due to my lack of energy and pain in my joints I still couldn't have the life I used to have. Because my energy was low, any strain caused me to take a severe turn for the worse. Being careful not to let my situation deteriorate, I had acupuncture or chiropractic treatments whenever the pain became intolerable. Still, it got worse whenever I caught a cold.

"In 1999, my rheumatism returned again after a cold. I'd had a ganglion on my right hand for about two years, and it was always hot.

At my check-up, the doctor told me it was unnecessary to treat it since I didn't have pain, but it grew bigger, from the size of a bean to a walnut shell. About 25 years had passed since my disease first broke out, and I was hopeless.

"Around that time, I learned from a health magazine about the autonomic immunotherapy practiced by Dr. Minoru Fukuda, which didn't require any medication. Since I was tired of using medicines, I decided to try the treatment, and I went to visit him.

"I felt little pain at the first visit as he put needles on my fingertips and the tips of my toes. I didn't really feel the effect at first. But the morning after my second visit the following week, I noticed a little change. The swelling in my fingers was completely gone. I could even move my wrists, which used to be in pain. I continued to visit him once a week, and most of the pain in my wrist was gone at the sixth visit.

The rheumatism that had been torturing me for such a long

time got much better in two months. I was simply surprised. On top of this, the ganglion on my right hand got smaller with each session, and now it's much smaller than it used to be.

"At one point, even an easy errand at home caused me to struggle, but now, with the pain in my hands gone, I could move more smoothly and do things faster than before. The suffering I had experienced since my forties seemed like a bad dream. Now I'm an old woman, but I've pained back a normal, healthy life thanks to the treatment. I'm going to keep doing the treatment to maintain my health."

SOLVING THE PROBLEM OF BACK AND KNEE PAIN

The number of people troubled by back and knee pain has been growing. Although this problem isn't fatal, it is hard to heal. In the journal of the Doctors Association of Japan, a doctor of orthopedics was quoted as saying that back pain accounts for 9.3 percent of the health problems reported in Japan. It tops the list, with all other diseases far below that number. About 20 percent of Japanese elders aged 65 and over have back pain. This means that one in every five seniors suffers from back pain. I commute by bus and see many old women during my trips because there's a general hospital on the route. I listen to their conversations, and they often complain that their backs or knees hurt. Some of them I see once or twice a week, but others I see every day. The seriousness of their conditions may differ, but it's a fact that many Japanese elders have back and knee problems.

The journal article goes on to say that physical therapy and nerve block therapy are now as commonly used by doctors to treat back pain as internal anti-inflammatory painkillers. But at the same time, the orthopedist also states that back pain is very difficult to heal—so much so that he practically thinks of it as divine work to eliminate back pain. By this, I assume he means that it's so difficult, only God can do it. Based on this article, I believe he is saying that alternative treatments—not anti-inflammatory painkillers—are less effective. Doctors generally prescribe internal medicine or external poultices for back pain, but the truth is that these don't really help. Back pains usually worsen over a long period of time—years or decades—so initially people don't take it very seriously. But as a result, many of our elderly patients come to orthopedic doctors with back and knee pain.

From what I understand, most orthopedic doctors don't hesitate to prescribe anti-inflammatory painkillers. But as I studied the white blood cells' control over the autonomic nervous system, I began to think it might be wrong to use anti-inflammatory painkillers for back pain. I came to understand the mystery of back pain in terms of immunology.

MECHANISM OF BACK AND KNEE PAIN

Why does back pain occur to begin with? Young people sometimes have acute back pain, but it's usually the middle aged or elderly who really have problems. There are two reasons: 1) their muscle strength grows weaker over time so that even normal movements begin to wear down muscle; and 2) during unusually heavy exercise, the body's energy- producing process creates a lactic acid chemical byproduct that remains in the muscle areas, causing pain and tissue discomfort once the muscles are finally able to relax. Together, this growing tendency toward muscle weakness and the gradual build-up of lactic acid deposits create the beginnings of back pain. The pain starts out mild, so patients can bear it initially, but over time they can't take it anymore and most likely end up in the hospital. Once they go to the hospital, the first treatment they're given are anti-inflammatory painkillers, which of course suppress the painful symptoms. For some people, one out of every ten or twenty, the pain really does go away after taking these medicines for a short period of time. But for most, although the medicines suppress the pain symptoms, they cannot heal or resolve the problem, which slowly grows more serious.

Why does it hurt when you relax after exercising your muscles? This is the key to understand how back pain begins. When you feel pain after exercising, it means that your bloodstream is trying to eliminate some of the lactic acid byproducts in your body as part of the recovery process. Even young people, when they perform unfamiliar physical labor, have this lactic acid muscular stiffness and discomfort, including back or knee pain, the next day or the day after. Both professionals and participants in modern physical fitness programs recognize this. When lactic acid builds up during exercise, it's stored in the hard-working muscle tissue. This increasing concentration of additional chemicals puts pressure on the blood vessels, interfering with the normal fullness of blood circulation in the stressed area. As a result, the amount of blood needed to remove this lactic acid cannot flow. Once the exercise is over and the muscles are allowed to relax, however, blood circulation recovers, the blood vessels expand to their normal size, blood pressure returns to normal—and this process begins to cause pain. In order for vasodilation (expansion of the blood vessels) to occur, prostaglandins must be released. This is an exothermic (outside the blood vessel) requirement that helps the affected tissue flex even more to create the space needed for blood vessel expansion, and this too causes pain. This necessary expansion of the blood vessels can on its own cause a fever when dilation occurs quickly, and the pain and discomfort from this can be very strong. In some cases of knee pain, one can see that the tissue around the knees has become red and swollen and feels hot to the touch (in other words, feverish), which means that blood circulation has been restored.

If you recognize these symptoms of recovery, you'll understand that discomfort and pain are simply part of your body's biological reaction as it helps you recover from muscle fatigue. The muscles, bones, and joints are all part of the mesenchyme system, with the same blood vessel and nerve structure. So, when muscle fatigue is very severe, constricted blood circulation extends beyond just the muscles that are being worked to affect the associated bones and joints as well. If this pressure goes on too long, tissue damage can result—its intensity dependent on the particular individual's starting strength and muscle flexibility. As the body's normal healing activity begins to help these stressed areas recover, blood comes rushing back, also accompanied by pain. Remember, because pain is the reaction of muscles and joints to the repair process, it should not to be stopped, but rather endured. Many pains will stop on their own if you just allow yourself to rest and increase blood circulation. For example, perhaps you've experienced muscle pain after skiing that became magically better after soaking in a hot tub. You relax in the heat from the water, and this relaxation and warmth help your body get rid of muscle fatigue very quickly. This is proof that your back and knee pain are calling for more heat and blood flow in the affected areas. They're asking you to give them good blood circulation to help them recover on their own.

How do anti-inflammatory painkillers work, on the other hand? They prevent the production of prostaglandin, the substance required to widen your blood vessels. So instead of helping your body recover, these medicines actually constrict the ability of your blood vessels to bring fresh blood to the damaged area. Because they further reduce blood flow and cover up the pain-causing effects of lactic acid, the pain seems to disappear for a moment. But because they inhibit blood circulation, anti-inflammatories actually interfere with and prevent the restoration of tissue health. They cool down the body by reducing blood circulation, preventing the production of the necessary prostaglandins, and slowing down or even stopping the body's own natural healing activity. As a result, there can be no recovery from fatigue or restoration of tissue, and no return to health. Anti-inflammatory painkillers stop inflammation and stop pain, and they also prevent tissue from healing. That's the truth about anti-inflammatory painkillers.

ANTI-INFLAMMATORY PAINKILLERS CAUSE CONSTITUTIONAL DISEASES

The doctor who wrote the journal article that I discussed earlier seems to have no doubt about anti-inflammatory painkillers. That's how back and knee pain is treated today, and that's precisely why back pain never goes away completely and never heals.

Anti-inflammatory creams, which are prescribed to treat back and knee pain, also work by reducing blood circulation in the affected areas, spreading their influence throughout the entire body. They're absorbed through the skin and enter the blood vessels, suppressing blood circulation and narrowing blood vessels throughout the entire body, and causing high blood pressure as a side effect. One or two weeks of this normally won't do much damage, but if high blood pressure continues for more than a month (and in some cases it can continue for up to half a year), it causes severe sympathicotonia—a condition in which the sympathetic nervous system dominates the general functioning of the body organs, causing vascular spasm, heightened blood pressure, goose flesh, and ciliospinal reflex. In fact, the use of anti-inflammatories and painkillers is one reason people end up with symptoms like high blood pressure and insomnia. And obese people who use these medications, which can increase the rate of sugar metabolism, are at greater risk of developing diabetes. Sympathicotonia can be useful as long as it periodically alternates with parasympathetic nervous system dominance. However, if sympathicotonia continues, it causes constant fatigue. Patients are so exhausted that they feel sick all day.

This constant fatigue, of course, brings about various other problems and symptoms, causing patients to return to the doctor and receive more medications to deal with each symptom—just as with collagen disease, explained earlier. Many old people come home with a pile of medications so large, it will barely fit into their bags. And all of this begins by taking a "simple" anti-inflammatory. Many people must have unknowingly damaged their bodies by taking them.

When you have sympathicotonia (sympathetic nervous system dominance), your pulse is faster because you're excited all the time. A heart rate averaging 80 beats per minute will damage heart muscle and cause enlargement. The additional stress narrows blood vessels, reducing blood flow and the availability of the blood's heat throughout the body, so the body becomes cold. The fingertips are always cold. Patients get so cold that they have to wear socks even in the summer. In the worst cases, their toes turn purple and may decay at the tips. Patients with sympathicotonia have a much higher risk of contracting various diseases. So, you need to be careful when taking anti-inflammatory painkillers.

Anti-inflammatory painkillers may take the form of poultices (such as a cream), internal medications (such as pills), or suppositories (rectal insertions), but they all have the same effect. So, if you don't see any improvement after you stop taking an internal form of anti- inflammatories, make sure you're not also using them externally.

It may sometimes be necessary to use an anti-inflammatory with ice to cool an area in a case of severe inflammation caused by injury. In these sorts of sudden and intensely acute cases, there is absolutely no problem in using an anti-inflammatory for a very limited amount of time. Anti- inflammatories only become a problem when used for a long period of time for chronic pain. Damage from long-term use of anti-inflammatories usually begins within five or ten years. Side effects include a reduction in the functioning of the body's digestive system, causing a loss of appetite and weight, faster aging, and eventually death. Anti-inflammatories are frightening medicines. Patients need to know what they're taking so they don't take them for too long.

ORTHOPEDISTS AND ALTERNATIVE MEDICINE

Some orthopedic doctors have begun to realize that the treatments they commonly use are not helpful. While this isn't just a recent development, the last ten or twenty years has seen a gradual increase in the number of doctors with this enlightened awareness. How have these doctors changed their practice? They've adopted chiropractic or arthrokinematic approaches: treatments that eliminate pain by fixing distortions in the bones, joints, and spine. Neither of these types of treatments depends on medicine. An increasing number of orthopedic doctors have adopted these kinds of treatments and they are becoming more successful. I'm very glad.

Orthopedic treatments of back and knee pain have not been taken seriously for several reasons. General medical professionals tend to ignore basic joint, spine, and bone problems because, in serious cases such as car accidents, the problems are so great that surgery by an orthopedic specialist is required. These specialists have a reputation for performing elaborate surgeries. They tend to focus their healing passion on treatments and procedures that provide immediate and visible improvement.

But back pains can be very inconspicuous. It's understandable that doctors don't want to commit their careers to studying back pain in the elderly when other medical fields are more glamorous. Many orthopedic doctors are very active, with a background in judo or other sports, and are therefore less interested in studying inconspicuous areas like back pain. And doctors of chiropractic have been regarded as a very strange minority. That's why the study of back pain treatment hasn't advanced much, and why waiting rooms are currently flooded with old people with back and knee pain. It's a pity that we're allowing our elderly to be treated like this after they've worked hard for such a long time.

HOW TO HEAL BACK AND KNEE PAIN IN MIDDLE-AGED PATIENTS

As our aging muscles grow weaker and start hurting due to

lack of exercise, what kinds of treatments are helpful? First, you need to spontaneously increase your blood circulation. Take a warm or hot bath to warm your body so that blood circulation can increase. Perform light exercises regularly to keep your muscles functioning at a level that allows you to conduct your daily activities. Some people have back problems when they're in their Sorties or fifties. The cause may vary: some work at a desk all day, some have weakened their muscles by putting on excess weight, and some are so overweight that their muscles are wearing down. Doctors need to determine whether a particular patient needs to strengthen their muscles, lose weight, or both. In some cases, an individual with generally strong muscles may play a strenuous sport that their muscles are unfamiliar with and find they don't have the strength to play for long or may experience muscle fatigue and back pain. I recommend that middle-aged people with chronic knee pain lie on their backs and move

their legs. Moving the legs without putting weight on them increases blood flow. For patients with back pain, I recommend bending forward and back.

I explained previously that back pain is caused by a decrease in blood circulation due to substances produced when muscles are worn down. When blood circulation is low, the surrounding tissue is affected as well. Tissue that surrounds an area of poor blood circulation is the first to be damaged. If the area of low blood circulation is around the spine, the spinal disks lose their elasticity; eventually, this can cause one or more slipped disks. Ligament damage can also cause slip disks, because the ligaments are no longer able to support the necessary connections to the bones. Underestimating these symptoms—assuming it's just fatigue or tired muscles—can cause more serious damage. Back pain shouldn't be treated lightly.

BONE DISTORTION DOES NOT NECESSARILY CAUSE PAIN

Fortunately, damaged tissue can be restored if there's enough blood circulation. I seldom see old women with their backs bent ninety degrees the way I used to. Women with this condition must have worked at farms, doing the weeding and planting, for a very long time. Following damage and repair, their backs grew into that bent-over alignment because they continued to have the same posture. The x-rays of spines like that are surprising, and young and inexperienced doctors are often shocked to see them. The lumbar is so crushed that it's almost amazing anyone can survive in that condition. However, even in older adults, the tissue can slowly recover as long as there is enough blood circulation—that's why these patients are fine like this. I would assume that they did something to support stronger, healthier blood circulation following the damage to their back—perhaps healing hot springs. Because they accepted that their backs were bent like that, their tissue recovered and adapted to the shape of their body, and they could lead their lives with a bent back but without pain.

Therefore, we cannot necessarily conclude that distorted bones are the cause of pain. If the bone is stable, it won't cause pain even if it's distorted. Pain generally occurs soon after the damaged tissue recovers. Once blood circulation is fully restored, muscle fatigue heals in several days, and damaged tissue in only a few weeks.

NEVER USE ANTI-INFLAMMATORY PAIN KILLERS TO HEAL CHRONIC BACK. KNEE PAIN

How do we treat patients who have taken a great deal of medication during many years of back pain? My colleagues instruct them to stop taking all medications, to take lots of hot baths, and to exercise well. Anti-inflammatory painkillers slow down and, at times, stop the functioning of the digestive systems, so if you stop taking them you'll have more appetite. When you eat, your parasympathetic nervous system is stimulated, and your blood vessels relax; more blood flows through the circulatory system; and damaged tissue recovers more quickly—usually within three weeks or so. In many cases, the pain has been known to subside completely once the parasympathetic nervous system became more active and healing began. Patients are often quite surprised by the speed of their recovery, after all those years of suffering.

Other things can also prevent healing. For example, tight garments such as corsets or girdles limit the ability of the body to move, thus reducing blood circulation. But the best way to heal is to stop taking anti-inflammatory painkillers.

Some chiropractic doctors don't understand the harm of anti-inflammatory painkillers. The bones may be fixed to reduce strain on the body, but the patient still doesn't recover because anti-inflammatory medicines cancel out the effects of the chiropractic treatment. But many of these patients recover extremely quickly with chiropractic treatment alone, once they quit using medication.

Another reason I don't recommend anti-inflammatory painkillers is that they can damage the stomach and lead to other problems. Anti-inflammatory painkillers slow down blood circulation, causing sympathicotonia. The increased influence of a more active sympathetic nervous system results in an automatic increase in granulocytes. When granulocytes increase, they rush to the mucous membranes. When they reach the stomach, they can damage the stomach lining. These results are quite easy to notice in the stomach, but they're actually simultaneously

happening all over the body. Granulocytes don't increase in just one area; they increase throughout the entire body. As this increase in granulocytes speeds up, damage to the tissue in the area of the pain increases. So, if anti-inflammatory painkillers upset your stomach, you can't just take stomach medicine and leave it at that. When your stomach is damaged, other mucous membranes in the digestive system and tissue throughout your body are damaged as well. Even if your stomach symptoms subside, these other parts of your body won't be healed. Digestive aids will not solve your problem.

USE ANTI-INFLAMMATORY PAINKILLERS FOR ACUTE PAIN ONLY

Anti-inflammatory painkillers are prescribed too easily for diseases other than back pain. One such painkiller—amino salicylic acid—is prescribed for ulcerative colitis, or Crohn's disease. Dispensed under the name Salazopyrin or Pentasa, these medications take the form of enteric- coated tablets, meaning they dissolve in the intestines. But using anti- inflammatories makes ulcerative colitis difficult to heal. Ulcerative colitis is caused primarily by stress. Teenagers, for example, often get ulcerative colitis as a result of sympathicotonia due to the stress of studying for exams. In Crohn's disease, sympathicotonia causes an increased number of granulocytes, which attack the mucous membranes in the large intestines. In order to recover and avoid damage to the mucous membranes, the body activates the parasympathetic nervous system, which stimulates activity in the digestive system, and diarrhea often results. The parasympathetic nervous system reflex eliminates the elements that cause pain. During this natural healing process, patients may experience a different kind of stomach pain, along with diarrhea and hematochezia (internal bleeding) from damage previously done to the mucous membranes by an increased number of granulocytes. Since stomach pain is very obvious, people tend to treat it allopathically using anti-inflammatory painkillers. These anti- inflammatories create tension in the sympathetic nervous system, easing the symptoms and associated pain. But diarrhea is a healing reaction for a patient with ulcerative colitis, which is itself caused by the tense sympathetic nervous system. So, if you keep taking anti-inflammatories, diarrhea will keep occurring as a healing reaction. In order to heal ulcerative colitis or Crohn's disease, you need to understand which kind of stress is causing tension in the sympathetic nervous system and eliminate this fundamental stress. You need to consciously think about what's causing stress and manage this stress in order to heal; otherwise, true healing will never be attained. At the same time, you should stop taking anti- inflammatory painkillers and endure the stomachache, understanding that diarrhea is a healing reaction. This can lead to fundamental healing. Ulcerative colitis and Crohn's disease are not difficult diseases to manage and heal if you understand the problem. But as with other diseases, healing is more difficult if steroids have become part of palliation.

I've described the negative effects of anti-inflammatory painkillers in great detail. Yet, if used for only a very short period of time in order to manage unbearably acute pain, they can be of great value. As long as your physical strength is normal, your mucous membrane won't be damaged if you take anti-inflammatories for a week or so. However, if you take them for more than two weeks consecutively, tension in the sympathetic nervous system will continue and an increasing amount of tissue damage will occur throughout the body. Some obvious symptoms of this are fast pulse, anxiety, and stomach dysfunction.

The consumption of anti-inflammatory painkillers is

considerably higher in America than in Japan. That's because anti-inflammatory painkillers, by stopping the production of prostaglandin and creating tension in the sympathetic nervous system, raise metabolism and consume calories without exercise. So, Americans who are obese can take anti-inflammatory painkillers and aspirin to lose weight. Because the medication suppresses their appetites, they don't need to exercise to lose weight, so weight loss is easy. But if Japanese people who aren't obese take the same medication, the unwelcome side effects appear sooner, so we need to be more cautious.

ULCERATIVE COLITIS AND CROHN'S DISEASE

Drastic increases in granulocyte levels are observed in the blood in peripheral areas of patients with ulcerative colitis and Crohn's disease. In times of mental and physical stress, their symptoms erupt. In ulcerative colitis of the large intestines, granulocytes enter directly, causing purulent inflammation. With the small intestines, on the other hand, lymphocytes block the entrance of granulocytes; in this case, inflammation results from an overabundance of macrophages.

Our body tries to eliminate both physical toxins and mental toxins, such as sadness, through vomiting and diarrhea. So, the diarrhea and stomachache that occur during attacks of ulcerative colitis and Crohn's disease could be the body's response to healing. They can also be seen as reflexes of the parasympathetic nervous system.

Therefore, it's important to eliminate stress through therapy. When you're stress-free, the symptoms should disappear, and your granulocytes should stop increasing. If you eagerly use allopathic treatments, you'll just suppress the symptoms and you won't achieve true healing. In particular, amino salicylic acid drugs such as Salazopyrin and Pentasa will only make the situation worse. Aminosalicylic acid is a painkiller that causes granulocytes to increase and also interferes with blood circulation.

Steroids, moreover, cause lymphocytes to decrease drastically and granulocytes to increase, causing your situation to worsen more quickly. When you stop taking medication, your diarrhea, stomachache, or inflammation may temporarily become worse. But remember that you cannot achieve healing without those true healing responses. If you understand this, you'll know that even uncomfortable symptoms are a necessary part of the passage to healing. If you work with these symptoms, you'll find that you can bear the discomfort and win out over them.

HOW TO HEAL AUTONOMIC IMBALANCE AND MENOPAUSAL DISORDER

An increasing number of women are troubled by autonomic imbalance. More women are experiencing menopausal disorder before menopause. I'd like to introduce ways to correct this problem using immune power.

I've explained previously that pain occurs when blood circulation, previously inhibited by stress, begins to flow once the body finally relaxes. Autonomic imbalance and menopausal disorders happen through a similar mechanism.

Women are sensitive to stress and cold. It's easy to see why Okinawa, with its warmth, is always the state in which women live longest. When faced with stress or cold, the blood vessels constrict, becoming narrow and reducing the flow of blood through the body. This causes blood circulation problems. Individuals with this condition have cold hands and feet, and even their faces turn pale.

Once the stress or cold is relieved, the blood flow increases, and blood circulation is restored. This widening of the blood vessels is controlled by hormones such as prostaglandins or acetylcholine. These hormones stimulate the parasympathetic nervous system and bring about relaxation.

Prostaglandin also causes pain, and therefore can be accompanied by headache or stomachache. If blood circulation is restored too quickly, dizziness, ear ringing, or flushing can result. The body can feel dull and tired because the parasympathetic nervous system is extremely active, doing a great job of getting you relaxed. When this relaxation reaction is too strong and the blood resumes flowing too quickly, the resulting heat in the system can cause fever (during menopause, these are called hot flashes).

When young women have this kind of reaction, they're likely to be diagnosed as having an autonomic system imbalance. Older women undergoing menopause are diagnosed as having a menopausal disorder. But if you understand what's really happening in the body, as I explained earlier, you can guess that the usual medical treatments used to eliminate these symptoms will fail.

Because all of these conditions have poor blood circulation in the background, it's important for patients to regulate their blood flow. They need to learn to deal with stress, to manage a cold environment by dressing warmly, to avoid strong air conditioning, to wear an extra jacket if necessary, and to exercise or bathe as needed to maintain good blood circulation. It's also important to eat brown rice, which moderately stimulates the parasympathetic nervous system, and to eat enough vegetables, fiber, and mushrooms to prevent constipation.

If you report these types of symptoms at a hospital, you'll be prescribed medications that suppress blood flow; in other words, medications that increase tension in the sympathetic nervous system. These medicines may temporarily suppress your pain, dizziness, and flushing, but your symptoms will only worsen in the long run, because you're increasing the levels of stress that are causing problems in the first place.

A decrease in the availability of the hormone estrogen is one cause of menopausal disorders. By avoiding stress and cold, you can deal with this problem. Many treatments commonly practiced today supply estrogen, which is contrary to the principle of nature, because estrogen is supposed to decrease during menopause. While taking estrogen can help reduce symptoms, it can lead to more serious problems later on.

Estrogen is a substance with cholesterol, so it's hard to eliminate and is easily stored in the body, potentially causing aging or cancer. This excess estrogen can lead to sympathicotonia, in which case high blood pressure and insomnia can be added to the list; therefore, you'll hardly be living a healthy life.

UNEXPECTED WAY TO HEAL A STIFF SHOULDER

Since we've now solved the "female" problems, let's go on to solve the "male" problems. Stiff shoulders are very common among men. The cause remains unknown even today, so there's been little choice but to treat the condition allopathically. Anti-inflammatory painkillers are almost always administered, and as a result, stiff shoulders have become very difficult to heal.

My colleagues and I, however, came to understand the problem after interviewing many patients and getting detailed backgrounds of their diseases. Some have stiff shoulders because they always sleep on one side, either right or left, which regularly places pressure on the shoulder joint and arm. If you always sleep with your right arm on the bottom, for example, blood circulation in the right shoulder and arm will be impaired and tissue damage will occur. Some people sleep on both sides, although this is less common, with a resulting stiffness in both shoulders.

Therefore, to heal a stiff shoulder it's important to sleep on your back as much as possible. Every time you wake up, return to your back. It may take some getting used to. In some cases, people have stiff shoulders because they've developed bad posture, which in turn prevents the flow of blood to the shoulders and arms. Therefore, it's important to analyze yourself, looking for any distortion in your lifestyle that could cause bad circulation. This is particularly important for people who sit at the computer all day. Being tense and hunching over while you focus on whatever project is on the screen creates a tension habit that, over the long run, can result in stiffness throughout the body.

If you have a stiff shoulder, you should move it as much as possible to increase the blood circulation. Taking a hot bath helps increase blood flow to the area and can hasten the healing process. The very worst thing to do is to take oral anti-inflammatory painkillers or apply anti-inflammatory ointment or cream to your skin. These medications slow the blood circulation even more, thus increasing the number of granulocytes—which continue to damage tissue even when you can't feel the pain.

When dealing with diseases whose cause is unknown, it's very important that one not depend on allopathic treatments, which are the opposite of healing.

QUESTION THE FUNDAMENTAL BASIS OF ALL ALLOPATHIC TREATMENTS

TESTIMONIAL 7

Managing To Break A Long-Term Steroid Dependency *(Male, 68 Years Old)*

"In April of 1978, I had an attack of acute hepatitis C due to major stress and exhaustion. Apparently, I had been exposed to the hepatitis C virus in surgery when I was young, and the latent virus became active when during my extremely weak and tired state. The symptoms were severe, and I had to stay in the university hospital for forty days. Once the symptoms calmed down, I went home, but they returned in November of the same year during a time when I wasn't feeling well, and I ended up staying in the hospital for four months. That's when I had my first dose of steroids.

"My condition was unstable after I left the hospital, so I visited a different university hospital two months later. Here, I learned that my hepatitis C was an autoimmune disease called lupoid hepatitis. Just breathing was painful, and I was so weak I couldn't lead a normal life. The doctor told me that my chance of survival was 10 percent. Since I was eager to recover, I stayed at this hospital for five months, receiving large doses of steroids. Although the amount of steroids was gradually reduced, I wasn't allowed to move from 7:00 a.m. to 2:00 p.m. while receiving the medication, nor did I feel like moving around because I was weak. I spent my entire day in bed.

"At the beginning of spring they stopped giving me large doses of steroids. I was allowed to walk around in the building, and in summer I was even allowed to walk outside. In the fall, I was allowed to take a bath twice a week, and I gradually made my way back to normal life. I finally left the hospital in December 1980, but the doctor made sure that I would take the medication, 5 milligrams of steroids, every day. I also started taking Imuran, an immunosuppressant. For work, I traveled to fix electronic machines, but because my family also owned a store, I was fortunate to be able to spend most of my time at home. For over ten years, I always had one hour of rest after each meal. In some instances, my GOP or GTP went up, but I could suppress the symptom by taking medication.

"Looking back at that time, I now know that I was very careful about my body and my lifestyle—more so than people normally are after an occurrence of hepatitis. But I unexpectedly found out that I had another disease in March of 2001. At a check-up near my birthday, the doctor said I might have cancer. I didn't have any symptoms that I could detect, but after the echogram and CT scan test, it was certain. At the doctor's recommendation, I went back three months later to the university hospital and had an operation to remove a cancerous tumor. The doctor told me that the tumor was about 25 by 30 millimeters in size, and that they took out about 50 by 60 millimeters of tissue, to 40 millimeters in depth. They also cut out part of the cholangial (bile duct). They also tested my liver at the time of the operation, determining that my hepatitis was chronic but had not yet advanced to cirrhosis.

"Although I was shocked to be diagnosed with cancer, I was still able to maintain a positive attitude and do whatever possible, probably because I had been living with a disease for so many years. My liver cancer surgery was difficult, but I was still able to feel fortunate that I didn't have cirrhosis. Looking back, I feel lucky that I didn't have to take anti-cancer drugs. The doctor had initially planned to give me internal chemotherapy, injecting ethanol into the cancer, but that plan was rejected because the site was too close to my lungs and too risky.

"Three months after the surgery, the area where the cancer had been was found to be completely recovered, so I returned to my normal life. But I didn't feel good all the time. I was dull and weak because I began taking steroids again. I wondered if there was any way to make my body better. Then I learned about autonomic nerve immunotherapy, as practiced by Dr. Keisuke Tajima. Since I often used my arms and hands to fix electronic equipment, I had chronic pain in my elbows and fingers, which prevented me from working fast. I was looking for a doctor who could help me with the elbow and arm pain, and by coincidence learned about Dr. Tajima.

"At the Tajima clinic, they treat elbow or arm pain with needles. There are also many cancer patients there, recovering. Since I'd had all kinds of treatments in the past and was ready to do anything, I asked for a treatment. I started visiting the clinic every other week to have shiraku treatment.

"The effect of the shiraku treatment showed up right away. My color came back. The weakness that I had felt throughout my body disappeared. Of course, the pain in my elbows is almost gone now. I told Dr. Tajima that I felt the effect really quickly. He told me that I had a strong intention to heal my problem, and that it's easier to activate immunity when someone has an attitude like that.

"Because I improved so much, I finally quit taking steroids. That made my body feel even lighter. It's been twenty years since my hepatitis began, but this is the healthiest time in my life right now."

Most medicines prescribed by doctors and in hospitals—not just painkillers—are allopathic. Stopping pain or diarrhea is an allopathic practice. I'm not saying that all allopathic treatments are wrong: they can help people who have a normal amount of physical strength deal with non-serious problems for short periods of time. However, you need to understand each disease, think carefully about the negative side effects of the medicines you choose to take, and be willing to reconsider your decision if the allopathic treatments don't improve the problem. In the final analysis, each individual patient must understand their body, how it works, and what they need. It is my hope that not just my patients, but patients everywhere will make an effort to understand their diseases as well as their doctors. Unfortunately, however, doctors sometimes treat several or even hundreds of patients, and it is physically impossible for them to fully understand the problems of each patient. When they're busy and under pressure, they may only be able to think about providing relief from visible symptoms. Patients, on the other hand, can totally commit themselves to thinking about their problems. They need to have knowledge and develop their own internal good sense in order to acknowledge that something is wrong if their condition hasn't improved after several months of allopathic treatment. If patients don't pay attention to their own body's feedback, and if they don't communicate their understanding and symptomatic changes to their doctors, they cannot heal.

In the past, people did not have access to as much information or knowledge of diseases as doctors did, so they weren't in a position to complain to their doctors. Because doctors were regarded as gods who healed people, it was just common sense for patients to listen to them and do what they said. But today, ordinary people have access to almost all the medical knowledge that's available through books, magazines, and the Internet. I hope that patients choose to study up on their own diseases so they can be active participants in the healing process and stop treatments when the results are not going well.

OTHER DANGEROUS YET FAMILIAR DRUGS

TESTIMONIAL 8

Pain and Tinnitus Disappear After Stopping Immunosuppressants and Beginning Aka Treatment *(Female, 50 Years Old)*

"I've suffered from severe shoulder stiffness since my twenties, and I began having pain on my left neck in my late forties. In April 2000, I began to suffer from tinnitus (ringing in the ears). The "zeeeee" noise in my ears never stopped. It was worse before menstruation and when my body was tired. I went to an otolaryngologist, who diagnosed a slight sensorineural deafness in my left ear, but no other problems were detected by examinations, including an MRI.

"At that point, they found out that I had iron deficiency anemia and high blood pressure. I began taking immunosuppressant and medication for anemia, which improved the condition. But the noise in my ears was still there.

"A year after the noise began, I was looking for some way to treat it and learned about AKA treatment. I began visiting the Kondo Clinic once a month. When I had a treatment, the pain in my neck disappeared and the noise diminished, but the effect only lasted a week or two before the symptoms came back. I was then introduced to the Hirota Physical Therapy Clinic for testing.

"At Dr. Kondo's clinic, I had a fabelle test in which they stretched and rotated my hip joints to see if anything was blocked or if there was any pain. If there was pain or a blockade, there could be sacroiliac problems or arthritis. In the course of this test, I realized that I had pain in my right kidney. The pain in my neck and kidney disappeared after AKA treatment, but the kidney pain came back a month later, and I again had back pain four days before the following visit. Two months later, the kidney pain became worse and the AKA treatment didn't even work much.

"I was worried that the AKA treatment might not help me heal completely. But Dr. Hirokazu Kondo, of the Kondo Clinic, and Dr. Setsuo Hirota, of the Hirota Physical Therapy Clinic, discussed my lymphocyte and granulocyte data and decided that I should stop using immunosuppressant.

"The results were dramatic. First, the AKA treatment was more effective than before and the kidney, back, and neck pain disappeared. Moreover, my lymphocytes, which had decreased due to the immunosuppressant, started to increase visibly.

"According to Dr. Kondo and Dr. Hirota, the immunosuppressant were unexpectedly causing severe tension in my sympathetic nerves, causing an increase in granulocytes. That may have caused the various kinds of arthritis I was suffering from. When it comes to arthritis like mine, which pets worse in AKA treatment, it's important to consider the influence of the medications you take.

"I have been feeling much better in every way since I stopped taking immunosuppressant. Moreover, I no longer have blood pressure problem, even though I quit taking my medication. My symptoms aren't completely healed yet, but the noise in my ears and the neck and kidney pain are almost gone and I'm able to lead a normal life."

Allopathic medicine regards symptoms as bad because of the discomfort they cause. I believe that other modern pharmacotherapies are problematic as well. I'd like to discuss a few.

One of these problematic treatments is prescribing depressants to people with high blood pressure. Modern medicine doesn't know the real cause of high blood pressure, which it calls "essential hypertension." But if you interview patients diagnosed with high blood pressure, you'11earn that they all have something in common: stress and hard work.

When you work too hard, your blood pressure rises because of tension in your sympathetic nervous system. So instead of treating the problem by taking medication, you need to lessen the amount of work. Better yet, find out why your work causes so much stress and then resolve the stress so that you don't go through the same habitual response. That's the best treatment when your sympathetic nervous system is overactive in response to stress. If you take medication to reduce blood pressure without reducing your workload or releasing the stress in some other creative way, your body won't have the blood pressure it needs to function, you'll feel bad all the time, and your health will go downhill.

Oral medications for diabetes are problematic as well. Like high blood pressure, diabetes is a response to the pressure of working too hard. Two mechanisms—stress and hard work—underlie the development of diabetes. First, tension is created in the sympathetic nervous system due to hard physical work. This tension constricts the blood vessels, reduces blood flow, and, in the body's attempt to keep warm enough to function, metabolizes stored energy, which can raise blood sugar. When the sympathetic nervous system is tense, adrenalin is secreted. If administered to a human or a mouse, adrenalin increases blood sugar levels to between 400 and 500 milligrams per deciliter. Moreover, when the sympathetic nervous system is tense, it suppresses secretion, and as a result the secretion of insulin in the pancreas is also suppressed. This accelerates the increase in blood sugar. It's therefore clear that diabetes can be healed by reducing the stress patterns associated with working too hard. If you're thin or of normal body weight, your disease will worsen if you try to control diabetes through diet (this isn't true for overweight or obese people). That's because starving creates additional stress on your sympathetic nervous system, increasing the essential tension. Oral diabetes medication is dangerous because the already weary pancreas, which has been suppressed and has stopped creating insulin as a result of excess tension, is now forced to secrete insulin. This forced stimulus totally exhausts the pancreas.

In fact, oral diabetes medication usually works for only a week or two. I've never heard of anyone being healed from this medication. Continuing to take the medication after it stops working is even worse, because the pancreas will be completely damaged, and without a functioning pancreas, diabetes becomes incurable. We can conclude that oral medication is one reason the number of permanent diabetic patients is increasing.

Another growing problem I'd like to discuss is the current

insistence on administering diuretics to patients with liver malfunction. Diuresis (the production of urine by the kidney) is controlled by the parasympathetic nervous system. When you have a problem getting rid of liquids, it means that your sympathetic nervous system is tense. In order to be able to urinate, you need to reduce your stress and ensure that you have good blood circulation. Again, just as with the pancreas, if you use diuretics to chemically force the liver to function, your already exhausted liver will receive such strong stimulation that it will be damaged to an even greater extent. This damage can get so bad that dialysis is needed. Dialysis patients are increasing every year due to the thoughtless use of diuretics.

You can begin to see that there's a cycle: diuretics—dehydration-thickening of the blood—bad blood circulation—fast pulse or increase in granulocytes—damage to the liver. Diuretics are used not just for liver problems, but for many other diseases as well, such as glaucoma, dropsy, or abdominal dropsy. Those who take diuretics often report severe thirst and feel that they're in bad shape. Their health starts to fail. Because dehydration causes tension in the sympathetic nervous system, it suppresses the functioning of the digestive system, preventing the body from absorbing water even when the patient drinks a lot. As a result, the body becomes even more dehydrated.

If the number of patients with a particular condition continually increases, it means that the treatment being used is not effective in healing the disease, and we need to question it. If patients are totally dependent on their doctors because everyone uses the same treatment or because a particular medication is prescribed by a famous doctor, even curable diseases can become incurable. To save your own body, you need to sharpen your personal intuition—your animal instinct—and learn how to tell whether the treatment you've been given is really going to work for you and your body, enabling you to truly heal.

Chapter 5
New Immunology

THE MECHANISM THAT CREATES IMMUNITY

Everybody today knows that immunity is important. But we barely understand where it comes from or how it's produced. Most people know that immunity is created when the body learns how to handle a foreign substance, and that once we have that immunity we will be immune (i.e., no longer intensely reactive) to the future presence of that substance. But for the most part, people don't really understand the mechanism of immunity.

Our body consists of cells with many potential capabilities, but most cells use only a few of these inherent capabilities during their normal functioning. The abilities that cells do use are quite one-sided: intestinal cells have the ability to absorb and transfer liquids from one area of the body to another; nerve cells have the ability to transfer perception through a linked network; and reproductive cells have the ability to produce ovum or sperm. But some cells have multiple functions, just like those of single- celled organisms. These are the cells that have to do with immunity.

Think of the amoeba, a single-celled organism. Amoebas manage to perform all of their organic activities—taking in nutrients, moving, digesting or eliminating foreign objects that enter the body—all within one single cell. There are actually cells like this in our human body—the white blood cells. White blood cells travel throughout our bloodstream, watching for and eliminating foreign objects as soon as possible. They're the essential center of our body's protective defense system—although when they become cancerous, these white blood cells can cause leukemia

HOW WHITE AND RED BLOOD CELLS ARE FORMED

In order to understand the many kinds of white blood cells and the functions they serve, it's helpful to have a basic appreciation of where they begin and how they're related to each other. The best way to show this is through a diagram.

All blood cells, whether white or red, are created from our

own personal supply of stem cells (about which we hear quite a bit these days) and are first released in the bone marrow. As these blood cells mature, they migrate to the rest of the body, taking up their separate "adult" tasks as the ever-changing condition of the body calls for them.

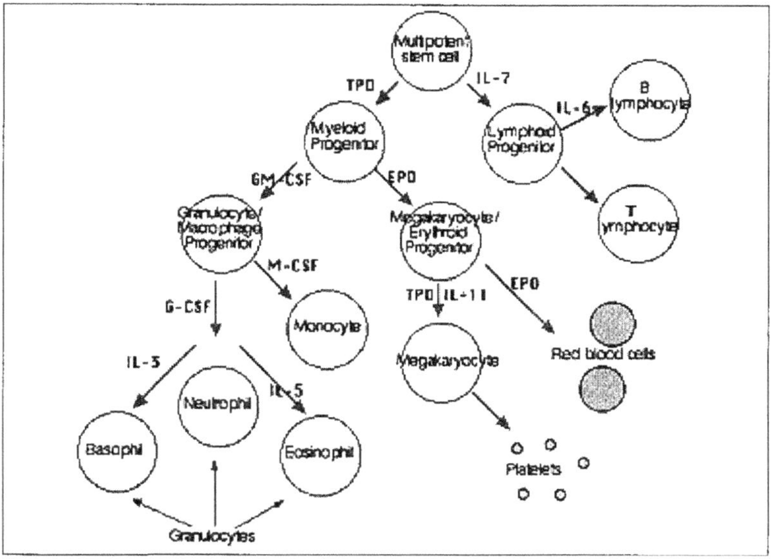

http://iisers.rcn.comfibimball.ma.iiltranet/BiologyPages/B/Blood.html

Figure 1. Blood Cell Formation and Relationship Structure.

As you can see in Figure 1, the basic bone-marrow stem cells create two different types of cells.

Major Elements in Blood & Their Functions

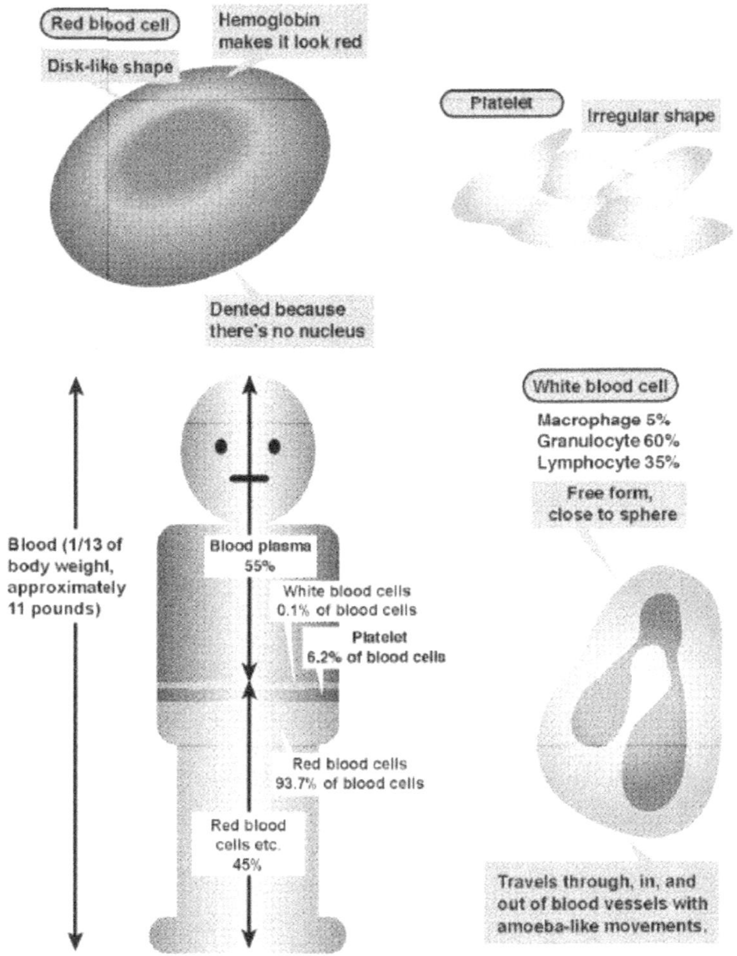

Substantial matter	Size	Number in 1 square ml of blood	Main function
Red blood cells	8/1000 ITIITI	4 million to 5 million	Transport of oxygen
White blood cells	10-15/1000 mm	4000-8000 Macrophage 200W00 Granulocyte 240m48oo Lymphocyte 1400-2800	Disposal of bacteria, immunity
Platelets	2-5/1000 mm	300,000	Blood clotting

** White blood cells make up only about 0.1% of all blood cells.*

The first, the ancestral lymphoid (lymph) cell, then divides into the B-type lymphocytes and the T-type lymphocytes.

The second, the myeloid progenitor (ancestor), separates out into two other progenitors. The first of these, the megakaryocyte/erythroid progenitor, in turn creates (a) the red blood cells (erythroids) and (b) the actual megakaryocytes, or clear blood platelets. The second type of cell created by the myeloid progenitor is the granulocyte/macrophage progenitor. From these come the "monocyte," or amoeba-like cells, and the three types of granulocytes: the basophils, the eosinophils, and the neutrophils.

MACROPHAGES: SOURCE OF WHITE BLOOD CELLS

As we've seen, there are three different kinds of white blood cells: monocytes, granulocytes, and lymphocytes. Because macrophages produce all three, I'd like to begin by explaining macrophages.

Macrophages are type of cell whose function is to absorb foreign objects, just as amoebas do. In fact, macrophages function very similarly to these single-celled organisms. Through the evolutionary process, many human cells became specialized for certain functions. White cells, however, including macrophages, retained their original form as cells that function in a primary way.

Macrophages, which are found throughout the body, have different names depending on where they are. This is the result of years of research. Medical science evolved from the study of pathology, a field in which "fixed" cells are studied under the microscope. The first documenting pathologist named the cells "macrophages" after watching these very large white cells among other, much smaller cells in the surrounding tissue. Because the cells were "fixed," researchers didn't see or understand macrophages as living objects moving and existing in different areas with different shapes. But in fact, macrophages have unique shapes depending on the tissue in which they exist. That's why the various macrophages were once thought to be different kinds of cells. Through years of different researchers finding different shapes in various locations, macrophages came to be called different names.

Starting from the top of the body, macrophages in the brain are called glia cells. These same cell types in the lungs are called alveolar macrophages; in the liver, they're called Kupffer cells. Macrophages that travel through the blood, called monocytes, are round. (Like amoebas, macrophages have pseudopods, or "false feet," that can extend or shrink, enabling them to move or stop. But because these "feet" could stick to blood vessel walls, making it difficult to flow in the blood, macrophages found in the blood system pull their pseudopods in, becoming round.) Histiocytes are macrophages grown in the bone marrow, which are unevenly distributed throughout the tissue as part of the Langerhans. Macrophages in joints are called joint macrophages.

These various macrophages were once considered different cells. But when we observe them closely, we can see that they all have characteristics similar to amoeba-like cells that absorb foreign objects and travel quickly to areas of inflammation. Researchers came to realize that macrophages, like amoebas, spread and change their shapes according to the space available in each particular body organ. Because their similarities were not noticed for some time, early researchers gave each type of macrophage a different name. But macrophages are the basic monoclonal (single) cells of the white blood cell family.

MACROPHAGES ALSO CREATE BLOOD AND BLOOD VESSELS

Other hemocytes (blood cells) evolved from macrophages as well. Amphibians, reptiles, and fish have red blood cells that carry oxygen and have a nucleus. But human red blood cells don't have a nucleus (are "denucleated") and have shapes that are very different from those of macrophages. The purpose of blood cells is to contain as much hemoglobin as possible in order to carry the maximum amount of oxygen; having a nucleus in a red blood cell is an obstacle to this. That's why the red blood cells of mammals developed without a nucleus.

Platelets are also derived from macrophages. Platelets are very small fragments of cells that coagulate blood. There are a great number of platelets: 100,000 to 200,000 in one microliter of blood. When newly formed in the bone marrow and still clustered together, platelets are called megakaryocytes. As they mature and leave the bone marrow, they separate out into the fragments we call platelets.

Like hemocytes, vessel endothelial cells were created from macrophages. Before organisms became highly evolved, they didn't have blood vessels. They had blood-forming tissue and a heart, but they merely sent blood to the space between each cell without the use of blood vessels. As organisms became more complex, this process of using simple heart pressure to force liquid among all the cells that needed blood became too inefficient; hence, blood vessels were developed. That stream of red blood cells evolved into a process that created its own blood vessels.

As they evolved from macrophages, monocytes maintained the ability to absorb foreign objects in order to eliminate them from blood. If we inject Indian ink, for example, into blood, monocytes will take care of it. Indian ink particles are very fine: they have a diameter of0.1 micron when suspended in water. Once these particles enter the blood vessels, vessel endothelial cells absorb them and throw them out of the bloodstream. Macrophages then come to absorb the expelled particles. Because the ink particles aren't a nutrient for macrophages and can't be decomposed by oxygen, they're transported either to the intestines, which eliminate solid material, or to the lungs, which surround them with a thick liquid called sputum, which we cough up and spit out.

THE DIVERSIFICATION OF WHITE BLOOD CELLS THROUGH EVOLUTION

Like amoebas, macrophages process foreign objects by swallowing them whole—a function called phagocytosis. White blood cells, which evolved from macrophages, have this same function. But as organisms evolved, their living environments changed. This change in turn gave rise to more complicated structures, and a greater variety of foreign objects to deal with as well. That's why protective cells began to specialize into different functions. Although basic macrophages remained the same, there also came into being granulocytes, which enhance the ability to eat other cells (phagocytosis), and lymphocytes, which administer immunity and cause phagocytosis ability to degenerate.

When we study the human body today, we observe that the number of granulocytes and lymphocytes are greater than the number of macrophages. This is particularly dramatic in the white blood cells, which are made up of about 5 percent macrophages, 60 percent granulocytes, and 35 percent lymphocytes. Granulocytes and lymphocytes, which evolved from macrophages, now play a more important role in the blood, overshadowing macrophages in number.

Granulocytes enhance the ability of macrophages to perform phagocytosis, so they're good at taking care of large objects such as bacteria. They swallow bacteria whole and use digestive enzymes and active oxygen to decompose them. Phagocytosis takes in foreign objects by wrapping them in a film. This film is then destroyed and the particle, whether cell or foreign objects, is crushed.

Large foreign objects like bacteria are about 100 times smaller than cells. But particles that enter the body are not always as big as bacteria. Some dangerous objects are much smaller. There are, for example, viruses, very small microorganisms like Rickettsia, toxins produced by bacteria, different proteins segmented by digestive enzymes, dangerous microorganisms in the air, pollens, and particles from the bodies of ticks composed of microorganisms. These must be dealt with as well. These small objects are about 10,000 times smaller than cells. Because they're too small to trigger the swallowing function of macrophages, they must be caught by bonding. Lymphocytes are white cells that have evolved to catch these foreign objects through adhesion molecules by causing phagocytosis ability to degenerate.

Protein molecules such as integrin, selectin and immunoglobulin are some of the adhesion molecules that exist in lymphocyte film. Antigens are cohered by combining several of these. These adhesion molecules are also used to bind cells. For example, macrophages use these molecules to stick to certain types of tissue. These molecules exist throughout our body.

B cells create antibodies and send them out to the lymphocytes. Because they're too big to travel through blood vessels fast enough when a foreign object enters the body, B cells instead send small protein molecules—adhesion molecules and antibodies—into the blood and body fluid to handle the object. Lymphocytes release these antibodies by separating the adhesion molecules in correspondence to the particular antigen that's present. These antibodies are even sent to the intestines, mucus, or secretions.

In sum, this mechanism to protect our body from harmful objects has developed as our organism has evolved. Primitive beings had only macrophages for protection, but evolved beings have two white cells in addition to macrophages: granulocytes, which have the ability to swallow foreign objects, and lymphocytes, which catch small objects by using adhesion molecules.

GRANULOCYTES PROCESS LARGE OBJECTS BY SWALLOWING THEM

Granulocytes have the ability to not only swallow foreign objects but to digest them as well. This power is generated by numerous granules (hence the name "granulocyte") in the cytoplasm. These granules are made up of various lysosomal enzymes. Many lysosomal enzymes, such as granzyme and lysosome, are crammed into small bags in the cytoplasm. That's why they can digest large particles such as bacteria. This is the elimination system of granulocytes. Large amounts of active oxygen are used in this process.

LYMPHOCYTES PROCESS SMALL OBJECTS USING ADHESION MOLECULES

Lymphocytes, on the other hand, appear to have no cytoplasm, but just a nucleus when observed under the microscope. I'll discuss this in more detail later, but basically, when lymphocytes are removed to be looked at under the microscope, they're hibernating. So, when pathology and histology were studied primarily through microscopes, lymphocytes were thought to have no purpose. They were believed to have a nucleus and some genetic information, but no functional intracellular micro-organella. Active cells usually need mitochondria to breathe, granules to store lysosomal enzyme for the digestion of foreign objects, granular endoplasmic reticulum to synthesize protein, and golgi body to gather protein. All cells have these intracellular micro-organella to perform various activities, but none are found in lymphocytes. Therefore, lymphocytes were considered to have no purpose until the 1960s, when the study of cell immunity began. Up until that point, the relationship between lymphocytes and immunity was unknown.

At one time, it was even believed that lymph nodes were just bags in which useless cells were locked.

The Functions of Granulocytes

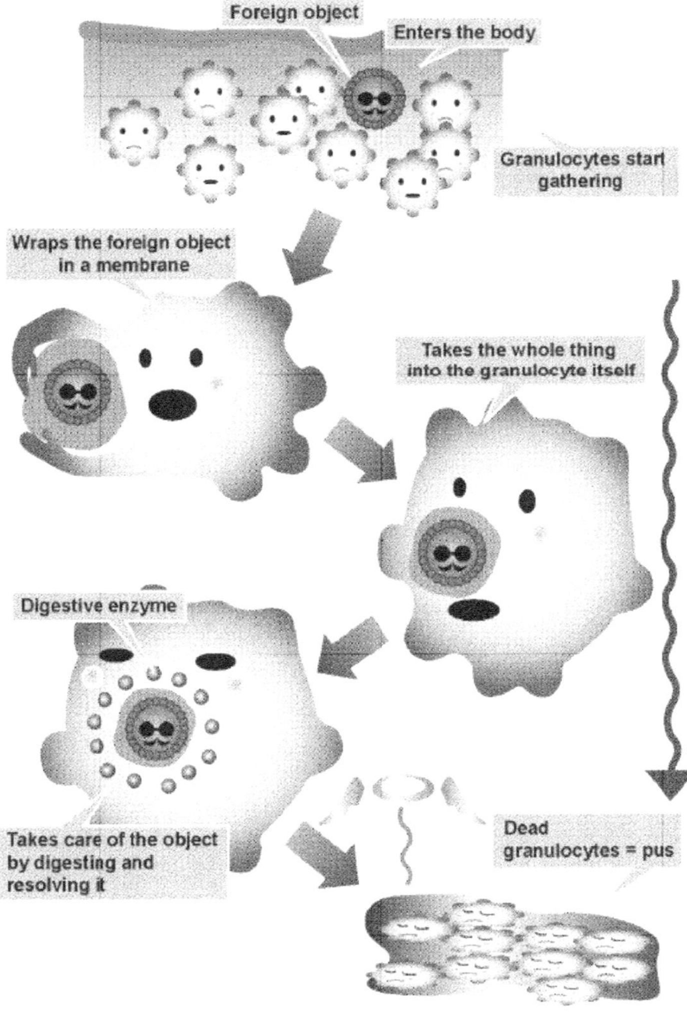

Battle Against Foreign Object = Suppurating Inflammation

As immunity research progressed, we began to realize that lymphocytes hibernate until corresponding antigens enter. Antigens are small foreign objects that react to antibodies. Lymphocytes awaken when they sense antigens entering the body. They then produce intracellular micro-organella to correspond with the antigens, as they split, creating clones. Lymphocytes are quite small when hibernating in the lymph nodes, composed of only a cell membrane and a nucleus. Once they awaken to fight antigens, however, they become larger. One lymphocyte will divide ten times, resulting in 1,000 times more lymphocytes upon battle. Diseases caused by contagious viruses usually have an incubation period before they erupt. That's because it takes a while for the hibernating lymphocytes to wake up and produce enough clones to fight against viral antigens. When you catch a cold, it's a few days before you start getting a fever and feeling really sick. That's because lymphocytes are usually resting and prepare for a battle only when antigens enter the body. Unlike granulocytes, which come quickly to fight against bacteria, lymphocytes need some time to prepare.

MACROPHAGES INSTRUCT LYMPHOCYTES

How do hibernating lymphocytes learn that antigens have entered the body? A substance called cytokine—a macromolecule of the active substances in a living body—transfers information between macrophages and lymphocytes or between lymphocytes. About fifty cytokines are known to us, including interferon, interleukin, and TNF.

All white blood cells produce cytokine, but macrophages do this in the most basic way. When an antigen enters the body and causes inflammation, macrophages discern the antigen's property and produce the appropriate cytokines to command the other white cells, the lymphocytes and granulocytes. If the antigen is bacterial, granulocytes come; in the case of a virus, lymphocytes fight it, depending on the instruction. In other words, lymphocytes can't act without instruction from macrophages. As proof, if you put lymphocytes alone in a test tube with an antigen, there will be no sign of an immune reaction. They don't work unless macrophages are there to read the antigen send the appropriate cytokines. This is how important macrophages are.

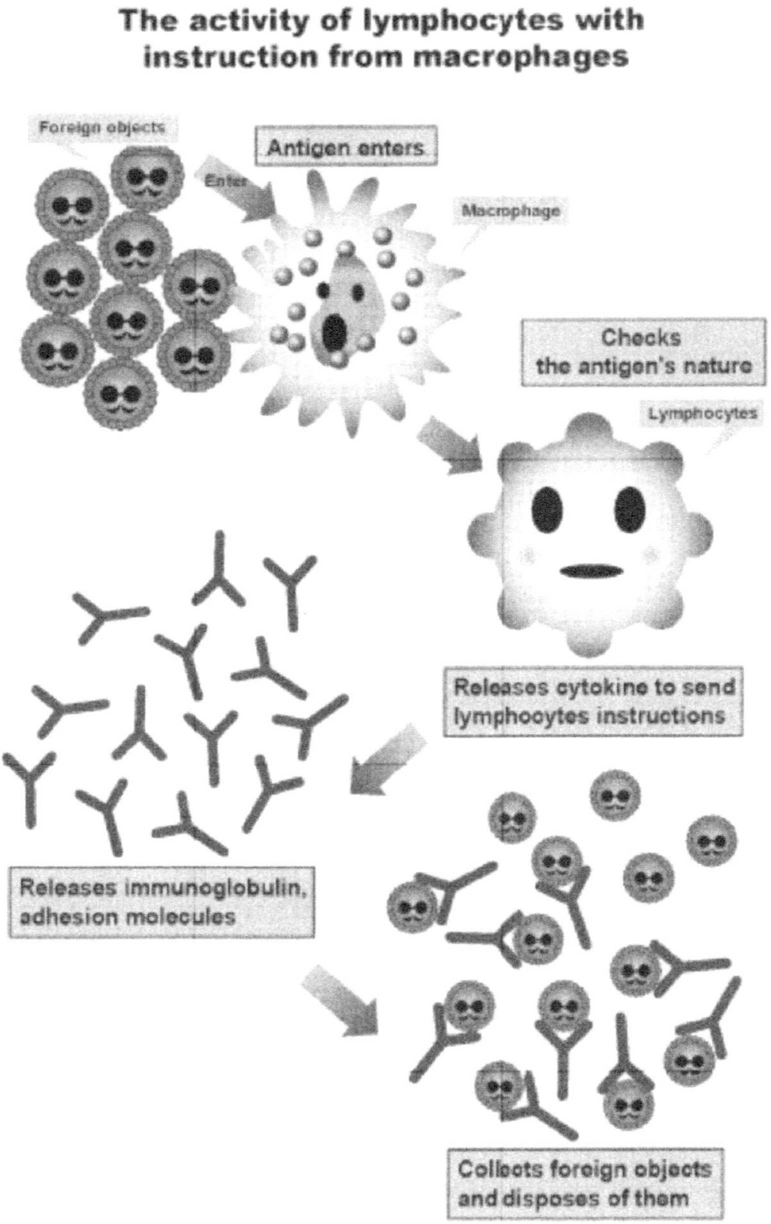
The activity of lymphocytes with instruction from macrophages
Foreign objects
Antigen enters
Enter
Macrophage
Checks
the antigen's nature
Lymphocytes
Releases cytokine to send
lymphocytes instructions
Releases immunoglobulin,
adhesion molecules
Collects foreign objects
and disposes of them

Lymphocytes split and grow in number under the direction of cytokines. But not all hibernating lymphocytes become active. Only those that have the protein or antibody corresponding to a particular antigen increase; others remain in hibernation. When an antigen enters for the first time, macrophages allow it into their own protein molecules, or MHC (which I'll explain later), where it's acknowledged by the lymphocytes. These helper T cells then transfer the information to B cells. The B cells increase through cloning, producing enough antibodies to fight the antigen. But a portion of the B cells rest, registering information about the antigen once the battle is over. If that same antigen returns, the lymphocytes recollect it and are able to produce so many clones quickly that the inflammation stops before disease can occur. That's how immunity functions against almost all antigens. Of course, different antigens are easier or harder for the body to cope with; but this is in general how we handle diseases for which immunity is relatively easy, such as parotitis or measles.

After the lymphocytes and antigens have battled, there's wreckage to take care of. This is again the job of the macrophages. Macrophages function as commanders at the beginning and cleaners at the end. It's believed that this is because macrophages are the basic models for other parts of the white blood cells. Macrophages are, in other words, the bosses of the white blood cells.

MACROPHAGES: BASIS OF THE IMMUNE SYSTEM

Our understanding of the mechanism of the immune system began only about forty years ago. The study of lymphocytes began to advance in the 1960s, when we began to understand the function of immunity. Because of this very short history, the public learned about the mechanism of immunity in a rather roundabout way, and it was even seen by some as a sort of sudden "wonder power." But in my many years of research, I've come to see that the immune system's protective quality has evolved according to the principle of ontogeny recapitulating phylogeny.

First, macrophages processed foreign objects by swallowing them, like amoebas; then granulocytes were created; then lymphocytes evolved to catch smaller objects using adhesion molecules in the cell membrane.

But it's the macrophages that instruct the granulocytes and lymphocytes, and that repair and manage the antigens and other infected and damaged cells that the granulocytes and lymphocytes catch.

We can therefore conclude that macrophages are the basis of immunity. Immunity wouldn't function without macrophages. Researchers often remove lymphocytes and place them in test tubes to study immunity, but if macrophages are taken away from lymphocytes, immunity-related activities rarely occur. From this, we know that macrophages control the activities of immunity.

Moreover, a fetus that lacks lymphocytes or granulocytes can manage to survive after delivery, but a fetus lacking macrophages can't. They're also closely related to the cells that form bones, such as osteoclasts, so the body of a fetus won't be complete without macrophages. If an infant lacked lymphocytes or granulocytes, they would be very vulnerable to infection and would therefore be put into a sterile room and given antibiotics to survive. But they could still come out of the womb. A fetus that lacked macrophages could not even build a body. That's how important macrophages are.

GRANULOCYTES HEAL INFLAMMATION WITHOUT FORMING IMMUNITY

I hope you now understand the protective role of macrophages, granulocytes, and lymphocytes. I'd now like to explain how the granulocytes and lymphocytes that receive instructions from macrophages work to protect the body.

White blood cells are 60 percent granulocytes and 35 percent lymphocytes, with the balance made up of macrophages. Why are there more granulocytes? It's because granulocytes are more often needed for battle. Of the foreign objects that come into our body, bacteria are predominant. That's why we have more granulocytes. When granulocytes and bacteria battle, purulent inflammation results as part of the healing process. When a wound from injury or surgery testers, that's the granulocytes battling. When the intestinal membrane is inflamed or ulcerated, it's usually caused by granulocytes battling where there are normal bacteria.

But battles between granulocytes and foreign objects don't necessarily result in immunity. In the case of pimples, for example, there's no guarantee that they won't come back. It's the same with food poisoning, a type of viral infection. It doesn't mean you'll never have food poisoning again. Granulocyte inflammation, unlike lymphocyte inflammation, can happen many times.

So, granulocytes, which make up about 60 percent of our system of protection, heal problems without generating immunity. If you don't understand this important point, enhancing immunity to evade disease won't make sense. Most books about immunity teach that the immune system protects our body, but they don't explain the function of granulocytes. They ignore the work of granulocytes, which make up more than half of our system of protection. Studying immunity without understanding granulocytes creates the misconception that all diseases are healed by lymphocytes immunity. But that doesn't explain the essence of the matter.

I believe that it's critical for a full understanding of immunity to acknowledge that 60 percent of inflammation is dealt with by granulocytes. And, as I'll explain later, granulocytes increase not just to manage inflammation caused by bacteria but also when we're under a great deal of stress. As we'll see, this point can help solve the mysteries of a number of diseases.

LYMPHOCYTES CAUSE SEROUS INFLAMMATION

Let's now look at lymphocytes, which make up 35 percent of our white blood cells. Lymphocytes cause a condition called catarrhal inflammation, which produces a thin fluid called serum. As I mentioned previously, lymphocytes battle with viruses. When you catch a cold and have a runny nose, for example, the inflammation that accompanies the production of serous fluid is a sign that lymphocytes have begun to battle. Lymphocytes also cause phlegmonous inflammations, which get red and swollen but don't fester, such as those that follow the bite of a toxic bug or the sting of a jellyfish or bee. The phlegmonous inflammation that results when tuberculosis is tested with tuberculin is caused by lymphocytes, as is what we usually call allergic inflammation.

In short, it's easy to tell whether granulocytes or lymphocytes are at work because the difference is obvious: inflammations caused by granulocytes are purulent inflammations that damage tissue, and ones caused by lymphocytes are catarrhal, phlegmonous, or allergic inflammations. Interestingly, no matter where an inflammation is, you can see changes in the blood. Doctors test your blood when you have an infection because inflammation in some areas of the body affects the blood. That's why checking the white blood cells can help diagnose whether infection is present.

WHITE BLOOD CELLS ARE CONTROLLED BY THE AUTONOMIC NERVES

As I discussed previously, the ratio of granulocytes to lymphocytes is 60:35, with the balance made up of macrophages. But this ratio is not always fixed. As I studied the daily and yearly rhythm of this proportion, I realized that some regular rhythmic changes occur, although the range is small. I began to wonder what caused these changes and learned that the white blood cells are under the control of the autonomic nerves.

I was not the first to discover this. It was Dr. Akira Saito, a lecturer of mine at Tohoku University, who discovered, reported, and outlined this theory. About fifty years ago, Dr. Saito discovered that granulocytes are controlled by the autonomic nerves and that lymphocytes are controlled by the parasympathetic nervous system. Because he was my lecturer, I continued my research, hoping to advance his theory. That's how I realized that periodic rhythms and changes in quantity have something to do with the autonomic nerves.

The autonomic nerves are adjusted through the opposition of the sympathetic and parasympathetic nervous systems. The sympathetic nervous system becomes active when we work, exercise, feel emotional, or worry; in other words, when we're excited. The parasympathetic nervous system, on the other hand, creates a state of relaxation when we rest, eat, or sleep. The autonomic nerves, which consist of these two opposing systems, control the functions of almost all cells—and the circulating white blood cells are no exception.

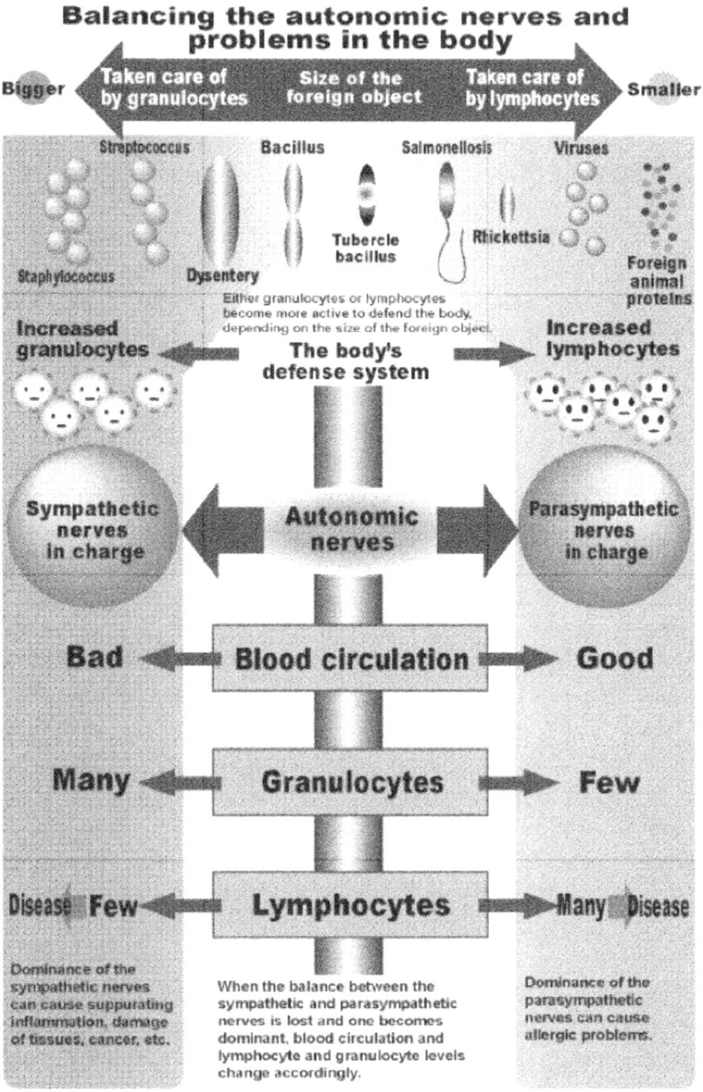

The autonomic nerves were the first nerves to evolve, and they work unconsciously. That means we can't intentionally try to tense the sympathetic nervous system or relax the parasympathetic nervous system. But we can tense the sympathetic nervous system by getting exciting or let the parasympathetic nervous system dominate by resting. Most cells are controlled by autonomic nerves. When we're excited, the sympathetic nervous system gives cells the instruction to work, and they create a cooperative system that helps us function. When we eat, the parasympathetic nervous system becomes active, instructing the cells of digestion and absorption to work and letting other cells rest.

Through testing, I confirmed that even the circulating white blood cells are controlled by the autonomic nerves. The autonomic nerves have a certain rhythm whereby the sympathetic and parasympathetic nervous systems gently switch in the course of a day. The sympathetic nervous system gradually becomes dominant from the time we wake until evening, and the parasympathetic nervous system becomes dominant at night when we rest. I tested how the proportion of white blood cells is linked to these changes by taking a blood sample every four hours.

These samples exhibited a pattern: the number of granulocytes increases when the sympathetic nervous system is dominant, and the number of lymphocytes increases when the parasympathetic nervous system is dominant. We also know that the sympathetic nervous system tends to be dominant during the winter, and the parasympathetic nervous system during the summer. I tested to see whether these yearly changes also affected the white blood cells, and the result was the same: there are more granulocytes in the winter and more lymphocytes in the summer.

There's a reason that the white blood cells are controlled by the autonomic nerves. In general, we're excited when we're active. Our hands or feet can get injured, and bacteria can enter. Granulocytes increase so we can protect our body from these bacteria. During the process of digestion and absorption, on the other hand, there's a danger that small particles can break down and enter our tissue, so we need more lymphocytes. Lymphocytes evolved to work with the digestive system because there was a need for them. The digestive system is controlled by the parasympathetic nervous system, so it's active when the parasympathetic nervous system is dominant. This activates lymphocytes as well. So, you can see that, in order to protect us, there's tremendous cooperation between the digestive and immune systems.

It's said that immunity can be enhanced when we rest. But when we rest, the parasympathetic nervous system becomes dominant and lymphocytes become active, which enhances the immune system. If we understand that white blood cells are controlled by the autonomic nerves, that granulocytes become active when the sympathetic nervous system is dominant, and that lymphocytes are active when the parasympathetic nervous system is dominant, we can prove scientifically what we already know from experience and from how we feel. The white blood cells are controlled by the autonomic nerves. I'd like you to remember this principle.

For several years, I said that lymphocytes have acetylcholine receptors and granulocytes have adrenalin receptors, as if lymphocytes do not have adrenalin receptors and granulocytes do not have acetylcholine receptors. I've since realized that I need to explain this more accurately. All the cells in our body have both adrenalin receptors and acetylcholine receptors, and lymphocytes and granulocytes are no exception.

The smooth muscles in the intestines are controlled by the parasympathetic nervous system. They become active when stimulated by the parasympathetic nervous system, and activity is suppressed when they receive stimuli from the sympathetic nervous system. In a similar fashion, lymphocytes are activated by stimuli from the parasympathetic nervous system and suppressed by the sympathetic nervous system. Granulocytes are just the opposite. So, the important point here is not which there are more of and which there are less of, but which stimuli activate or suppress them.

AUTONOMIC IMBALANCE CAUSES DISEASE

The fact that all cells, including white blood cells, are controlled by the autonomic nerves enables us to be in good physical condition and be prepared and protected. Sometimes, however, we strain ourselves, worry too much, or eat too much food without exercising. This can burden the sympathetic nervous system and cause the parasympathetic nervous system to be overactive. Anyone can suffer from autonomic imbalances at times, when these imbalances affect our health or defense systems. In other words, too many granulocytes due to an overactive sympathetic nervous system or too many lymphocytes due to an overactive parasympathetic nervous system can create adverse physical conditions or disease.

Functions of the autonomic nervous system

The sympathetic and parasympathetic nerves in the autonomic nervous system have opposite functions, but they are in balance when the body is healthy.

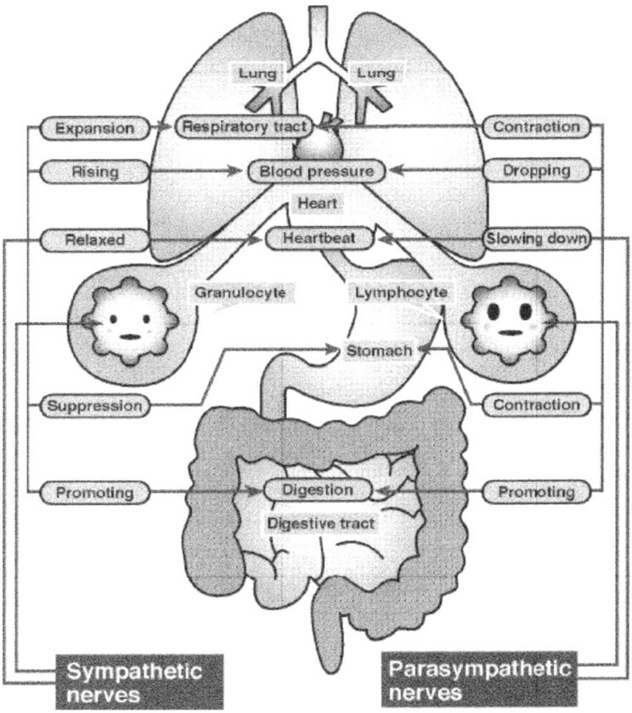

Nerves for physical movements, made tense by adrenalin. When active, they activate the functioning of the heart and lungs so that one can move more actively.

Control breath, digestion, and circulation. Have opposite functions from the sympathetic nerves. When they are more active, they support the digestive process, making the digestive organs more active.

When there are too many granulocytes due to an overly dominant sympathetic nervous system, they attack normal bacteria, which can cause purulent inflammation. Moreover, granulocytes commonly destroy old tissue, making them an active force of metabolism. Too many granulocytes may attack tissue unnecessarily and speed up metabolism too much. Granulocytes are narrow in the middle, with a strangely shaped nucleus. Our bodies are made up of countless kinds of cells, but only Granulocytes have this type of nucleus. When a cell dies, the nucleus twists and splits, in a process called apoptosis; granulocytes look as if they're dying even when they're alive. That's why they have short lives. Brain cells can live as long as we do, but granulocytes die after about two days.

EXCESS GRANULOCYTES: A FACTOR IN ULCERS

When granulocytes die and their nucleus breaks, the active oxygen in the cell is released, oxidizing the surrounding tissue. Too many granulocytes can kill the surrounding cells and damage tissue. That's how stomach and duodenal ulcers are caused. The sympathetic nervous system is overactive when you're stressed or worried. That causes granulocytes to increase and attack bacteria in the body and tissue, eventually leading to ulcers.

It was once believed that hyperacidity caused stomach ulcers. Helicobacter pylori, a type of bacteria, was also thought to be the cause. But study has shown us that stomach ulcers are actually caused by excessive granulocytes due to an overactive sympathetic nervous system. Granulocytes increase when there's stress, and spread to mucosa all over the body, including the stomach. When they're stimulated by helicobacter pylori and other substances, they produce active oxygen and damage mucosa tissues, leading to stomach ulcers. Tests show that helicobacter pylori is not the main factor in mucosa damage: in one example, a young man in his twenties with almost no helicobacter pylori developed a stomach ulcer when exposed to intense stimulation and fear. As a result of tests such as these, we've disproved theories that stomach acid and helicobacter pylori cause stomach ulcers. In fact, a paper I wrote on this particular study was published several years ago in the American journal Digestive Diseases and Sciences.

An awareness of the phenomena caused by excessive amounts of granulocytes or lymphocytes can help you to understand the mechanisms behind a variety of diseases. Many people think diseases are caused by genetics or some unknown biological factor, but neither of these reasons explains how disease comes to be in our bodies. By studying granulocytes and lymphocytes, though, we can see that 90 percent of all diseases are caused by an excessive reaction in the autonomic nerves (the sympathetic and parasympathetic nervous systems) and the white blood cells (granulocytes and lymphocytes). We can then look at just how this excessive reaction on the part of lymphocytes causes disease.

EXCESS LYMPHOCYTES MAKE BODY TOO SENSITIVE

When there are too many lymphocytes, we become oversensitive to antigens, which causes allergy problems. I'd like to further discuss lymphocytes in order to explain this mechanism.

Lymphocytes did not suddenly lose their reliance on phagocytosis and develop adhesion molecules; rather, they reached this stage through many steps. Lymphocytes are derived from macrophages, like granulocytes. There are many varieties of lymphocytes, such as T cells produced outside the thymus, T cells (Th1 cells, Th2 cells, cytotoxic T cells), and B cells (B-1a cells, B-1b cells, B-2 cells), and NK (natural killer) cells, widely known to attack cancer cells and the first type to be created.

NK cells, also called large granular lymphocytes, evolved from macrophages, with which they share a similarity in shape. Macrophages move about on their "feet" like amoebas, have intraplasmic granules and kidney- shaped nuclei, and digest foreign objects by swallowing them. NK cells, while not as large as macrophages, are the largest of the lymphocytes. They have granules, as you can tell by their name, granular lymphocytes, and, like macrophages, have kidney-shaped nuclei (the other evolved lymphocytes have round nuclei). It's clear that NK cells were produced from macrophages.

Yet, no one else in the scientific community acknowledges that this is the case. To illustrate my theory, I performed tests on NK cells in 1985, in which I observed them swallowing bacteria under various conditions. In one test, I added serum to yellow staphylococcus, a type of bacteria, and witnessed the NK cells swallowing the bacteria. I realized that, even though they're lymphocytes, NK cells will indeed begin to swallow bacteria under certain conditions. Usually, lymphocytes catch foreign objects using adhesion molecules, but the NK cells swallowed them just as macrophages do, though to a lesser extent. So, depending on the situation, NK cells will process objects by swallowing.

Therefore, it's clear that recently evolved lymphocytes still retain some characteristics of macrophages. Look at their shape: NK cells still have granulated powder in their cytoplasm; evolved lymphocytes are round and have no granules. This shows that it hasn't been long since NK cells evolved from macrophages. These results were published in the American Journal of Immunology.

TCELLS PRODUCED OUTSIDE THYMUS: WATCH DOGS OF ABNORMAL ACTIVITY WITHIN BODY

After NK cells came T cells produced outside the thymus. T cells administer cellular immunity, an immune reaction that occurs when cells attack foreign objects, rather than producing and releasing antibodies. The "T" in T cell stands for thymus, which is where the cells are produced. The thymus is made up of very soft fat-like tissue and is located behind the ribs. The T cells produced here protect our body from outside antigens, such as viruses or other foreign objects.

Following their discovery in the thymus in the 1960s, it was believed that T cells were produced only in the thymus. But in 1990s, I discovered that they are produced in other areas as well, such as the liver and the intestines tube cuticle. These cells are referred to as T cells produced outside the thymus, as distinguished from T cells produced in the thymus, called thymus-produced T cells. I also discovered that T cells produced outside the thymus are old cells that evolved soon after NK cells, and that T cells produced outside the thymus and NK cells watch not for outside antigens, but for abnormal activity within the body.

NK cells and T cells approach antigens and initiate an immune reaction. Their receptors acknowledge foreign objects entering cells and kill the infected cells by spraying substances such as dialytic ferment, which they store in their own cells. Because T cells react with antigens by approaching them directly, this reaction is called cellular immunity.

B cells are another type of lymphocyte. The "B" derives from the bursa of Fabricius, a specialized organ in birds, where the cells were first discovered. Mammals, including humans, do not have a bursa of Fabricius, and it's believed that human B cells are produced in the bone marrow. B cells have immunoglobulin, receptors that perceive and gather foreign objects. But B cells don't travel to these objects. Instead, they release receptor-equipped antibodies into the body fluid. The antibody then flows through the body fluid, sticking to the foreign object and reacting with the antigen. This immune reaction is called liquid immunity, as distinguished from cellular immunity. So, T cells and B cells process foreign objects in totally different ways.

I believe that, like lymphocytes, B cells diversified in three stages: B- 1 a, B-1 b, and B-2. Among lymphocytes, the comparatively newly evolved NK cells and T cells produced outside the thymus exercise self-response: they respond to cell disorder. NK cells that kill cancer cells are one example. Similarly, in the B cell group, the newly evolved B-1 cells release auto-antibodies that correspond to inner disorder. If you look at each kind of lymphocyte, you can see that our basic immunity evolved from their role in eliminating abnormal cells within the body.

Most studies that the public sees focus on immune responses against antigens and foreign objects from outside the body, such as viruses. These studies have therefore emphasized that the basis of immunity is the differentiation of self and foreign object. But if you study older types of lymphocytes that haven't evolved as much, you'll realize that the basis of immunity is not the acknowledgement of outside antigens. Rather, immunity evolved out of recognition of the self and disorder within the body.

DEVELOPMENT OF THYMUS IN LAND-BASED ORGANISMS; ROLE IN FIGHTING ANTIGENS

The evolution and diversification of immune cells is closely related to the evolution of organisms. When organism moved from the ocean to the land, they created organs such as the thymus and bone marrow in order to produce highly evolved lymphocytes such as T and B cells. I believe that the thymus enabled organisms to create a system to acknowledge foreign antigens. The variety of available antigens drastically increased once organisms moved to the land. There are many more antigens in the air than in the water, and more chance of getting injured on land. Land-based organisms needed to develop a system against foreign antigens. That's why the thymus developed.

Another factor that greatly furthered the evolution of the immune system was the increased metabolism that resulted from living on land. The amount of oxygen inhaled from air is much greater than that from water. This broadened the types of activities organisms could engage in by giving them more energy for moving around, coping with gravity, and so forth.

The amount of oxygen in the air has made the concentration of oxygen in arterial blood five times greater. Water contains 1 percent dissolved oxygen, whereas air is 20 percent, so the amount of oxygen in a land-based environment is twenty times greater, which increased the oxygen in the blood by five times. With five times as much energy available, metabolism advanced and allowed for more movement. This created more opportunities to be exposed to antigens. Organisms have had develop enhanced immune systems to fight foreign antigens in order to survive.

The thymus originally evolved from gills. Once organisms moved to land and began breathing with lungs, their gills degenerated but did not disappear completely. Because antigens often attacked fish at their gills, these organs contained a lot of lymphocytes. As organisms moved onto land, the expansion of the lungs pushed this area down to the thorax, to become the thymus. The thymus still maintains this system against foreign antigens, which originated in the gills.

This is a very big transformation in the evolution of organisms. I'd like to explain a little more about how this system came to be created. When our ancestors lived under water, 95 percent of the lymphocytes in the gills were self-responding (watching for inner disorder), and only 5 percent responded to foreign antigens, because there were far fewer antigens in the water. But as organisms moved out of the water, the gills evolved into the thymus, the self-responding lymphocytes (the 95 percent) were discarded, and the lymphocytes that dealt with foreign antigens (the 5 percent) were maintained. These lymphocytes continued to replicate and divide, creating a huge immune system in the thymus whose sole purpose was to fight foreign antigens.

In other words, the immune system that fights foreign antigens is a newer system that resulted from evolution. Yet, throughout the history of research immunology, scientists determined that the purpose of immunity is to recognize foreign antigens. That's because they only studied the evolved immune system. They believed that immunity was a system to acknowledge self and non-self. But as the study of auto-antibody-producing cells such as T cells produced outside the thymus, NK cells, and B-1 cells has advanced, we've come to realize that immunity is something that takes place within our own bodies. First, our defense mechanism attacks and eliminates abnormal cells within us; second, we have a very fine and clever system that evolved to fight foreign antigens. This second type of immune system is a rather new one that came about when organisms moved onto the land.

OUR ORIGINAL IMMUNE SYSTEM SOLVES THE MYSTERY OF DISEASE

Unfortunately, typical immunology textbooks focus primarily on the new immune system and rarely mention the differentiation of immune cells outside the thymus, which I discovered. They mention that NK cells kill cells with disorders such as cancer cells, but their descriptions of this process are brief. But from this perspective, you can't solve the entire mystery of immune system functioning and the mechanism of disease. That's because you need to work with old lymphocytes in order to understand immunity against difficult diseases of unknown origin, such as cancer; autoimmune diseases; some geriatric conditions; pregnancy; protozoan infections that parasitize cells, such as malaria; and GVH (graft vs. host) diseases following transplant.

When you have one of these difficult diseases, autoantibodies are produced, and the self-responding type of T cells are activated. The more highly evolved new cells, such as the T cells and B cells produced in the thymus and bone marrow, don't deal with problems such as these. While a great many of these evolved T cells and B cells occupy the lymph nodes and spleen, the old immune system is particularly important when it comes to these difficult diseases.

Where are the cells of the old immune system located? There are almost none in the lymph nodes and spleen, nor in the thymus or bone marrow. Instead, they are located around the digestive tract; around the liver, which evolved from them; around the exocrine glands, such as the salivary and submandibular glands; and around sexual organs such as the uterus, which form secretions.

I believe that the old immune system developed around the digestive tract because digestive enzymes cannot break foods down to the level of an amino acid. A block of peptides and a group of connected amino acids could function as an antigen, making the immune system particularly important in this area. Another reason is that the immune system may be needed to deal with the viruses that can enter the body with food.

MHC: UNIQUE TO EACH INDIVIDUAL

In order to understand the evolution and function of lymphocytes, it's important to also understand the major histocompatibility complex antigen, or MHC. MHC is a protein molecule that displays antigens, but each person differs in their particular arrangement of amino acids. This difference in protein molecules is why rejection often happens in transplants.

Only 1.3 percent of our DNA differs from that found in monkeys, while 20 percent differs from mice. Mammals are very similar when it comes to their protein composition; in fact, there's humans are 99.9 percent the same, so there's almost no difference. But in a transplant, rejection can happen if just one cell has a different protein molecule. That protein molecule is MHC.

About a hundred thousand kinds of human genes and protein molecules are produced. But most molecules are similar among individuals. Only with MHC is there a slightly different arrangement of amino acid in each person. The name MHC derives from its discovery as a very important major protein of histocompatibility that determines whether or not rejection occurs in transplantation.

Because rejection can occur because of differences in MHC, it's necessary to use immunosuppressant in transplants. In bone marrow transplants, for example, an individual must be found that matches a patient's MHC. If a different MHC is transplanted, the immune system acknowledges this different protein as one it does not have and attacks it, causing rejection. This is just one example of an immune phenomenon caused by the reaction of the lymphocytes.

Because MHC has a very quick metabolism, it is destroyed and produced more quickly than other proteins. All the cells of our body have it, so rejection will always be a factor in transplantation. However, if you suppress immunity throughout the body through immunosuppressant, you can prevent rejection in areas with less MHC, such as the kidneys or liver. That's why there have been many successful cases of transplantation in these areas. But because patients must keep taking immunosuppressant, some problems can continue after surgery. They can catch cold easily, and even small cuts can fester. They're likely to develop cancers as well.

Skin transplantation and lymphocyte transfusion, on the other hand, rarely succeed because there are so many MHC proteins in the cells and lymphocytes of the skin. Even with the use of immunosuppressant, skin cannot easily be transplanted to another person.

MHC ENABLED US TO SURVIVE

Why did MHC become so diversified that it causes rejection in transplants? The reason is survival of the species. Dangers from foreign antigens such as bacteria and their poisons have frequently threatened extinction of the species. Many species have already become extinct for this reason. Mammals, however, which are physically weak to begin with, have undergone intense diversification. This diversification of MHC has helped us survive by creating both strong and weak cells to battle each dangerous antigen.

One example is plague, which spread throughout Europe during the Middle Ages. It's said that about three-quarters of a village's population died when plague reached their community. But not everyone died. Those who survived the infection did not have severe symptoms. The symptoms of a disease can be part of the body's immune reaction against it. A strong immune reaction can cause high fever or encephalitis, which can themselves damage the body. But a weak immune reaction allows antigens to harm the body. So, an immune reaction that's neither too weak nor too strong is the key to healing. The individuals who survived the spread of plague were those who's MHC did a moderate job.

This diversification in MHC enabled the species to survive and prosper by changing the strength of the immune reaction.

Because MHC diversification is also observed in mice, it's believed that this process began in an early stage of mammalian evolution. Humans evolved from primates about five million years ago, but MHC diversification is said to have begun about thirty million years ago—way before we were primates. Mammals already existed as long as fifty million years ago, around the time the dinosaurs became extinct, but they were insectivores or nocturnal. They wouldn't have been able to survive if all the members of the species ate the identical toxic food. In order to sustain the species, mammals began to diversify the proteins that attached to antigens, and eventually, humans evolved. It's ironic to discover, as we develop the science of transplantation, that these diversified protein molecules reject each other.

THE OLD AND NEW ORIGINS OF MHC

Interestingly, our bodies contain both new MHC, which has evolved through diversification, and old invariant MHC, which hasn't diversified. As I noted earlier, the more advanced T and B cells are located in the lymph nodes and spleen and produced in the thymus and bone marrow, while old lymphocytes such as NK cells are located in the digestive tract, liver, exocrine glands, and uterus. Similarly, old and new MHC can be found in different areas. The old MHC, which didn't evolve, remains in our body along with new MHC, which evolved some thirty million years ago—a fact that was discovered only about fifteen years ago.

The old MHC is expressed in the digestive tract, liver, exocrine glands, and uterus.

Thus, we can theorize that the evolution of MHC, the proteins that display antigens, occurred simultaneously with that of lymphocytes during the evolution from macrophages in amoebas. That may explain why organs that were left behind in the evolutionary process continue to maintain the old type of lymphocytes and still recognize the antigens that enter the old type of MHC. New lymphocytes, on the other hand, recognize antigens that enter the new type of MHC. Even among protein molecules, they divide their roles in order to watch for both inner disorder and foreign antigens.

THE OLD AND NEW IMMUNE SYSTEMS REVERSE ROLES IN THE ELDERLY

Throughout our lives, our old and new immune systems play different roles, varying in their importance. The thymus, the center of the new immune system, grows larger from birth until about age twenty and from that point grows smaller. When we're young and the thymus is large, our lymph glands and spleen are filled with evolved T and B cells. As we age, the thymus starts to shrink, and the lymph glands and spleen grow more obsolete. That's when the intestines, liver, and lymphocytes in exocrine glands awaken into greater activity.

Stress can cause the thymus to shrink regardless of age. In the presence of stress, glucocorticoid steroid hormones are secreted, causing the thymus to shrink and the lymph glands and spleen to atrophy. This activates the old immune system, rather than the new one, and causes lymphocytes in the digestive tract and liver to increase. In other words, the old immune system is the one that recognizes these antigens entering the body. Stress causes the functions of the two immune systems to reverse.

This is actually a well-developed system. As we age, our bodies contain a greater number of abnormal self-antigens. Oxidization of protein and fat occurs as well, giving us wrinkles and spots on our skin from stored waste matter. It's best to destroy and eliminate cells that have become less functional or that carry waste. That's where the old lymphocytes—the self-responders — come into play. They sense disorder in the body and produce or activate auto-antibodies in order to eliminate abnormal areas and help the body deal with the problems of aging.

THE OLD IMMUNE SYSTEM PROTECTS CENTENARIANS

Before the advancement of immunology, it was believed that immunity decreased and became weaker as we aged. But this isn't so. The old lymphocytes are just as active and functional when you're old as long as you're healthy. To prove this, I conducted research with my colleague Hisami Watabe, currently a professor at Ryukyu University, and other professors at the university. We studied the lymphocytes of people over 100 years old in Okinawa, where there's a large concentration of centenarians. We observed that the organs of the old immune system, such as the digestive tract and liver, were filled with old lymphocytes, which spread through the blood and protected the body. On the other hand, we noted fewer lymphocytes in the lymph glands and spleen and in the receptors of the new immune system, such as the thymus.

OUR OLD IMMUNE SYSTEM PROTECTS OUR BODY IN TIMES OF STRESS

In an emergency, stress can cause emphasis to switch from the new immune system to the old one. When we're under stress, granulocytes increase, tissue damage occurs, cells become disordered, and the secretion of waste matter is suppressed. If the stress continues, we become gaunt as the damage, disorder, and build-up of waste accumulates throughout the body. In a case like this, the problem is within the body itself, rather than from external antigens, so the old immune system is called upon to deal with the abnormal cells and waste.

If stress continues, a virus infection will occur. Viruses don't just come from outside; many lurk in our body. One well-known example is herpes. When the new immune system goes down due to continued stress, the suppressed herpes viruses that have hidden in our body begin to emerge, damaging tissue and causing inflammation. The old immune system is needed to fight against the abnormal cells that are created in this type of situation.

The old immune system is also closely related to autoimmune diseases such as collagen disease. Collagen diseases often occur after a severe cold. The new immune system may have been weakened, possibly due to stress, at the time the cold was contracted. In fact, my collagen disease patients often tell me that they have had some sort of stressful experience just before an outbreak. In the case of autoimmune diseases, it's the old immune system that defends the body.

THE OLD IMMUNE SYSTEM SUPPORTS HEALTHY PREGNANCY

The old immune system plays a major roll not just in negative situations such as stress and autoimmune diseases, but also in pregnancy. Once the fertilized ovum settles and begins to grow in the uterus, nutrition must be transferred to the fetus. This causes stress and creates tension in the sympathetic nervous system. It shrinks the thymus and increases the number of old lymphocytes in the liver and uterus and can sometimes cause autoantibodies to be produced. If these autoantibodies become prominent, a disease called ketosis can occur, though in a healthy mother the number of autoantibodies released is usually not a problem. After delivery, the old immune system becomes weak, the thymus grows larger, and the new immune system begins to function again.

Why does this phenomenon happen? As I've discussed, the old immune system targets abnormal cells. In areas of the body where cells reproduce frequently, disorders are more likely to occur. Cancer cells, which are just one type of abnormal cell, generate from cells that reproduce continuously. The tissue of the skin, intestines, and glands are in a state of constant reproduction; that's why adenocarcinoma occurs. Cancer is more likely to appear in an area of propagating cells.

A fetus growing inside its mother is also made up of propagating cells, which propagate as fast as cancer cells. It's possible for cells from the fetus to flow into the mother through the umbilical cord, which connects the fetus and the mother at the placenta. But old lymphocytes prevent this from happening. In keeping the fetus' cells from entering her body, a pregnant woman uses the same types of self-responding old immune system cells—such as NK cells and T cells produced outside the thymus—that are used to attack cancer cells. If the system fails, the woman may develop a benign hydatidiform mole, or a malignant choriocarcinoma. Both of these phenomena happen because of cells from the fetus. So, a healthy pregnancy can't happen unless the old immune system is activated.

However, if the sympathetic nervous system becomes severely tense during the pregnancy, not only does the new immune system get weaker, but the old immune system also becomes excessively active. The old lymphocytes then attack the fetus, recognizing it as abnormal cells. This is ketosis. Ketosis causes high blood pressure and nephritis, as well as a phenomenon that can lead to miscarriage called gravid kidney, in which the old lymphocytes attack the fetus. Listening to the stories of people who developed ketosis, I learned that they had all experienced stress— whether from straining during the pregnancy, from a sad occurrence, or from a pre-existing heart condition—which caused their new immune system to diminish too much. To conclude, even though a mother's thymus grows smaller during pregnancy, the pregnancy will be normal as long as old immune system becomes moderately active. If it's not active enough, the mother could end up with choriocarcinoma; and if it's too active, she could develop ketosis.

As we now realize, understanding the function of the old immune system helps us understand the mystery of disease. I find this matter so profound that I have no interest whatsoever in schools of thought that neglect it. The old immune system solves the mystery of pregnancy, aging, stress and autoimmune disease, and collagen disease. Most diseases that are little understood and difficult to treat occur in the realm of the old immune system. It's a pity that this is barely understood. If we know the mechanism of this old immune system, we can come up with fundamental treatments for all the most difficult diseases to cure.

CONCLUSION: IMMUNOLOGY THAT FOCUSES ON OLD IMMUNE SYSTEM IS KEY TO FUTURE

I'd like to summarize the foundation of the type of immunology that I advocate. First, our body is protected by white blood cells consisting of lymphocytes and granulocytes; therefore, it's not lymphocytes alone that protect us from disease. Granulocytes defend us from large foreign objects such as bacteria and rid us of about 60 percent of the external enemies that invade our body. When we think of immunity, we tend to think only of lymphocytes, but remember that it's granulocytes, not lymphocytes, that heal tissue damage. People tend to focus on the aspects of immunity that fight very fine foreign antigens such as viruses. This indeed plays a very important role when the body is young and the thymus active. But during stress, aging, or phenomena such as pregnancy, the thymus shrinks and the active lymphocytes change as a result; then the old immunity, which is produced outside the thymus, becomes active and protects the body through self-response, in which the old lymphocytes recognize antigens by putting them in the old MHC. If you understand this basic process, the mystery of difficult diseases will be solved one by one.

Unfortunately, the old immune system does not get enough attention. Most researchers focus on the advanced immune system, which is a very large and interesting area on which to conduct analytical research, and on which many research dollars are spent. But through my own research I came to realize that the mystery of difficult diseases could not be solved without conducting research on the old immune system as well. I've heard of no research on the advanced immune system that has solved these mysteries, unfortunately. While much of this research is very advanced, it has not succeeded in healing a single immune disease, much less the autoimmune diseases. That's because the new immune system deals with foreign antigens only, not with diseases caused by self-abnormalities within our own body and tissue.

Chapter 6
Your Lifestyle and Disease

During my study of the autonomic nerve's dominance over white cells, I came to understand that various cells in our body are influenced by the autonomic nerves. White blood cells, which travel around the body, are also dominated by the autonomic nerves. The purpose of this system is to create conditions that enable our body to go about its various activities. My years of research convinced me that most organic reactions are good for our body. It's natural for organisms to react to change by adjusting their condition, even if uncomfortable symptoms result. This system is certainly not meant to cause disease.

When we think about why we get sick, we can see that we are under various types of stress. Throughout life, we get infections, we have worries, we strain ourselves at work, and so on. The stimulation of all this stress creates an extreme bias within the autonomic nerves, making the cells of our tissue or the white blood cells that protect our body too active, and damaging the body. This is the fundamental mechanism of disease.

Looking at disease in this framework, we can see that it's essentially our lifestyle that determines whether or not we get sick. Humans strain themselves in order to survive hardships and challenges that create stress. We can endure this to a certain point, but there's a limit. If we keep straining ourselves, our bodies will cease to tolerate the reaction to strain. In order to maintain your health, it's very important to know your body's limits. For example, when young people stay up all night, they can recover after a short rest. But if they continue this behavior for a few days, their body will be damaged. And if someone in their fifties stayed up for even one night, their body could be severely affected, unless they're in very good condition. I believe each person's limitations are different depending on their age and physical strength, so we all need to know how much our own body can tolerate.

The same can be said for mental strain and stress. If you carry around too much sadness, sorrow, or hardship, you will create tension in the sympathetic nervous system and cause tissue damage. Stress literally undermines our body. Our lifestyle isn't just about how we live—it's also about our attitude toward life. If you want to have a healthy life, it's important to eliminate stress in the mind.

A LIFE THAT'S TOO EASY CAN ALSO CAUSE DISEASE

If stress is bad for us, should we therefore try to live a completely easy life? Not at all — too much relaxation can harm us by causing stress in a different way.

The best examples I can find are obesity and lack of exercise. Excessive obesity harms our body. Obesity creates a relaxed condition in which the parasympathetic nervous system is active, but too much obesity can cause stress and phenomena like loss of breath or fatigue. In a situation like this, just a little strain can over activate the sympathetic nerves, which can cause disease.

As I mentioned in my explanation of allergic diseases and atopic dermatitis, being relaxed and having too many lymphocytes can make the body too sensitive. In some people, just a little stress can cause an allergic reaction, such as hives. And due to the parasympathetic nervous system, women's blood vessels tend to widen when they're too relaxed, causing their body to swell.

Being relaxed and having a lot of lymphocytes doesn't mean you won't get sick. While it's true that cancer and collagen diseases are caused by an overly dominant sympathetic nervous system, some people get sick despite having lots of lymphocytes. About 20 percent of patients get sick even though their parasympathetic nervous system is active and their condition relaxed. This group of patients needs to activate their sympathetic nervous systems by pursuing a more active lifestyle, exercising, improving their diet, and so on.

YOUR MIND CREATES YOUR PHYSICAL CONDITION

I mentioned previously that certain temperaments make people more prone to cancer. Trying to do your best is a sign of responsibility, which most people would consider a positive trait—but overworking is not necessarily good for you. Many people get sick because they work too hard and their sympathetic nervous system becomes overactive. Trying to accomplish everything yourself is not something to be proud of. People sometimes find themselves in situations in which they have no choice but to complete a certain amount of work, but they're unwilling or unable to find someone they trust to share the workload. Too much diligence or perfectionism can cause sympathicotonia. Each individual is different: some work too hard and some relax too much. To maintain health, you need to understand your own personality and tendencies, and avoid extremes. That's something we all can and should do.

Of course, certain hardships are inevitable at times, and they can certainly cause stress. It's very difficult and very sad when a family member is sick or when you lose someone close to you. Such pain is hard to overcome. But you need to consider whether spending your days endlessly grieving is good for you or for the people around you. Strong emotions always affect the body. Being too sensitive, worrying excessively over little things, or getting caught up in jealousy can harm you. When you carry around negative emotions or try to cause harm to others, your mind and your body both become distorted. The mind is a very important factor in the prevention of disease.

IMPORTANCE OF EATING FOR ACTIVATING PARASYMPATHETIC NERVOUS SYSTEM

Food consumption automatically activates the digestive tract and stimulates intestinal bacterial flora. Making your digestive tract work by eating something is the easiest way to activate the parasympathetic nervous system. That's because the digestive tract, which consists of all the body's organs from the mouth to the anus, is the largest system that directly connects to the parasympathetic nervous system. That tells you just how important diet is.

In fact, the ability to eat certain foods directly determines the effect that immunity revitalization treatments have on cancer patients. Oftentimes, cancer patients have a dominant sympathetic nervous system and need to activate their parasympathetic nervous system to correct the imbalance, so it's important that they eat. Even if they're weakened by anti-cancer drugs or surgery, they can still recover as long as they're able to eat on their own to some degree.

Of course, what they eat is important as well. One reason that an increasing number of geriatric diseases are showing up in Japan today is that our diet has become westernized. In a pamphlet called Shizenshoku (Natural Food) News, a nutritionist raises the point that Japanese people, who are used to a diet consisting of rice and fish, may end up with a variety of physical problems if they radically change their diet to include meat, dairy, and eggs in imitation of Westerners. I agree. The Japanese have a long history of adaptation and evolution. Changing our diet all of a sudden puts strain on our bodies. In fact, many cancer patients who have recovered or are in the process of recovery choose diets based on brown rice and traditional foods.

IMPORTANCE OF BREATHING TO CONNECT CONSCIOUSNESS AND UNCONSCIOUSNESS

Along with the digestive tract, the respiratory organs are one of the largest systems in the human body. When humans are anxious, our breath is fast and shallow; when we're relaxed, it's slow and deep. Breathing is the only activity in our body that's both conscious and unconscious. In other words, it's controlled by both the sympathetic and parasympathetic nervous systems. We breathe even if we don't want to or forget to. It's an automatic function because it's controlled by the autonomic nerves. That's why it gets faster or slower, depending on our thoughts and emotions. When our sympathetic nervous system is tense, our breath is faster, and when our parasympathetic nervous system is dominant, our breath is slower.

But at the same time, we can consciously control our breathing to some extent. It's impossible to be aware of your breathing from morning till night, of course, but for limited periods of time, we can correct our breath. For example, we can breathe in deeply and out slowly. If we repeat this several times, the autonomic nerves receive the information that the body has taken in a lot of oxygen. The parasympathetic nervous system will then be activated to slow down the breath. Our body reacts this way so it won't take in too much oxygen; that's why we feel relaxed after taking deep breaths. Our physiology encourages us to take relaxed breaths following deep breaths that give us lots of oxygen, because there's a connection between our consciousness and unconsciousness. If we understand the relationship between breathing and the autonomic nerves, we can see how much we benefit from deep breathing.

MUSCLES ARE MEANINGLESS UNLESS THEY'RE USED

In our evolutionary process, humans acquired large amounts of complicated muscles. Without exception, these muscles will fail if they're not used. Where our muscles are more prominent, we need to exercise in order to keep up with them. Because humans stand up instead of relying on all four extremities for walking, we have more muscles in our legs than in our arms. Therefore, when we exercise, our focus should be on walking.

Like the muscles of our legs and arms, the muscles that support our spine are very large. The back and stomach muscles are a major part of our musculature. Since half of our weight is in the upper body, and since we must fight gravity to keep upright, the muscles in the back and stomach are prone to straining. These muscles work hard, slowly moving our upper body as we perform our daily activities; the energy of exercising strains them even more. That's why muscles sometimes get hurt through acute or sudden movements. So, if you don't exercise the muscles in your stomach and back, they can fail unexpectedly.

However, exercising and weight training until your body becomes extremely muscular is also hard on the body, based on the balance of the autonomic nerves. The more muscle you have, the more oxygen must be taken in to maintain them, causing tension in the sympathetic nervous system and creating a condition that's ripe for disease. But letting your muscles atrophy by being too relaxed is not good either. As your muscle decays, it will cause diffuse atrophy, and even normal daily activities can exhaust the muscles, causing pain and other problems in the back, knees, shoulders, spine, and other areas.

THE BODY SHOULDN'T BE COLD

Thus far, I've explained that many diseases are caused by poor blood circulation. Blood circulation is controlled by the parasympathetic nervous system, which regulates relaxation. Therefore, you shouldn't cool your body too much, and you should exercise as frequently as you can in order to maintain good blood circulation.

It's also important to keep the body from getting cold by avoiding cold substances. It's best to refrain from drinking or eating cold things. It's also important to avoid exposure to too much air conditioning. Instead, do things that keep your body warm. Increase your body's ability to move stagnant blood by exercising more or by taking hot baths.

Dr. Katsunari Nishihara, formerly a lecturer at Tokyo University, insists that an increase in the number of opportunities to eat cold food (thanks to the development of the refrigerator) has become a major factor in many diseases. When there was no refrigeration, a watermelon chilled in the well was as cold as food could get. But we now have access to extremely cold juices, sodas, and milk, and people get ice cream at the convenience store even in the winter. Cold food is everywhere.

When you eat something cold, it cools down your mouth, esophagus, stomach, and finally your intestines. Cold food remains in the stomach for a while, where peristaltic movements warm it up a bit before it goes on to the intestines; but cold liquids go directly to the intestines after passing through the stomach only briefly. They cool down the intestines immediately, as well as the large lymphocyte system in the intestines that regulates mucosa immunity. This system can't function in the cold, and disease can result. Because of this, Dr. Nishihara recommends taking milk or juice out of the refrigerator about half an hour before drinking to bring them to room temperature.

Cold beer is tasty, but if it's very cold it can overstimulate the intestines.

People who are particularly sensitive to this may feel pain. It's actually a very dangerous drink. In fact, Dr. Nishihara drinks warm sake instead of cold beer. He believes that cold drinks make people aggressive, which does make some sense. When your body is stimulated, the sympathetic nervous system tenses up and you're ready for battle. In the movies, Yakuzas (Japanese mafia) drank cold sake before attacking their enemies. That's actually very practical. The Yakuzas may have used cold sake to force themselves to fight, because when the sympathetic nervous system is extremely tense, you become unaware of yourself or your fear.

IMPROVING MODERN MEDICINE: EXPANDING TREATMENT CHOICES THROUGH ALTERNATIVE, COMPLEMENTARY MEDICINE

Today, there are increasing attempts to approach medical treatment using tools other than modern medications, even among doctors. We're seeing more meetings and conferences regarding alternative and complementary medicine, for example. I believe that people are seeking options to counterbalance the negative aspects of Western medicine. Western medications are very strong and can produce an immediate effect, but they can also cause strong side effects, which create tremendous problems for some patients. These patients are beginning to choose alternative or complementary medicine because they produce fewer or no side effects. Alternative and complementary treatments include such practices as herbal medicine, acupuncture, moxa, aromatherapy, and homeopathy, all of which gently, but slowly, stimulate the body's natural biological responses that promote healing. They support healing by strengthening immunity, improving circulation, and facilitating better elimination. Alternative medicines utilize natural biological responses, so they work more slowly compared to Western medicines, which work directly on suppressing the symptoms that we have learned to call disease. Alternative practices are related to the ways of healing that humans have used naturally throughout their entire history to recover from disease and injuries. I believe that this connection will make alternative and complementary medicine very attractive to patients.

Of course, Western medicine has brought us many important advances. Precise observation and examination is possible because of Western medical developments, and it was Western medicine that enabled us to overcome many of the deadliest infectious diseases. It has made enormous contributions to our health. But there are negative aspects as well. Because its focus has been too much on the analysis of disease, Western medicine no longer looks at the health of the body as a whole. And pharmaceutical research has created very strong drugs. These drugs are effective because they target specific symptoms, but their makers stopped questioning them far too soon. As a result, there's no understanding of whether these drug applications actually improve the health of the body as a whole or contribute to true healing.

Chemotherapy, for example, can shrink cancer. But shrinking cancer doesn't necessarily heal it. You're healed only when you begin to regain a healthy life. If you have to lead life with a failing body due to the side effects of therapy, the medical treatment can't be good, even if the cancer area itself is smaller. This is the limit that Western medicine now faces as a result of its narrow vision.

As I've observed cancer patients, I've come to believe that cancer treatment has really reached a turning point. Most patients rely on Western medicine at the beginning of their treatment, but many turn to alternative medicine once Western medicine has done everything it can. Modern medicine is not yet comfortable enough with itself to consider both types of treatment equally important from the beginning. By the time many patients come to me and my colleagues, they're physically exhausted from taking Western medications and have lost all hope of healing. That's a pity. Alternative medicines heal slowly and naturally using the body's built-in biological response system, so your body won't heal unless you maintain enough strength to allow the biological reactions to function correctly. Many patients would have healed completely and quickly if they had tried alternative treatment sooner. Once patients become exhausted and have little or no energy, even alternative medicines can do little more than reduce the pain a bit or give them a little more time to live.

I therefore hope that more people become aware of alternatives that exist beyond Western medicine. The more you know, the better able you are to make effective choices. You may choose to deal with a problem quickly using Western medicine—often the choice of young people who have a lot of strength, or patients in the midst of an acute attack of a disease. But with chronic diseases or problems that have been around for a while, which take longer to heal, you may wish to try alternative medicine in order to enhance and increase your body's own healing power.'

EXPANDING THE FUTURE OF MEDICAL SCIENCE THROUGH EASTERN PHILOSOPHY

Alternative medical treatments are often effective for diseases that require the prolonged and potentially harmful use of Western medicines, such as cancer, collagen diseases, and allergies. These diseases can become ongoing, chronic problems, meaning that the autonomic nervous system, the immune system, and the circulatory and digestive systems are all out of balance. That's why alternative medicine, which corrects such imbalances by focusing on the entire body, is much more effective. So, if Western medicine can't heal you, I think you should give it up quickly and try alternative medicine.

I believe that Eastern philosophy lies at the foundation of alternative medicine. The basis of alternative medicine is to deal with disease by understanding why the whole picture is the way it is. Eastern medicine is sometimes called holistic medicine, in contrast to Western allopathic medicine, which is called analytical medicine. The Eastern medical process is good at grasping the body in its entirety. But Eastern medicine has its weak points too. If only Eastern medicine existed, the chemical and biological mysteries of all the different organisms wouldn't have been uncovered. Eastern medicine and Western medicine have moved in very different directions because of the differences in their underlying perspectives. Up to this point, there's been no way for them to cooperate with each other, because they developed from points of view that totally dismissed the other.

But I think it's possible for these two to contribute to human health together and avoid conflict, if not cooperate outright with each other. I think it's especially possible in Japan. Japan has developed for the past hundred or more years by accepting both Western and Eastern philosophies. This has to be possible in the field of medicine as well, especially when our entire society is moving in that direction. I think that, of all the world's nations, Japan has the most potential to create a point of view that blends the holistic treatment methods of alternative medicine with the truly excellent aspects of Western medicine, which have contributed so much to the advancement of medical knowledge throughout the world. Thanks to Western medicine's attention to detail, practitioners with an Eastern holistic perspective can now see how those details work together and can begin to use their wisdom in a more focused manner to support a quicker return to balance for the whole person.

CREATING SOCIETY WITH LESS DISEASE

Despite our effort to lead a peaceful life with a calm and stable mind, humans do not have the power to deal with and adapt to everything. Modern man seems to have forgotten this. The power of nature is great indeed. Even today, we can't totally control our entire environment, including such elements as air pressure and temperature. Since the beginning of time, our natural environment—the clean environment within which we grew—has had a direct influence on our lives. When pollutants, such as those we have unthinkingly let loose during the past 150 years, dissolve into the many layers of the environment, the effects are beyond our imagination. We are, after all, part of nature. Selfishly trying to use nature, with the attitude that science controls everything, simply doesn't work.

If we change the way we think, though, we may be able to accept and use this powerful force without fighting it. Perhaps everyone has at some time had a deep concern in their heart that they couldn't solve. When this type of concern affects our health, nothing goes right, even if we fully understand that eliminating worry can help our tense sympathetic nervous system recover. We can't heal our disease because we get so caught in concern, and it comes to rule our reality. There are some things we can't solve if our minds are preoccupied our daily lives.

Sometimes, accessing our deeper selves through the natural human activity of prayer, or by returning to traditions, can make us feel better when times are rough. In Japan, we have ceremonies for overcoming sorrow or for building and supporting our minds as we pray for a peaceful future. Going to shrines on New Year's, remembering the deceased at Bon Festival, or attending funerals are formal ways to focus on a life event and gain closure. Even if it's not yet scientifically proven that these processes give us respite from pain and heartache, we can commit to doing what we can. I think we should return to our culture and traditions if they help us solve our problems and bring us peace of mind.

LIVING ACCORDING TO THE RHYTHM OF NATURE BRINGS ULTIMATE HEALTH

When I was younger, I discovered that the sympathetic and parasympathetic nervous systems alternate switching on and off during the course of a day. I presented this research in a study of the daily rhythm of the autonomic nerves and white blood cells. As my research continued, I discovered that the autonomic nerves are influenced by changes in air pressure; that their rhythms last about seven to ten days; and that they change at different points during the year as well. In short, the autonomic nervous system is being shaken, changed, and moved all the time. Because it changes according to variations in the natural environment, if you fight its rhythm, you're also fighting nature. If you have an unreasonable lifestyle that ignores this natural rhythm, your struggle will invariably result in failure. As I see increasing numbers of cases like this, I believe it more and more.

Some people can't rest at night unless they've been active enough during the day to exhaust themselves. In some cases, a person's stimulated daytime state continues through the night, leading them to stay active all night and reversing the rhythm of their sympathetic and parasympathetic nervous systems. Our physical rhythm can become different from that of nature. Some drugs stimulate and maintain nervous activity and cause insomnia. Anti-inflammatory painkillers and steroids can do this, as I've discussed, as well as antihypertensive, drugs for Parkinson's diseases, anti-anxiety agents, sleeping pills, and others. None of these should be taken for a long period of time, because they cause the natural biorhythmic cycle to fail. High atmospheric pressure creates tension in the sympathetic nervous system, and low atmospheric pressure activates the parasympathetic nervous system; therefore, it's natural to work harder and be more active and sociable when it's sunny, and to want to spend quiet, reflective time alone on a rainy day. I believe that following your natural sense in this way is a valuable tool for good health.

The balance between the two sets of autonomic nerves changes from day to day and from season to season throughout the year, so it's natural for your life to change a bit accordingly. It's easier to work during the winter because the sympathetic nervous system tenses when we need to endure cold. And it's best to rest during summer vacation because the parasympathetic nervous system is dominant in the low atmospheric pressure of summer. It's ideal to take a month of summer vacation if possible.

Look at the natural rhythm of our activities throughout history: during the hot summer, man worked hard on the farm, thus activating his sympathetic nervous system. So, the work and activity required to grow our food helped balance the parasympathetic nervous system dominance caused by the seasonal warmth. The need to work offsets our preference to rest and relax. In winter, on the other hand, our bodies tend to be tenser because cold creates tension in the sympathetic nervous system. Historically during the winter, we spent more of our time indoors, where we tended to be quiet and get more rest. This helped balance the stressful demands of the cold weather.

With diseases such as cancer and collagen disease, which are caused by tension in the sympathetic nervous system, it's most important to create a relaxed situation in which the parasympathetic nervous system can be dominant until healing occurs. But if a healthy person begins to live in ways that allow the parasympathetic nervous system to become dominant, their life will start to feel flaccid and idle. If this occurs too often, they'll become susceptible to allergies and other health challenges.

To be happy, we need a lively, vibrant lifestyle. There's a time to be active and aggressive, and a time to relax and rest. The best guideline is to live according to daily rhythms, barometric rhythms, and yearly rhythms: the rhythms of nature. Living this way—with periods of activity and periods of rest in moderation—enables us to maintain our best physical and mental health.

Healing Your Healing Power

By

Dr. Kazuko Hillyer Tatsumura
Ph.D., OMD

THE WIND AND THE SUN

From the sky, the wind and the sun had a contest to remove a man's coat.
The wind said, "I can take off the man's coat easily."
The wind started to blow hard on the man.
The more fiercely the wind blew, the harder the man clutched
onto his coat and did not let go.
The sun smiled, and started to send the man warm, kind light.
Soon, the man felt very warm and took off his coat by himself.
— The Philosophy of Holistic Healing

INTRODUCTION

I am very humbled and honored that Dr. Toru Abo has given me his permission and encouragement to add this chapter to his earthshaking new book. Originally published in Japan in 2003 under the title "Immunity Revolution," this book caused quite a sensation in Japan and is still on the best-seller list. It has inspired many people, both sick and healthy, to consider taking a holistic approach to disease and health and has revolutionized people's thinking in Japan.

Below, I describe some of the safest and most effective holistic healing methods currently being used at the Gaia Holistic Health Center in New York. The Gaia Holistic Health Center was formed by caring, egoless people in the wake of the World Trade Center tragedy on September 11, 2001. Gaia aspires to transform trauma and pain into a collective quest for the real meaning of life, holistic health, healing, consciousness, compassion, and social responsibility, empowering us to share, heal, and serve each other. Later in this section, I describe a selection of some of these methods that are in line with Dr. Abo's theory of Restoring Self-Healing Power by healing the immune system.

Some of the main practices at the Gaia Holistic Health Center are:

Far-Infrared Onnetsu Therapy: This therapy is the crown jewel of Dr. Abo's theory. Patients who have not healed successfully through Western medicine often find complete recovery with far-infrared treatments. This is due to the fact that this method actually heals one's own healing power, as described by Dr. Abo's theory. Please see page 187 for more information on this remarkable therapy.

Detoxification: Through kinesiology and other techniques, we test each patient to determine which herbs or drugs they're taking are making them weak and which are making them better. A mild detoxification along with their Onnetsu therapy releases heavy metals and other toxins.

Herbs: Individual treatment plans are prepared to restore the patient's strength and self-healing power.

Tibetan Medicine: Traditional Tibetan diagnosis and herbs.

Japanese Hari Acupuncture Treatment: Compared with traditional Chinese acupuncture, the Japanese Hari method is somewhat less aggressive and relatively more refined. Intuition and energy healing techniques are emphasized.

Spiritual Harmony with Nature: We teach and encourage patients to maintain a daily practice of meditation, chanting, prayer, yoga, breathing exercises, and reflective practices that focus on gratitude.

Technical trainings: We train our patients and our practitioners in Onnetsu therapy, moxa, and Japanese Hari without needles for home and clinical use.

Benefits of Western Medicine: Eliminating or conquering illness, treating symptoms or parts of the body, scientific

There's been a tendency recently in the field of holistic medicine to blindly reject Western medicine, and vice versa. But it should not be this way.

The continuous progress of Western medicine is amazing and admirable. Western medicine is absolutely necessary and essential in emergencies and for special surgeries. It can also provide a diagnosis that is universally understood by all Western doctors, helping them determine their patients' conditions realistically and in detail. Even in cancer research, the so-called "three major treatments" are constantly changing and being re-evaluated. According to new findings, chemotherapy drugs are improving, radiation dosages and durations are changing, and constant advances in surgery are being made.

Western healing focuses on dealing with symptoms as quickly as possible, and its medications are developed for the purpose of reducing or eliminating symptoms. So, it's very good for treating patient discomfort. But these medications often cause side effects, causing doctors to prescribe other medications to treat these new side effect symptoms, and so on, and so on. This is very difficult for patients. Perhaps it would be best if Western medications and other treatments were used primarily for emergencies rather than for long-term, continuous treatments in order to reduce the risk of side effects. While it could be a difficult process, it might be a good idea to look into alternative methods once you've used Western treatments for a while, so that you can begin to heal yourself and gradually reduce your reliance on Western medicine.

However, patients are still being shuffled from one test to another, test after test, exhausting their energy when they're already sick to begin with. Some of these tests are even physically harmful, though they may be necessary (such as radiation). This system also causes patients' spirits to suffer anxiety, uneasiness, uncertainty, and worry, and can lead to depression.

A lot of money is spent on studies and research in Western medicine. I hope that this amazing research and development will be for the good of the world in accord with the law of nature, not just to benefit humans or make more money for the drug industry and medical profession. It's my hope that the Western medical community learns about holistic medicine too and realizes that there are more choices than what is learned in Western medical school.

Benefits of Holistic Medicine: Balancing, harmonizing, negotiating, treating the whole body and even the mind, rather nonscientific

Holistic diagnosis can often reveal the real, original cause of illness because it's based on understanding the relationships of each organ and body part and sometimes even emotions. Western medical tests discover and diagnose the manifestation of conditions in the body, or just in one part of the body. Asian diagnosis looks at why this manifestation has appeared by studying the whole body—even a person's state of mind. In other words, it looks at the human being as a whole, not just at the parts that are troubled. Watch out if someone says, "There's no scientific proof)." Really, who cares? The proof is in the pudding! Perhaps Western science is not highly developed enough to prove the thousands of years of healing that humans have experienced. This is a total disrespect of our own healing power! I believe that scientific proof is needed for new drugs or procedures developed by Western medicine, but not for traditional methods that have been proven experientially for thousands of years.

In our practice at our center, and in my life experience, I have seen many cases that have baffled Western medicine. Through our ability to approach healing holistically and to help inspire people to heal themselves with their own natural healing power, great results are achieved. Time and time again, our patients return to health—often to the best health of their lives. Key to this improved health is making sure that our patients understand that each and every one of us is responsible for our own health. Ultimately, no one can do our own work for us—and this is a very great thing! It means that this ability to improve, to be healthy and happy, is always within us. It is given to us when we are born and is with us for as long as we live. We always have this choice available, each moment of every day.

In my opinion, this is where Western medicine falls short. Ultimately, it's not up to anything outside of our own selves to "fix" us. While I think that Western medicine is a great help in many ways, pharmaceuticals can cheat us of our healing process by masking illness and leading us to believe that we're on the path to health when the medications are working. In reality, these medications are only stopping the symptoms, which people often mistake for recovery. However, without our own active input, it can be very difficult to make real progress in our healing process. With Western medicine, we often think we're on the path to improved health, but in truth we're often standing still, or even slipping backwards. This is evident in the harmful side effects that can occur.

On the other hand, holistic/Asian diagnosis is totally harmless and doesn't cause fatigue or damage to the cells. It doesn't require tests with machines, but rather utilizes a highly trained practitioner's deep knowledge and keen sense of intuition. Because of this, people sometimes find it hard to accept the diagnosis. It may be considered "nonscientific." But holistic/Asian diagnosis often reveals what Western medical tests can't, because it looks at the condition or illness as part of the entire being. Ideally, one should have both a Western medical diagnosis with machines and tests and a holistic diagnosis, because often the real, or original, causes of illness are hidden and not revealed in Western medical tests.

In healing, the most important thing is the mind—a mind of thankfulness and gratefulness, at every moment, toward all occurrences around us: air, food, family, friends. This humbleness miraculously brings enormous, positive healing *Ki* energy.

Holistic diagnosis can reveal the root cause of disease, but recovery from symptoms might take longer than with Western medicine

A woman came to my clinic and said that her eye doctor had told her she would lose sight in her left eye unless she had an operation immediately, due to advanced glaucoma. She was sad and crying. I looked at her face, skin color, and complexion, and immediately knew that her liver was not healthy. My pulse diagnosis also revealed weak liver energy and overactive lungs, with insufficient kidney energy. I told her, "You may want to postpone the surgery for a couple of weeks to see what we can do together holistically. It's totally your decision."

She chose to listen to me, and we tried Onnetsu therapy. This is used most significantly to boost the immune power in order to self-heal. We worked on the extremely hot spots on her liver, gallbladder, kidney, and eye points on the back of her head. I also recommended a detox program for the liver. I told her my opinions and outlook toward health and well- being, and about her own healing power—how to boost her immune system and self-healing mentally and physically.

I told her to trust herself—that these therapies are merely helpers for her own healing power. I said, "Ultimately, you are the best healer, you are the best doctor." She came about three times a week. A few weeks later, her eye was completely well, and she was very happy that she had been able to avoid surgery. Her testimonial ("My eyes") is at the end of this chapter.

This is just one example of the many cases in which holistic diagnosis helped find the original cause of illness. It also shows how the liver is related to the eyes. Believe it or not, our kidney energy relates to our ears and our knees, too. So, when a patient presents with knee pain, we often look at the condition of their kidneys. Western doctors might laugh at this.

According to Dr. Abo's theory, all body disorders start with an imbalance in the autonomic nervous system—the essential vital health mechanism, which gives us our immunity and our self-healing power. Our health is guided by the balance of and relationship between the sympathetic and parasympathetic nerves in our autonomic nervous system.

This is where our challenge begins. If Dr. Abo's theory is true (and this writer believes it is 100% true!), how can we find these imbalances and correct them to achieve balance? And more importantly, how can we strengthen and stimulate the function of our autonomic nervous system? This part of the book attempts to show some important holistic ways to solve this matter.

WHY WE GET SICK

Illness, or the failure to be healthy, comes from some kind of imbalance that we ourselves create. This can come about in a number of ways, including the following: constant unnatural posture or muscle movements; insufficient or unsuitable exercise; too much stress concerning work, relationships, or money; mental anxiety; depression; eating too much rich food or the wrong combination of foods; and spending time in a harmful environment. Illness occurs when we don't live according to the law of nature—when we are in dis-ease with nature. It's time for us to take responsibility for ourselves instead of blaming others or outside circumstances.

- Mind-heart imbalance. The following contribute to an imbalance of mind-heart: stress, negative thoughts or attitudes, overwork, over-achieving mind, greed, grief, complaining mind, unsatisfied mind, ungrateful mind, anger, irritation, agitation, constant judgmental mind, and not taking any relief from the above.
- Imbalance in the body, muscles, bones, and organs. The following contribute to an imbalance in the body, muscles, bones, and organs: bad habits in movements and posture (standing or sitting); not taking care of fatigue in a timely manner; over- exercising; not fully recovering

after an accident, illness, or surgery; chronic lack of sleep.

- Intake imbalance (food, air, water). (Note that "good" food means whatever is suitable for you now. This will be covered in greater depth later.) We believe that every living being has its own life force energy and a strong wish to sustain its life. Therefore, when we take in food, we are sacrificing other life forces so that we may allowed to live. With this in mind, let us ask forgiveness and give thanks to all life forces, each grain of rice, each leaf of vegetable, when we receive a meal. We should prepare food with caring thoughts in mind for the raw materials and with the total health of the person who will consume the food.
- Environmental imbalance. This subject is so enormous that people sometimes believe they're powerless to do anything about the condition in which we live on the planet. But if every individual doesn't think and act now, our planet will experience a disaster through global warming, flood, drought, and poisoned air and water. Natural disasters will continue to happen. Although it hasn't been proven, the unusual hurricane, flood, and tsunami of recent memory might very well be connected with the unusual melting of arctic glaciers. Each one of us must consciously work toward the goal of creating a healthier earth. Turn off the lights and use less electricity in your daily life. Reduce your use of chemical detergents and soap, cosmetics, and synthetic furniture and rugs. Use public transportation instead of cars, recycle as much as you can, and don't throw out items that are still usable. Take a moment to think about containers and plastic bags. In Europe, plastic bags are not given out routinely; instead, people carry reusable bags with them when they shop.

All of these imbalances cause our *Ki* (in Chinese, *Chi*) to stagnate. When *Ki* doesn't flow smoothly throughout our body, we get sick. So, what is *Ki?*

WHAT IS *KI?*

Everything on the planet contains *Ki*, which is essentially a vibration unique to that object. *Ki* is vibration and light. *Ki* is life force

Ki runs through our body, more or less like electricity. Just as a perfect machine such as a computer can't run without electricity, no sentient being can run or function without *Ki*. Like electricity, *Ki* is usually invisible to the human eye, but on occasion or by some people, it can be seen, and it has sometimes been recorded in photographs.

In humans, *Ki* often has its own consciousness independent of that person's consciousness. Just as people vary, *Ki* in humans varies. Different forms of *Ki* can be very different from one another. These different types of *Ki* can be categorized as Sinki (good, helpful *Ki*) and Jaki (bad *Ki*, which creates disturbance). When good, healthy *Ki* is abundant and flowing smoothly throughout the body, one is healthy and happy. When *Ki* clogs or stagnates in spots, one becomes sick or unhealthy. In fact, the Japanese word for sickness or illness is written with a character that means "the *Ki* is sick." We don't say our body is sick. When we're in good health, we say that the *Ki* is in its original state. We constantly use the word *Ki* for everything: kuki, tenki, kiko. In other words, *Ki* is in every aspect of our lives. We say of a person who feels good, "That person's *Ki* is so good." We call our child Mujaki, meaning innocent, without bad *Ki* (Jaki). When we have a special, close sense of someone, we say, "Our *Ki* matches." When we feel something, we say that our *Ki* is responding. When we notice something, we say the *Ki* is attached or noticeable. What is all this *Ki*? It's an unconscious feeling, but *Ki* itself has consciousness and influences us.

Ki consciousness exists on different levels, relative to one's own consciousness. The *Ki* that creates unhappiness or sickness or causes accidents is called Jaki, or negative *Ki*. On the other hand, good *Ki*— positive *Ki*—can help us heal, make others happy, and make everything positive.

HOW TO GENERATE POSITIVE *KI* IN YOUR BODY AND ELIMINATE NEGATIVE *KI*

The attitude in our mind influences our body. Whether we overcome or give into sickness depends on our attitude, mentally and physically. On the other hand, physical illness can cause mental dis-ease. We must accept this relationship between the mind-heart and the physical body/ matter. We must really understand and feel that a change in mind-heart does, in fact, change our body/matter and our life. And vice versa. If we can learn and accept this, we have found the key to health, happiness, and wealth. We will speak more about this later.

PRACTICAL ADAPTATION OF DR. ABO'S THEORY IN A HOLISTIC WAY

It may be helpful to discuss the overall view of holistic healing, specifying certain points and modalities that are in line with Dr. Abo's theory, and which in my opinion are very effective. These various methods all contribute to our self-healing power. The goal is the same: the restoration or promotion of self-healing power. Dr. Abo's theory is, ultimately, about healing yourself through your own healing power—immunity—which lies in the spine and autonomic nervous system.

To summarize Dr. Abo's theory of the immune system in simple terms, two different patterns exist:

1. Stress → tension in the sympathetic nerves → bad blood circulation and increased granulocytes → diseases that damage tissue
2. Lack of exercise, apathy → overly active parasympathetic nerves → fatigue and increased lymphocytes → allergies and diseases such as depression.

One thing that's very important to understand is that the holistic way of healing takes much longer than the Western method of getting rid of symptoms because it deals with the real cause of disease in your being as a whole. In addition, you must be aware of the holistic healing reaction known as Kouten Hannou.

KOUTEN HANNOU (HEALING REACTION)

This Japanese expression refers to the symptoms that are the body's natural reaction during the process of healing, before conditions improve. Patients often experience one or more of the following symptoms.

- Fever, mild headache, fatigue, and mild cold-like symptoms are part of the healing reaction that occur when your immune system tries to send increased blood and lymph in order to fight and remove waste so that new, energized cells can begin to heal you. You're using extra energy, so of course you feel tired.
- Inflammation is the normal way our body responds to tissue damage by sending blood to the damaged area in order to repair it. Increased blood flow causes swelling.
- Diarrhea is a wonderful mechanism of nature that removes toxins from your body as quickly as possible through the digestive and eliminative systems.

These symptoms are important signs that you are healing yourself— all proof that natural healing is taking place in your body. But this only happens when there's no interference from Western medicine, so taking any medication to reduce these symptoms—any painkillers, any anti-inflammatories—is totally counterproductive to your healing and should be avoided as much as possible. Be encouraged if you notice the following signs, despite the seemingly "negative" symptoms, because they mean that your recovery is coming!

- You feel good when you wake up
- You have appetite and can eat
- You don't feel cold all the time
- You face is pinkish in color
- You eliminate well (no constipation)

HEALING IN THE HOLISTIC WAY

In terms of actual practice, one can accomplish this holistic healing in two ways. But before I continue, I must make one point clear. In Asian medicine, the mundane and transcendental aspects of healing (described below) are intertwined and work hand in hand, influencing each other. They are never separate from each other.

A. Supplying *Ki* energy: the mundane, practical, physical aspect (The word mundane is used here only to describe the mean and method; it's closely related to the transcendental aspect in the end. The mundane level concerns the physical body and taking care of the body in a physical way.)

B. Balancing *Ki* energy: the transcendental, spiritual, mind-heart aspect.

A. Supplying and promoting the flow of Ki energy and elimination: The Mundane Aspect

The word energy means life force (which can be interpreted as heat). All living things need this in order to survive. Energy is created in many ways. Some energy is created within us; other energy is taken from outside. Because energy is our life force itself, it promotes our blood flow, body fluid flow, and *Ki* (life force) flow. It also changes food to the nutrients our body needs.

WHEN OUR BODY TEMPERATURE FALLS, WE BECOME UNHEALTHY

In Japan and Asia, unlike in the U.S., inner body temperature is considered the key to health. We do everything we can to retain heat in our body. Today, inner body temperature tends to be lower than normal, causing imbalance and dis-ease. We have a traditional saying: "Upper cold, lower warm. Upper empty, lower solid." This means—contrary to what the Western world believes—that we should keep our feet and lower legs warm (especially the ankles), not the head or upper body.

RAISING OUR INNER BODY TEMPERATURE BY SUPPLYING HEAT FROM OUTSIDE THE BODY

A Japanese theory that has existed for thousands of years states that in order to be healthy, our inner body heat must be kept high. We believe that when the inner body temperature is low, cells are deprived of heat, which is energy, and that this prevents the cells and organs from functioning well. Based on this theory, the Japanese have developed many methods for raising heat and body temperature in order to heat the body's deeper areas. It's interesting to learn that Dr. Abo recently explained this through his scientific discovery that "a person with low body temperature can't activate the lymphocytes in his white blood cells; therefore, his immune system can't function well, even if he has enough lymphocytes and white blood cells." This is why people with a low body temperature get sick easily.

Low body temperature can be caused by:

- Lack of exercise.
- Excessive water intake. Asians view water intake quite differently from Westerners (especially Americans). We don't recommend taking in excess water, because we believe that doing so overworks and cools the kidneys and leads to bloating.
- Wrong food, wrong meal timing, irregular meal schedule.
- Stress, worry.
- Too many supplements, too much medicine.
- Smoking and drinking too much coffee and soda.
- An irregular lifestyle, not enough sleep, late nights, late mornings.

Even if we're just sitting motionless, we're still creating heat in our bodies. Even when we're sedentary, our muscles produce more heat than any other part of our body—about 25 percent of our body heat. So, as you can see, light exercise such as yoga, tai chi, and mindful walking are optimal.

ILLNESSES CAUSED BY LOW BODY TEMPERATURE

Low body temperature can cause a number of illnesses, including depression; bloating; swelling, women's problems, especially difficulties with menopause; headaches; dizziness; ringing in the ears; hair loss; age spots; wrinkles; aging skin; irritability; constipation; difficulties with urination; constant cold-like symptoms; cancer; diabetes; shoulder pain; lower back pain; ulcers; high blood pressure; infertility; diseases of the skin;

collagen disease; multiple sclerosis; arthritis; rheumatism; prostate problems. Heating the body helps eliminate these illnesses.

A low inner-body temperature often accompanies symptoms of swelling, which in Asian diagnosis may be interpreted as a sign of illnesses. When your lower body swells in the afternoon, a heart problem is indicated. When your eyelids swell, there's a kidney problem. When your stomach is filled with water, there's a liver problem. It's important to determine and treat the root organs that are involved. But it's also important to warm our body in cases of general swelling, because swelling is a sign of toxic build-up. Warming the body increases blood flow to the kidneys, stimulating elimination.

The mundane aspects of receiving healing energy into our body can be accomplished in two ways:

1. Supplied from outside the body
2. Created within the body

1. Means to Receive Heat From Outside the Body

DR. KAZUKO'S ONNESTU THERAPY

Based on my many experiences of helping people heal themselves from simple back pain, neck pain, sports injuries, and even difficult and "incurable" diseases, I consider this therapy to be the crown jewel of Dr. Abo's theory. I am so grateful that he has explained the scientific reasoning that shows why the beliefs and methods we have practiced for thousands of years are correct and effective.

The principal theory of the Dr Kazuko's Onnetsu far-infrared method comes from an old Japanese belief that unhealthy body cells are deprived of heat and energy and are therefore cold— colder than healthy cells— and constantly shoot cold energy out from inside, toward the surface of the skin. In the Dr Kazuko's Onnetsu method, these cells are warmed with far-infrared rays that originate from the sun.

WHAT IS FAR-INFRARED?

In the late 1960s, NASA reported that rays of sunlight between 5 and 25μ 'microns' (or 8-14μ) are most beneficial to the growth of life. Light in this range promotes the life force, rejuvenates cells, and repairs damaged cells. These rays fall within the infrared range (.75 to 1,000 microns of wavelength). Incredibly, the wavelength of a healthy human body is also within this range. This fact helps explain the phenomenon of hand healing, or energy healing by touch.

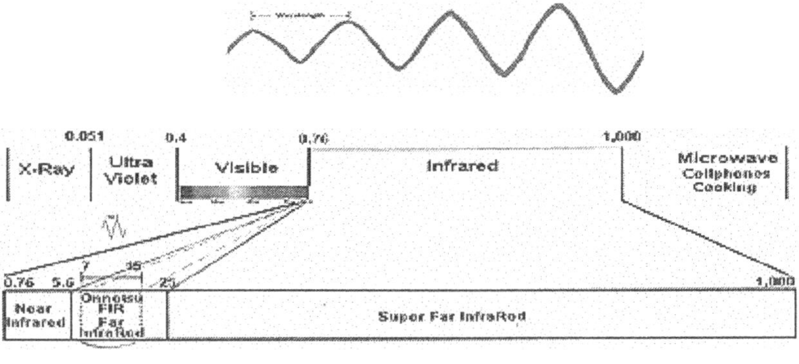

NASA's findings prompted a number of Japanese scientists to try to create tangible objects that would emit these kinds of rays constantly. After much research and experimenting, a number of scientists succeeded in creating objects composed of baked ceramic, various minerals, and stones. These baked ceramics were patented and developed into goods of many types. They were made into cotton and threads, and knitted into socks, shirts, and other types of clothing. They were made into mats, futons, and blankets. Healing lamps and other tools that emit rays in the far-infrared range of sunlight were created using these special ceramics.

WHAT IS DR. KAZUKO'S ONNETSU THERAPY WITH HEAT USING FAR-INFRARED, TERHERTZ?

Heat

Hippocrates' thoughts: "The Heat is the Ultimate Healing."

"Those who cannot be cured by Medicine
may be cured by iron (Knife).
Those who cannot be cured by knife may
be cured by fire (Heat). Those who cannot be
cured by Heat are to be considered incurable."
-- Hippocrates (460-370bc),
Father of Modern Medicine

Dr. Mitsui, an acupuncturist in her late seventies, had helped many people through traditional Japanese healing methods with heat. Dr. Kazuko, learning about far-infrared, came up with her own unique Onnetsu Therapy.

FAR-INFRARED VIBRATION

One characteristic of far-infrared is that the ray penetrates deep into the inner body from the surface of the skin—about four inches—reaching even to the organs. Dr. Kazuko believed that adding far-infrared ceramics to a heating mechanism would make a beneficial healing tool. In this way, Dr. Kazuko's Onnetsuki Therapy was born.

FAR INFRARED OF 8-10μ FROM SUNLIGHT

All living beings need Water, Air, Food and Sunlight. According to NASA, out of vast range of Solar Energy, only the narrow spectrum of 5-25μ helps to grow and heal. Dr. Kazuko's Onnetsu therapy is based on this NASA's finding of FIR but further narrowing down to 8-10μ for its effectiveness. Far infrared rays are indispensable for maintaining life in healing, rejuvenating. By combining with Terahertz, Far infrared waves penetrates to deeper cell levels of the body and can make the healing faster and more effective.

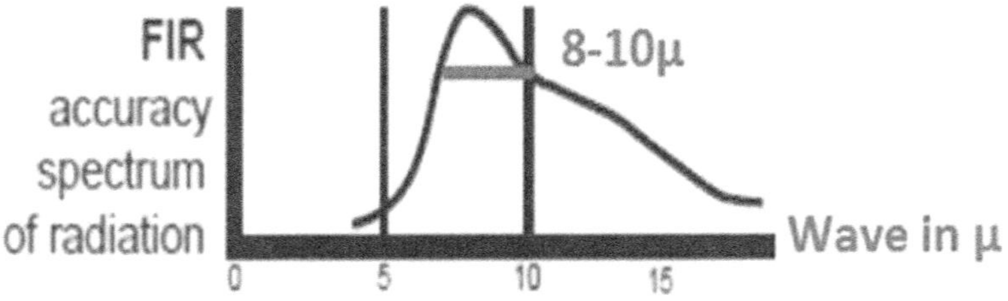

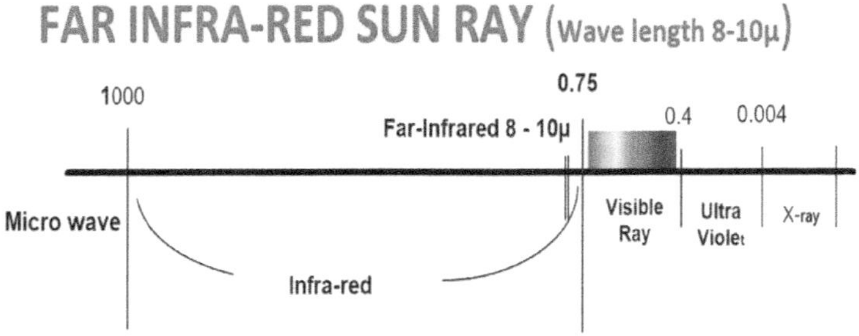

TERAHERTZ VIBRATION

The Onnetsuki is a handheld instrument that looks like a wand. It's remarkable in that it finds degenerated cells deep inside the body from the skin's surface. As I mentioned previously, the skin above these degenerated cells is cold. So, when the Onnetsuki is placed on that part of the skin, the patient's reaction is hot, hotter than in other places. The practitioner then chooses to treat this spot until the reaction is consistent with that in other areas. So, this new modality applies vibrations of far-infrared and Terahertz to the body together with heat.

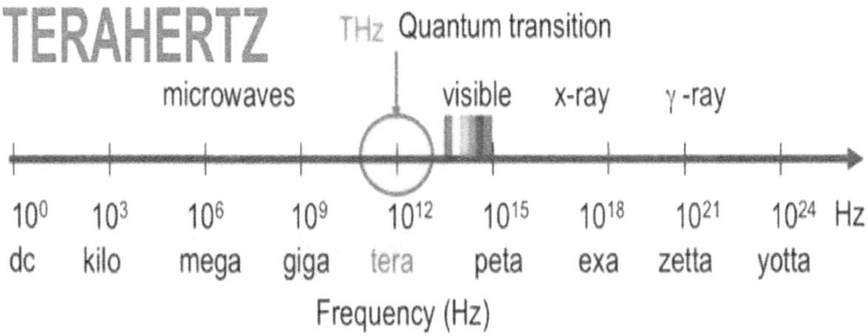

WHAT IS TERRAHERTZ?

Terahertz is extracted from active volcano rocks just like gold or diamonds. Everything on this planet carries vibrations including our body. Application of Onnetsu-ki to our body activates deep cells and vibrates water molecules. The Cold unhealthy cells start healing rejuvenating and reviving.

TWO PHASES OF DR. KAZUKO'S ONNETSU THERAPY METHODOLOGY

1. Fundamental Application to Promote Your Own Healing Power - Immunity

The general promotion of one's healing power through the spine -the home of autonomic nervous Increase self-healing power (Immunity) with Far Infrared Onnetsu Therapy system—which balances the sympathetic and parasympathetic nerves. According to Dr. Abo, this balance leads to the promotion of our immunity and self-healing power. Applying Onnetsuki to the spine and heating the spine area generates and improves the function of all the organs, including the heart, lungs, liver, gall bladder, kidney, bladder, spleen, stomach, pancreas, and large and small intestines. It also stimulates hormonal balance through the duodenum, thymus, and thyroid.

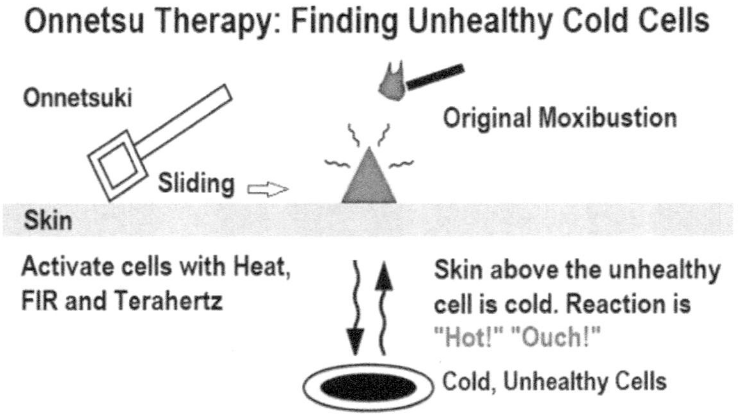

This spot is called the Cold Spot which is an unhealthy spot in need of treatment.

2. Local Application to Heal Problematic Points – Cold Spot Found from #1

Once problematic spots are found, based on the patient's reaction to the Onnetsuki, far-infrared waves and heat are applied at those locations with the Onnetsuki. This rejuvenates the degenerated cells at these spots. Application of the Onnetsuki is repeated until the reaction subsides and the patient no longer feels hot in that area. This indicates that energy is reaching the cells, that the area and the degenerated cells are warming up, and that recovery has begun.

The Japanese people use this theory and have developed many methods for raising the body temperature and reaching deeper areas of the body.

Here is one example of how Dr. Kazuko's Onnetsu Therapy works. This is the story of Lady 'A'. Her testimonial is at the end of this chapter *(see page 221)*.

A lady came to our clinic in terrible condition at the final stage of brain cancer. She said that all her doctors had given up on her.

She couldn't even walk, and her words were barely audible. Her right side, especially her arms and legs, were paralyzed. Her whole face and body were bloated. Her legs were very swollen, indicating kidney failure. I thought it would not be long before she left us, and that I could not possibly help her. So, I asked her, "Are you ready to die?" She cried and said, "No, I'm scared." I explained that dying is not such a bad thing. It's like changing old clothes for new ones. Your spirit will never die anyway, so don't fear death—simply be ready for it. Today you are alive, so make the best of it, without too much anxiety. Be positive that you'll live tomorrow as well, and the day after, and the day after, and so on... with full gratitude that you're alive.

We began daily Onnetsu therapy. just one week later, on September 14, her blood test showed remarkable changes in the proportion of white cells (lymphocytes, macrophages, and granulocytes). By September 20, her blood test indicated further improvement in the lymphocytes. I was excited because this is almost exactly what Dr. Abo's theory indicates. just as in Dr. Abo's explanation of the autonomic nervous system, the balance between her sympathetic and parasympathetic nerves had failed due to years of stress. Her sympathetic nerves were so overwhelmingly tense compared to her parasympathetic nerves that the proportion of her granulocytes had grown far too much in proportion to her lymphocytes, which were very weak.

White Blood Cell Differential	*Healthy Person*	*Lady 'A' Aug 30, 2004*	*Lady 'A' Sep 14, 2004*	*Lady 'A' Sep 20, 2004*
Lymphocyte	35%	7.2%	22.4%	31.2%
Macrophage	5%	6.4%	10.4%	7.3%
Granulocytes	60%	86.4%	67.3%	61.5%

I was amazed and encouraged and realized that there was hope for her healing power! She came for treatments practically every day. Her language ability and use of her hands came back. The unhealthy hot spots disappeared from her head. Her appetite returned. Her recovery was remarkable in every aspect. By early 2005, she was cancer free!

The doctors were surprised. She lived very happily and healthfully for almost one year. She began traveling and enjoying life.

But her story doesn't end with this happy outcome. Unfortunately, about one year after her recovery, she felt so good and so healthy that she decided to go back to work as a day trader. She was excellent at day- trading, an extremely stressful type of trading in the stock market.

Against my strong advice, she thought she would be all right. About six months later, her brain tumor reappeared, this time on the left side. This one grew very fast. When I learned of this recurrence, she was already in the hospital going through three Western treatments (radiation, chemotherapy, and surgery). I visited her, but a short while later she left us. We all have to go sometime, and this was her time. Every day, I thank her for the great opportunity and the remarkable teaching she gave me.

HOT BATH CURES

Hot bath cures include hot spring cures, dry and wet saunas, sawdust baths, hot sand, and herbal steam baths.

In Japan, we have traditional onsen (hot mineral spring) cures, in which we go to hot spring areas and take multiple hot mineral spring baths for a number of days. We regularly sink into hot water for long periods of time to warm the inside of our body. This is one of the very best ways to balance the autonomic nervous system. When you warm your body, you stimulate the elimination of body waste through the skin, stool, and urine; stimulate digestion; relax the muscles; and relieve physiological stress.

Thanks to volcanoes that line the entire length of Japan, there are more than 3,000 hot spring spots. Kouboudaishi, a famous sixteenth- century monk, discovered many medicinal hot springs all over Japan and promoted touji (healing with hot mineral water baths). Today, people visit these areas to recover from chronic illnesses. Touji is an extremely important part of Japanese healing, and very much a part of Japanese customs and culture. It's very popular for ordinary Japanese people to visit hot springs regularly to recharge, rejuvenate, recover from daily stress, and maintain their youth. The addition of mineral salts or citrus fruit together with heat from the springs provides excellent support for our body through the skin. Going to hot springs is healthy for the body, mind, and spirit.

Taking hot baths is healing tradition the Japanese should be proud of—and one that should be practiced all over the world. The Japanese bathe daily in their homes to promote their physical and mental health.

Hot baths are usually heated to about 7°F (4°C) higher than your normal body temperature. A customary regimen is as follows:

- Water temperature between 102° and 107°F for 20 to 40 minutes (stimulates the parasympathetic nervous system): This lower-temperature, warm bath should be taken for 20 to 40 minutes. It's good for high blood pressure, insomnia, excessive stress, chronic chill or coldness, physical fatigue, and arthritis.
- Water temperature 107°F and up for about 10 minutes (stimulates the sympathetic nervous system)

The Japanese are accustomed to much higher water temperatures. This temperature is much more effective—if you can tolerate it. Sink into a deep bath of 107°F or higher for about 10 minutes, repeating as desired. You can alternate hot and cold baths for an extremely yang bath. This is not recommended for those with heart problems or high blood pressure. This type of bath is very beneficial for arthritis, muscle and bone pain from physical activity, stomach ulcer, and hyperacidity. It also boosts energy and suppresses appetite and is followed by a feeling of total relaxation.

HEALTH BATHS YOU CAN DO AT HOME

Adding mineral salt, citrus fruit, or essential oils to the hot bath water allows these substances' healing properties to enter our body through the skin.

- **Mineral salt bath:** Stir about 9 to 10 ounces of natural salt into the bathtub. For moisturizing and stimulating perspiration, aches, stress, bruises, insect bites
- **Ginger bath:** Grate a piece of ginger into a mesh

pouch and put it in the bath. For constant chill, back pain, rheumatism, insomnia, and to prevent cold.

- **Garlic bath:** Grate a clove of garlic into a pouch and put it in the bath. For cold, anemia, stiff shoulder, dizziness, emphysema, and ear ringing. Do not stay in the water too long as Garlic may irritate the skin
- **Herb bath:** Chop 20 to 100 leaves (mint, eucalyptus, or labiate—fantastic if you can get it) into a mesh pouch and place in the bath. Begin filling the bath with a small amount of very hot water. For physical fatigue, mental fatigue, mental stress, heat exhaustion, and laziness.
- **Lemon or Orange bath:** Slice a lemon or orange into the bathtub for beautiful skin and to treat stress and insomnia. Don't throw away the skin of oranges—they're wonderful for a hot bath. Put them into a pouch and place in the bath. Begin filling the bath with a small amount of very hot water, adding slightly cooler water until you reach the desired temperature. The aroma itself will heal you.
- **Rose or flower essence bath:** Put several rose petals or a few drops of essential oil into the bath. For stress and hangover.
- **Milk bath:** It's said that Cleopatra took this bath every day for her eternal beauty! Dilute the milk in hot water, of course: one full glass for a big tub.
- **Footbath:** The feet are sometimes called the second heart. Heating the soles of the feet is wonderful for stimulation and circulation. In Japan, you find many beautifully constructed outdoor and indoor public foot bath areas, usually at hot springs, and you can see many people, young and old, enjoying foot baths.

The foot bath is one of the easiest to create. If you can tolerate it, the water should be a little bit hotter than in other baths. Put hot water into a large bucket or pail. Sink both feet in the water to the mid-calf. Add more hot water periodically. Relax, listen to music if you like, read a book that's not too taxing, or meditate. Your entire body temperature will rise.

DRINKING WARM BEVERAGES, ESPECIALLY HERBAL TEAS

Tea with ginger and caffeine encourages elimination. Ginger warms the body and strengthens blood flow to the kidneys. The most well-known Japanese recipe includes ginger, sour pickled plum (umeboshi), and a drop of soy source in bancha tea (or simple black tea). Sodas and coffee decrease our body temperature and should therefore be avoided as much as possible. Avoid drinking too much water, as well—especially with ice! It is simply a myth that you must drink eight glasses of water per day. In fact, in Japan we say, "Don't drink too much water," as doing so overworks the kidneys.

OTHER HEAT TREATMENTS: PACKS AND WRAPS

Loquat Onnetsu wraps, seaweed wraps, hot mud wraps, hot stone massage, ginger packs, mustard packs, potato packs, and other treatments are easy to do yourself. Here are some recipes.

- **Ginger packs:** Placing a ginger pack on your back at the kidneys increases blood flow to the kidneys and improves kidney function. The amount of urine will increase, decreasing bloat. A ginger pack is effective for stiff shoulders, back pain, rheumatism, joint pain, female problems, and bladder problems. If you put one on the bottom of your feet, it will make you sweat and you will feel good physically and mentally.

1. Grate about 5 ounces of ginger into a cotton pouch and tie it with string.
2. Put the pouch in a pot with 2 liters of water. Heat it to just before boiling.
3. Let it cool to about 160°F. Then soak a hand towel in the liquid and squeeze out the excess water.
4. Put the towel on a cold or problematic part of the body.
5. Cover with plastic wrap to retain heat, then top with a dry towel.
6. Repeat 2 or 3 times every 10 minutes.

- **Mustard packs:** The first time I visited the Soviet Union in 1966, I caught a severe cold accompanied by bronchitis and a high fever. I was taken to a hospital. There, a female doctor administered a mustard pack on my chest and back. It burned my skin, which was red for several days. But after just one treatment, I recovered completely. It was so effective; I didn't care about the burn.
- A mustard pack is very effective and easy to do at home and is especially beneficial when you have a cold accompanied by a steady cough. But be careful not to leave it on too long.

1. Put a tight-fitting t-shirt on the patient.
2. Mix 1/2 teaspoon mustard seed powder with 1 tablespoon flour. (You may use mustard seed powder, grind fresh seeds yourself, or use regular mustard.) Gradually add cool water to the mixture until it turns into a paste. Spread the paste onto a piece of old flannel (about 12" x 6").
5. Place the pack on the patient's chest and secure with the t-shirt.
6. Check occasionally to make sure the skin does not turn raw.

ABOUT MOXA (MOXIBUSTION)

Moxibustion is said to have originated in China more than 3,000 years ago, during the Shang Dynasty. The technique spread to other Asian countries, including Japan, Korea, and Tibet. Today it's practiced all over the world. Despite its Chinese origins, moxa has flourished in Japan more than in any other country. In fact, the root word moxa actually derives from the Japanese word mogusa, meaning burning herb.

In moxibustion, a stick or cone of mugwort or moxa is placed on the skin over a certain region of the body to treat both acute and chronic conditions. The moxa is burned, sending warm heat and the healing energy of the moxa deep into the body.

Moxa is often placed to correspond with acupuncture points, warming the degenerated cells and tissue in order to promote and improve the circulation of blood and *Ki* throughout the body. It enhances the quality of the blood, increases the number of blood cells, and raises immunity as well. When placed along both sides of the spine, as is traditionally done, moxa is especially effective in stimulating and balancing the autonomic nervous system and in promoting immunity. It can be very effective in balancing hormones as well. If done properly, it is safe and has no side effects. Moxibustion increases physical strength and changes the body condition more than treating or repairing acute problems. In Japan, moxibustion is often practiced together with Japanese Hari meridian therapy.

2. Creating Heat (Energy) Within the Body

SOME HELPFUL TRANSCENDENTAL HEALINGS: MEDITATION, AYURVEDA, AND AROMATHERAPY

MEDITATION

Meditation is an excellent way to create inner body heat, particularly in the autonomic nervous system. As you meditate, imagine a brilliant white light coursing through your body. Imagine the far-infrared rays shining on the top of your head, then moving through your chakras in the front of your body, from top to bottom. Then, beginning at the bottom of your spine, imagine the bright white light moving upward, shining on each vertebra all the way to the top of your head. Feel the heat warming your spine, the home of the autonomic nervous system. The light stimulates the autonomic nervous system to promote immunity. This is one of Dr. Abo's theories on healing.

Before I meditate each morning, and again before each class and each patient, I find it very important to prepare the following three secrets, which Master Oki taught me long ago and which are part of daily Buddhist practice. I know that this preparation helps me attain perfect balance in my autonomic nervous system, both physically and mentally.

ACUPUNCTURE

The recent interest in acupuncture deserves praise. Acupuncture promotes the flow of blood and *Ki* in our body and inner organs and can be used to treat both acute and chronic conditions. It also stimulates the immune system and activates the autonomic nervous system when administered at points along the side of the spine and in the head and neck areas. It stimulates the flow of *Ki* from one organ to another, pin organs to yang organs, and vice versa. This huge and very complex subject is beyond the scope of this text.

YOGA

This ancient Indian art hardly needs explanation, given its immense rise in popularity in the West over the last 20 years. All yoga poses promote health by creating heat inside the body and circulating *Ki* throughout the organs. Poses especially effective in stimulating the autonomic nervous system include the cat, cobra, arch, twist, forward and backward bend, triangle, fish, and grasshopper. These poses move and use our spine, making it very flexible and strong. Numerous books and classes in yoga and tai chi are available. We should incorporate these types of exercises into our daily routine in order to stimulate the autonomic nervous system and cultivate our immunity. For further reference, see Masahiro Oki's remarkable book Joy of Yoga.

TAI CHI & CHI GONG

Tai chi and chi gong can be described as controlled movements that promote the flow of *Ki* into the organs, stimulating their functioning and that of the autonomic nervous system. Historically, the most important figure in tai chi is Chang San-Feng, a Taoist monk in twelfth- century China who developed the initial set of exercises by observing and imitating the movements of animals such as the tiger, dragon, leopard, snake, and crane. Tai chi was originally a form of martial arts, practiced for self-defense and fighting. Over time, people began to practice it as a moving meditation and breathing system as well. So, the theory and practice have evolved in agreement with traditional Chinese medicine.

The Taoists felt that stagnation of *Ki*, or energy, was the cause of disease and aging. In tai chi, each movement flows into the next throughout the form. One practices the movements slowly and gently, with the mind focused on feeling the flow and the body remaining soft and relaxed at all times. The entire body is constantly in motion and at one with the breath. Tai chi exercises all the major joints and muscles while cultivating and circulating internal energy, or heat, within the body, stimulating and balancing the autonomic nervous system. It promotes flexibility, strength, and stamina, despite the fact that there is hardly any impact or strain on the body. While moving the entire body through the form, one also learns to cultivate the connection between mind and body, while enhancing balance and coordination. Today, tai chi is practiced worldwide for its benefits in maintaining health and enhancing self-healing power.

AYURVEDA

The field of Ayurveda is truly about taking total care of ourselves. Ayurveda operates on the principle that all things on the planet— materials of plant, animal, and mineral origin—have medicinal value. The medicinal properties of these materials have been used for centuries to cure illness and maintain health. Ayurvedic practices restore balance and harmony, leading to self-healing, good health, and longevity. According to Ayurvedic philosophy, an individual bundle of "spirit" uses satwa (subjective consciousness or psychic forces) to manifest sense organs and a mind. This spirit and mind then project themselves into a physical body that is created from the bhutas (the five great eternal elements). The sense organs then use rajas (activity) to project out of the body into the external world in order to experience objects. The body becomes the mind's vehicle, the physical instrument of sense gratification. The five elements combine into bioenergetics forces that govern and determine our health and physical condition. The three gunas - rajas, satwa, and tamas (gross energy or inertia) determine our mental and spiritual health. Therefore, one could say that Ayurveda is a holistic system of health care that teaches us to balance these energies in order to achieve optimum health and wellbeing.

Ayurveda (also called ayurvedic medicine) has been practiced primarily in India for 5,000 years. The word Ayurveda is a compound of âyus (long life) and veda (knowledge), and roughly translates as the science of long life. Ayurveda concerns methods for healthy living, along with therapeutic measures to create physical, mental, social, and spiritual harmony. Over the past 40 years, there's been a growing recognition of the value of Ayurveda. Today, ayurvedic hospitals and practitioners flourish throughout India and the world. The principles of many natural healing systems now familiar in the West, including homeopathy and polarity therapy, have roots in Ayurveda. The production and marketing of ayurvedic herbal medicines has increased dramatically, as has current scientific documentation of its benefits.

AROMATHERAPY

Aromatherapy is the holistic practice of using volatile and essential oils extracted from aromatic plants to enhance health, well-being, and beauty Used therapeutically, essential oils can help a wide range of problems, from stress and insomnia to acne, menstrual cramps, depression, fatigue, and even the common cold. Aromatherapy is a treatment that uses scent. Smell is the least understood of our five senses and yet is perhaps the most powerful. It's believed that simply inhaling an essential oil elicits an immediate olfactory response and allows for immediate absorption into the bloodstream. The olfactory membrane is the only place in the human body where the central nervous system is exposed and therefore in direct contact with the environment. When an olfactory receptor cell is stimulated, an impulse travels along the olfactory nerve to the limbic portion of the brain where memory, hunger, sexual response, or emotion is evoked. When inhaled into the lungs, essential oils have been found to provide both psychological and physical benefits. Not only does the aroma of the natural essential oil stimulate the brain, triggering a reaction, but the natural constituents (naturally occurring chemicals) of the oil are drawn into the lungs, also supplying physical benefits. If not done correctly and safely, however, essential oils can cause severe consequences.

Essential oils can be added to the bath or massaged into the skin, inhaled directly or diffused to scent an entire room. In this way, they can be used to relieve pain, care for the skin, improve digestion, alleviate tension and fatigue, and invigorate the entire body, as well as reduce anxiety and promote relaxation. In addition, oils can have antiseptic or antiviral properties. Pleasant smells such as peach and plum can reduce pain. Jasmine, ylang-ylang, and peppermint can lift depression. Geranium and bergamot can relieve anxiety. Rose and carnation can restore energy.

We constantly create heat within our body to some extent, even if we're not conscious of it. But if we apply Dr. Abo's theory consciously through certain practices, our health will greatly improve. These practices include acupuncture, yoga, tai chi and chi gong, breathing exercises, kampo, and the use of food and supplements.

BREATHING EXERCISES: BALANCING THE AUTONOMIC NERVOUS SYSTEM THROUGH BREATHING

Numerous breathing exercises can help balance the autonomic nervous system. Many of these can be found in the very helpful text Deep Breath Changes Your Body, by Osamu Tatsumura.

Deep, slow, soft breathing stimulates the parasympathetic nerves. Strong, short, fast, shallow breathing stimulates the sympathetic nerves. So, you can choose a breathing exercise based on your needs.

One of the healthiest ways to breathe is with hara, or abdominal, breathing. This type of breathing is very beneficial for your health and relieves pain. We use it in Onnetsu treatment.

When someone can't tolerate the heat, or a spot that's particularly hot is found, we ask the patient to use hara breathing. Remarkably, the breath allows the patient to tolerate the "ouch, hot, hot!" enabling us to go deep into the body for treatment. I'll describe the breath to you here, so that you can do it yourself.

1. Lie on your back with your chin pointed comfortably inward, without tension. Put your left hand on your chest and your right hand on or slightly under your belly button.
2. Breathe out all your air by pushing all the way down on your abdomen with your right hand.
3. Breathe in by pushing your belly button up fast, as if it were a large balloon. Make sure that only your right-hand moves, not your left. Your chest should remain stationary. Count to three.
4. Slowly shrink the balloon as if all the air were leaking out. Exhale.
5. softly on a sighing sound ("aaaaahh") as you count to nine (in other words, the exhale should be three times longer than the inhale). Allow the right hand to help by pushing the abdomen toward the spine until there's no more air.
6. When you can't push anymore, release the right hand. Air should come in naturally, without consciously forcing the inhale. Make another big balloon.
7. Throughout the exercise, the chest should remain stationary. You can observe this by watching the left hand, which shouldn't move.

This is the hara breathing technique. Once you find you can do this technique lying down, practice it sitting or standing. The benefits are enormous. Hara breathing forces your diaphragm to go lower, creating more space in the lungs—which you can then use for more air. In other words, hara breathing increases your lung capacity. It also eliminates pain.

KAMPO HERBAL MEDICINE

It's beyond the scope of this text to fully explore this incredibly wonderful but vast field. For present purposes, the only important remedy I'll mention concerns Kabbontoii. Kakkontou is a famous herbal combination remedy. When taken hot after being boiled, it is considered the most effective herbal medicine for heating your body from the inside. Many doctors and herbalists in Japan swear that it can cure all diseases, from the common cold to serious cancers. It can also be used to help treat pneumonia, bronchitis, headache, chronic shoulder pain, skin inflammation, rheumatism, hangover, dizziness with blurred vision, and toothache. It's most commonly used during the early and middle stages of the common cold or flu, where it treats symptoms of chills and fever without sweating, muscle aches, headache, nasal congestion, runny nose, postnasal drip, sneezing, coughing, diarrhea, wheezing, and loss of appetite.

Here's a recipe for this Japanese herbal formula.

- gm Licorice Root (gan cao)
- 15 gm Kudzu (ge gen)
- 3 slices Fresh Ginger (sheng jiang)
- 5.5 gm Ephedra (ma huang)
- 4 pieces Chinese Dates without pits (hong zao)
- 12 gm White Peony Root (shao yao)
- 12 gm Cinnamon Twig (gui zhi)

Boil all ingredients in about 6 to 8 cups of water and let simmer until about 80 percent of the liquid is left. Strain. Drink hot an hour after each meal.

FOOD: HOW AND WHAT TO CONSUME
(Good Food Means Food That Suits Your Needs Now)

Food creates heat (energy) in the body. Overeating certain foods, no matter how good they might be, or under eating certain foods, as well as exposure to contaminated food, air, and water can create imbalance in our bodies and deprive us of heat.

Here is the optimal way to consume food.

1. Natural foods. Use only natural ingredients and fresh, organically grown food with no artificial fertilizer. Never use artificial seasonings or additives.
2. Local and seasonal ingredients. Nature provides food suitable to each location, which contains the natural life force of the season. 1.
3. Small quantity, large variety. Use an abundance of different ingredients in small portions. In Okido, we believe that at least 36 different ingredients should be consumed each day.
4. Foods low in calories, fat, cholesterol, and salt.
5. Whole foods. It's better to eat a whole small potato than part of a large potato, or a whole small fish rather than the fillet of a large fish. This allows us to take the whole life force of the entity.
6. Food that corresponds to your roots. Consider where your ancestors came from. You can't tell an Eskimo to become a vegetarian. If you come from a meat-eating background, vegetarian food may not be good for you in the long run.
7. The quantity and speed of meals. People tend to overeat and eat too fast. When we eat too fast, we're not utilizing our very best enzyme, saliva, for digestion. And we overeat most of the time. Please stop when you're 70% full, not 1 00%! A recent scientific study has linked eating at 70*/o capacity to health and longevity. To eat less, take just a small spoonful of food each time and chew it at least 50 to 100 times. I guarantee that you will feel full after eating half as much as usual. I use the expression, "Drink your food and chew your water." This is the

best way to lose weight naturally. You should also know that it's very bad to drink water with meals. Instead, you should drink water 30 minutes before or after a meal so that the food won't swim around in your stomach. Your saliva should provide enough moisture.

8. Eat with deep gratitude. When we consume food, we must realize that we are sacrificing another life force in order to sustain our lives. Fish, chicken, carrots, each grain of rice—they all had the right to live, just as much as we have. We must therefore thank them for their life force, and not waste their energy. If you maintain this sort of attitude, their life force will live in you energetically.
9. Well-balanced foods. It's important to eat foods with a balance of all the various nutritional elements. It goes without saying that the five food categories of USDA pyramid and the U.S. recommended dietary allowances (RDA) should be observed. But in addition to these Western concepts, holistic medicine takes into account the yin and yang and five-element theories. The concept of food as medicine is important because foods influence and change your body and mind. The saying "you are what you eat" is exactly right. You become what you eat. Here is an explanation of food balance as contained in the yin and yang and five-elements theories, as well as in Dr. Abo's theory.

BALANCING YIN AND YANG IN FOOD

Remember that categorizing food in terms of yin and yang is a relative process, never black and white. Such groupings are never absolute. In general, we say that vegetables are more yin than fish; fish is more yin than poultry; poultry is more yin than meat; small fish are more yang than large fish; small potatoes are more yang than large potatoes; red wine is more yang than white wine or beer; and so on.

Here again, as with all other aspects of Asian medicine, there is no scientific proof, but rather knowledge handed down for centuries from teachers to students or known among wise folk.

Yin foods relax and cool the body, while yang foods tighten and warm the body. This is a very important subject in Asia. Everyone's energy is different and varies at different times. Some people are yin and others are yang. One is no better than the other, but when you're sick you're usually more yin than yang. We need to balance our type so that our energy doesn't become too yin or too yang. While we can adjust this balance through daily activities such as exercise and relaxation, it's also possible to control it through food. Here are some typical yin foods and yang foods. Remember that one can get sick by taking the wrong food at the wrong time.

YIN FOODS (cool your body, expanding)	YANG FOODS (warm your body, tightening)
Raw food	Cooked foods, pickled foods, dried foods, salted foods, fermented foods such as miso and soy sauce
Green, white, or soft foods	Yellow, red, dark, hard foods
White rice, white bread	Brown rice, dark bread
Vinegar, curry, refined salt, spices in general	Sea salt, rock salt
Milk, yogurt	Cheese
Vegetable oil, mayonnaise	Butter
Soda, coffee	Apple cider, black tea, green tea, herbal tea
Snacks, cookies	Some dark colored nuts and seeds
Beer, whisky	Sake, wine
Fish	Meat
Leafy vegetables (vegetables that grow above ground): tomatoes, cucumbers, eggplant	Root vegetables (vegetables that grow underground or directly on the ground): beats, carrots, burdock, lotus root, yams, potatoes daikon, radish, zucchinis, onion, scallions, leeks, pumpkins
Refined white sugar	Honey, maple syrup
Tropical fruits (bananas, mango, pineapple, etc.)	Strawberries, apples, cherries, prunes
Persimmon, watermelon	
Citrus fruits (lemons, oranges)	

FOODS THAT ARE BALANCED IN YIN AND YANG

Some foods are balanced in yin and yang. Of these, the very best is brown rice. Brown rice is the most complete food, which contains all the necessary nutrition and yin and yang balance. It's very important to chew it well by taking a very small portion in each mouthful. Together with our saliva, brown rice produces an enzyme that stimulates tremendous immunity in our body. Other great foods in this category include seaweed, nuts, and seeds.

BALANCING THE FIVE ELEMENTS IN FOOD

According to the five-elements theory of ancient China and Japan, there are five colors and five tastes for five organs. We should consider the relationship between these colors and tastes and the corresponding organs and eat according to your condition, or generally try to eat a balanced diet that includes all the colors and tastes.

1. Red and bitterness relate to the heart
2. White and spiciness relate to the lungs
3. Yellow and sweetness relate to the spleen
4. Green and sourness relate to the liver
5. Black and saltiness relate to the kidneys

BALANCING AUTONOMIC NERVOUS SYSTEM WITH FOOD

(from Dr. Abo's writing)

FOODS THAT ACTIVATE THE PARASYMPATHETIC NERVES

The parasympathetic nerves become activated when you're well rested, relaxed, and warm; when your blood flows well; and when there's movement in your digestive system. So, foods that stimulate bowel movement, warm the body, help blood circulation, or help us eliminate food are also those that help the parasympathetic nerves become dominant. Consuming an appropriate amount of sour or bitter food also helps activate the parasympathetic nerves. These include soy products, miso, pickles, natto (fermented soy), yogurt, green vegetables, mushrooms, seaweed, sesame, brown rice, other grains, beans, small fish, vinegar, and umeboshi (pickled plums). These foods:

- Improve the condition of the intestines (make the digestive organs work)
- Warm the body and improve blood circulation (don't cool the body)
- Promote elimination (contains lots of fiber; sour and bitter food)
- Provide a nutritional balance (perfect foods that contain all necessary nutrition on their own)

Today's children may be restless and lack endurance because they don't eat enough grains and rice. Many women don't eat rice or carbohydrates because they're dieting but going without these neutral foods for a long period of time creates imbalance in the autonomic nerves, which can result in mental imbalance, poor functioning in the immune system, and often a poor physical condition. In the past, Japanese people consumed 80% of the total daily calories from grains, but I think that, ideally, modern people should take in 40-50% of their calories from grains for optimal balance of the autonomic nerves.

FOODS THAT ACTIVATE THE SYMPATHETIC NERVES

It's not good to eat only foods that help the parasympathetic nerves. Eating nothing but vegetables relaxes your body, which helps the immune system—but it doesn't give you the power to do things. When you need to focus or work hard, you need foods that stimulate the sympathetic nerves, such as salt, coffee, beef, pork, chicken, red meat, fish, eggs, greasy food, and cold food. Meat, for example, is an acidic food that contains amino acids, and can be digested quickly. So, it's used right away for activities, and the sympathetic nerves become dominant. If you consume too much of these foods, though, your granulocytes will increase, and your immune system will grow weaker.

Foods that stimulate the sympathetic nerves basically lower your immune power and can also cause dependency and addiction. If you become dependent on them and consume them too much, your blood vessels will shrink, and you'll get excited physically and mentally. This further increases the number of granulocytes in the white cells, resulting in a decrease of lymphocytes and creating an imbalance in the autonomic nervous system.

NEUTRAL FOODS THAT BALANCE SYMPATHETIC AND PARASYMPATHETIC NERVES

Neutral foods—including brown rice, wheat, potatoes, corn, and grains—are not inclined toward the sympathetic or the parasympathetic nerves and consuming them is critical to maintaining balance in the autonomic nerves. These foods create mental stability and physical endurance, and so should

be consumed in the proper amount to reduce stress, since stress lowers immunity. Grains and carbohydrates help balance the autonomic nerves; therefore, a diet lacking in grain can affect the body negatively.

When your daily meals follow these nine guidelines, your internal organs will function better, you'll digest well, and you'll achieve your ideal weight naturally. You'11ook younger and more beautiful and feel more energetic. You'll build a healthier body and a happier mind. To a great extent, all illnesses are caused by, and can be prevented by, what we eat. You become what you eat. Food together with daily exercise affects both the length and the quality of our lives. As Hippocrates said, "Let thy food be thy medicine and thy medicine be thy food."

ELIMINATION

Elimination is the removal of unnecessary and negative elements from our body and mind, including the following:

- Body waste (stool, urine, sweat, body fluid, tears)
- Unnecessary heat
- Cluttered thoughts and clogged knowledge
- Extra or leftover energy and negative energy
- Poisons and harmful toxins

DETOXIFICATION (DETOX)

We live in a very toxic world. Our soil, air, and even ocean water are contaminated. We use toxic materials in daily life: in pesticides, cleaning detergents, shampoos, toothpaste, cosmetics,

Teflon pots, and so on. According to a recent study, we're surrounded by over 200 chemical toxins. Ninety-five percent of chronic diseases are caused by toxins. These toxins can cause autism and diabetes, even in newborns. This is shocking.

The topic of detox has become very popular in recent years. This is an excellent trend. Cleansing (especially of the large intestine and liver) creates cleaner blood and better circulation, which improves the quality of the blood and builds a stronger immune system. There are many traditional natural ways to detox the organs, such as olive oil and citrus fruit (grapefruit) for the liver, a method I learned from Russia.

Here are two extraordinary products we use in our center.

HYAKUDOKU-KUDASHI (HDK)

HDK cleanses the colon, purifies the blood, and enhances immunity.

HDK is recommended for any of the following: acid reflux, headaches, menopause symptoms, allergies, hemorrhoids, water retention, shortness of breath, hepatitis, poor concentration, cellulite, high or low blood pressure, poor digestion, cholesterol problems, joint pain, skin problems and wrinkles, constipation, low energy, uncontrollable weight, gas and bloating, low sex drive, hair loss, memory loss and deterioration of the mind... or just to keep young and healthy!

HDK has been produced for more than 430 years in japan by a company established in 1570 and located in the Mie prefecture. Also known as "100 toxins out," HDK was once available only to a privileged few, but later became treasured as a miraculous household medicine.

To this day HDK is not mass-produced, but rather created with great care and compassion by highly spiritual people, who still maintain a Medicine Buddha and Shinto medicine deity shrine in their private herb farm. HDK is also recommended by Dr. Andrew Weil. It's only available through personal import from Japan (visit www.gaiaholistic.com or contact kazuko@gaiaholistic.com or (212) 799-9711 for more information).

HDK cleanses the blood, enhances immunity, boosts your natural healing power, and gradually dissolves shukuben (fossilized stools that have been embedded in the creases of the wall of intestines for years). HDK's gentle stimulation encourages steady elimination of stool and gas, rarely causing stomach upset. Do not mistake this cleansing process for diarrhea.

NATURAL CELLULAR DEFENSE HEAVY METAL ELIMINATION (NCD)

The total load of toxins in the environment now exceeds your ability to adapt without health consequences. In recent studies of the umbilical cords of new mothers, the EPA has found over 200 toxic chemicals—an enormous increase since 2001. An average of 200 pollutants have been found in the blood of newborns as well. These chemicals are neuro- and endocrine toxic, lower libido and metabolism, stop absorption of nutrients, and destroy the immune system. There are 1,500 metric tons of toxic materials in the jet stream. U.S. industries pour 4.7' billion pounds of toxins and 72 million pounds of carcinogens into the environment annually. DDE, an immune-toxic herbicide linked to cancer, was found in 84% of foods tested by the FDA. Mercury alone causes 20,000 premature deaths and untold illness and suffering every year. What about the other 115 chemical poisons?

Natural Cellular Defense (NCD) is an extraordinary new product that detoxifies heavy metals. Odorless and tasteless, it comes in liquid form and is highly effective and easy to use. It's available at our website (www.mywaiora.com/86914 I). Produced by the company Waiora, it's made from zeolite, a mineral born when volcanic lava met seawater a million years ago.

NCD is widely known to:

1. Safely and effectively remove toxic heavy metals.
2. Trap and remove viral particles from your body.
3. Lower the risk of cold and flu infections.
4. Balance pH levels so that viruses and bacteria are less likely to survive.
5. Trap excess protons in the digestive tract, lowering the risk of acid reflux.
6. Improve nutrient absorption in the digestive tract.
7. Support a healthy immune system by removing toxins and chemicals.
8. Trap allergens in the bloodstream and digestive tract,

reducing symptoms.

9. Help stop diarrhea through its absorptive effect on the digestive system.
10. Produce amazing results in the improvement of m any life- threatening and debilitating diseases.

ABOUT SUPPLEMENTS

Today, there is altogether too much promotion and use of supplements. I routinely ask my patients to bring in all their daily supplements, and I am absolutely amazed. Some bring a large suitcase-full! Each one of these supplements may have shown good results in this or that clinical study in laboratories—but they may not be right for you at this time. Most people no longer even understand what's going on in their bodies from taking all these supplements.

It's important for people taking supplements to understand the following:

- It is impossible for our digestive mechanism to digest multiple supplements at one time – or even in one day. We use O-ring test by Drs. Omura and Shimotsuura to determine what is really good for you and what amount is good for you at this time. So, therefore, do not buy any supplements unless you confirm with us first. *You are wasting money!*
- Each of us is a distinct individual with our own distinct energy and distinct needs for supplements at different times and in different amounts. Furthermore, your body is constantly changing every month, every week—even every day. A supplement that's backed by great scientific data and works for some people may not necessarily work for you.
- One supplement may cause a negative effect if taken in combination with another supplement.
- One supplement may cancel some or all of the good effects of other supplements.

I believe the time has come to stop surrendering to the incredible commercialism of the supplement industry, and go back to basics—that is, taking in good food. Supplements, after all, are intended to supplement good, nutritious food. Of course, our food supply today is deprived of nutrition and isn't healthy enough, so we need some supplements here and there, now and then. But there's no need to spend a lot of money popping pills and liquids without knowing what they're actually doing for you—or to you. Our clinic patients who bring in large amounts of supplements tell me they're taking this one for this symptom, that one for that symptom, and so on, and so on. It's shocking! They tell me how much they spend on all these supplements, and they're reluctant to throw them out. But not only are many of the supplements ineffective—they could be doing them harm. And our ability to digest these pills? Forget it! We absolutely cannot digest all of these supplements—no way!

At our clinic, we use an O-ring test (a kind of Kinesiology) to study the supplements that our patients use one by one, carefully eliminating the ones that aren't beneficial or that could be harmful. Then, one by one, we test to determine the right quantities of each beneficial supplement and add them back in one by one to see if any of them cancel out the others. We go through this process periodically.

THE TRANSCENDENTAL ASPECT

In this section, I'll discuss holistic healing approaches that relate more closely to the psychological, neurological, and spiritual aspects of healing.

THE POWER OF POSITIVE POSTURE OF MIND (THE 3 P's)

1. Know the facts and accept the truth—accept the worst-case scenario and say, "So what?" to it. My late teacher Master Masahiro Oki, Japan's most important holistic healing master of all time, said in the 1950s, "Don't doubt, don't believe, but do verify (find out the truth)" Doesn't this sound like someone we know? (Ronald Reagan famously said "Trust, but verify," speaking of Soviet President Mikhail Gorbachev.) Then, once you've verified, accept the truth.

2. Laugh, be joyful, and smile all the time. In Japan, we have a saying: "The gate of laughter brings in good luck." Avoid all negative emotions. In the case of cancer, for example, being told by your physician that you will die in such-and-such a time can

be totally detrimental. Who is this person who dares to say such words about your life force? This shows absolutely no respect for your life force or your healing power. Don't take it to heart. They're just repeating a statistic—and one that's based only on Western medical procedures. Say to yourself, "So what?" You are you, from yesterday to today, one day to the next. Not much has changed, but their statements could cause you to change, mentally. Don't let this happen—it will immediately weaken your immune system and self-healing power. Let the power of positive attitude prevail.

To avoid letting negative emotions enter your mind and harm you, you must accept emotions, without denying them, and then say, "It's all right. So what? I'm alive today. Everything is and will be ok."

Remember, your current condition is the accumulation of many years of behavior that has been unnatural, unbalanced, or wrong according to the laws of nature. Think about what went wrong (maybe you didn't do anything wrong but were under too much stress, or your environment was unnatural), and think about changing your lifestyle. Maybe each day was like one drop of wrongdoing, and now it's become a river that has accumulated over the years, perhaps 10 years, without your awareness. To correct this condition, to recover, and to gain back your health may take six months to a year. It may never happen, if that's the will of the universe (or god). We all have to go sometime. Live with a good quality of life—laughing and being joyful, living each day, one day at a time. It's better that way, don't you think?

The fact is, you woke up this morning! That means your life force decided to live today. You've been given your life for today; you are allowed to live today. Be grateful to your life force and to everyone and everything around you that has made this miracle of today possible for you. Don't be so anxious about living beyond today. Everyone dies. You should be thankful that you've suddenly become aware that you're alive. You weren't so anxious about living when you were healthy, were you? You didn't even think about life and death. Now you're aware, thank god. You should even thank the doctor who gave you that prognosis.

No more being sad and depressed over things you can't do anything about (which is true most of the time)! Measure your life force today—just for today—by observing and knowing how you feel. Today, you're not too ambitious, not over-achieving—but not too lazy, either. Fear, especially fear of death, has an enormous influence on whether we heal or get sicker. According to Dr. Abo, the number of lymphocytes in your white blood cells and the white blood cell count itself drops fast when you're fearful. Don't go through test after test. Tests cause anxiety and are often harmful to the body. They can also be harmful to your mental state, if the results are negative. Even if the results are good, you can become overconfident and forget that you were ever sick, which could cause you to stop caring for your body and mind/soul. Instead, measure your health by asking your life force how you feel today. If you feel terrific, there's no more you need to know. Living today is all that matters.

THE LAW OF SYNCHRONICITY

Our consciousness is absolutely amazing. It works more or less like a tuning fork. When a tuning fork is rung, other objects in the room that have similar properties begin ringing at the same vibration pitch. Likewise, when we emit thoughts or consciousness, we cause other people (or situations or conditions) to vibrate with the same thought or consciousness. I always demonstrate this in my lectures, and audiences are always amazed. I call this the he of synchronicity. It works without your knowing.

Suppose, for example, that you're depressed today and feel that nothing is going right. You don't even feel physically well enough to go to the office—but you have to, so you go to work with this feeling. You emit feelings of depression everywhere, and the others you come in contact with (who may have been more or less depressed than you) join in. As a result, the depressed feelings create multiple vibrations, and keep multiplying and multiplying. You get more and more depressed as the vibrations are bounced back to you from the others. In a similar way, if you think something will go wrong, it does. That's because you're summoning the energy of "something going wrong" and emitting those vibrations. It's like a magnet. If you say, "I'm sick, I don't feel good," all the time, you will soon get sick.

There is a way out. The first step is to consciously say thank you for your situation. It doesn't matter how terrible it looks. Say "Thank you!" and invite any kind of positive thoughts, especially gratitude and thankfulness. First, smile and find gratitude in the little things that are right in front of you—like the fact that you were able to come into the office. Then thank everything around you—anything and everything you can think of! "I didn't have a headache today—thank you!" "I was able to eat last night. I didn't go hungry—thanks!" "I ate a delicious meal—thanks!" "I have enough money to live for today—thanks!" And so on. You'll be amazed that there are so many things to be grateful for. Then recall or visualize your happiest time by creating an image of it in your mind. I usually use memories from my childhood—trying to catch a dragonfly or butterfly with my brother, holding hands with my mother on the way to a festival at a nearby shrine—things like that. You begin to smile. Before you know it, you're sending out positive energy, and this time the positive energy from other positive people starts to vibrate with your consciousness, multiplying, multiplying, and multiplying. Soon, you're no longer depressed, and are all set for a happy day! Isn't this simple? Smile, smile, smile. Happy feelings attract more happy energy, which creates a happy situation.

This phenomenon—the law of synchronicity—means that you always attract the same kind of vibration that you emit. We often make friends with the same type of people. Or we think of someone and that person thinks of us at the same time and telephones us. We notice that a similar incident repeats itself—accidents, for example. We keep making the same mistakes, the same kind of fortune or misfortune happens to us repeatedly. These aren't coincidences, but rather the universe working within the law of synchronicity, which is the law of nature.

The first step is believing that everything and every thought on the planet carries the vibration known as *Ki*, and that we need positive *Ki* in our minds.

As long as you create and maintain positive *Ki* within yourself, it will overcome and change everything. You don't need to know how or why this happens. Just let it be. Someday, when human beings reach a higher plane, we may be able to explain this phenomenon. For now, just believe that it is always the case.

Secret One: Balance and Harmonize Your Body with Nature

Balance your posture with nature and the universe so that your life force can flow naturally. First, straighten your spine from the base of the spine to the top of your head, without tensing. Open and lower your shoulders. Tuck your chin slightly and keep your eyebrows apart (this can only be done with a slight Mona Lisa smile). Your eyes should be softly closed, or half closed. Focus on this hara point—the center of your body, about one inch under the belly button, inside the middle of your body.

Secret Two:
Balance and Harmonize Your Breath with Nature

Practice hara breathing (see page 198) to make your breath deep, quiet, and soft. This will calm your mind and enable your autonomic nervous system to work.

Secret three: balance and harmonize your mind with nature

Begin observing your breath, focusing your entire mind. Experience the sensation caused by each breath by placing your attention on the inside of your nose as you inhale, and on the outside of your nose (just above the lip) as you exhale. Make your mind sharper and sharper, focusing it like you would focus a camera lens, or a spotlight on a stage. Observe diligently any sensation your breath may cause at every moment. This is the beginning of meditation.

If you'd like to learn how to meditate, I recommend that you study Vipassana meditation, which is said to be the way that Shakyamuni Buddha himself taught 2,500 years ago. There are teaching centers all over the world where you're taught and given accommodations and wonderful vegetarian food—all for free. But you must go for 10 days. Ever since 1968, when this 10-day course was first taught by Goenka-ji (S. N. Goenka) in India, it has been traditional for "old" students (as students who've completed the 10-day course are known) to take care of "new" students. Not until you've finished your first 10-day course may you make a donation or provide volunteer service, if you wish. This is absolutely the very best meditation instruction available. I dare say that this 10-day teaching will be the most meaningful, most wonderful, and most beneficial 10 days you will ever spend in your life. Do try to go. And put your name on the waiting list, because courses often fill up. For more information, visit *www.dhamma.org*.

Conclusion

As the title *Healing Your Healing Power* indicates, this chapter has discussed ways to heal your own healing power holistically (meaning in a way that is harmless and that takes into account the entire being). Ultimately, only you can heal yourself. You are your own best doctor. You must become able to listen to your body's cry and joy.

In general, holistic practice is non-aggressive and kinder than Western medicine. It not only helps acute and chronic conditions, but also prevents illness and promotes general health, both physically and psychologically. These treatments, or modalities, are based on thousands of years of knowledge, and are astonishingly effective. Holistic/Asian diagnosis can often reveal the causes of illnesses by examining the relationship of the organs and other parts of the body. Using holistic treatments based on this knowledge, you can help heal yourself.

Western medicine and holistic/Asian medicine should work hand in hand. Patients need to know that they have alternatives. Most importantly, we should try our utmost to avoid anything that can damage our body, cells, and mind, and promote any method that helps our immune system.

In 1998, When Dr. Mitsui and I wrote a book called Overcoming Cancer and Other Diseases in a Holistic Way, this was a very new and unusual concept. I hid the book from mainstream booksellers, fearing negative consequences and repercussions. But the books sold out through word of mouth. Since then, many changes and developments have occurred in Western medicine, as well as in holistic medicine. Both fields are narrowing in on each other. Today, many people go to alternative practitioners in addition to Western practitioners.

Acupuncture has almost become the norm. Yoga, tai chi, and Pilates classes are booming. Good nutrition and diet are on people's minds. Positive things are happening in the field of prevention as well. People are aware of the dangerous effects we have on our environment.

I think the next step will be a return to living by the law of nature, even with our knowledge of scientific advancement. There will be no conflict. Science will help us think and live by the law of nature, rather than preventing us from doing so. This will be the true science that human beings will create.

There's still a long way to go before we may humbly realize that any disease is a dis-ease of our whole body and whole being, physically and mentally. I hope the next stage of understanding will come in the next 10 years, so that we can come to understand that we are only a tiny part of the universe. We must find a way to obey and live in accordance with the law of nature, rather than with the notion of "conquering" the universe.

We must realize that anything that disturbs or blocks the law of nature (God almighty? Some great entity?) causes dis-ease in the earth's environment, in where we live, and within our bodies and organs. This is a real cause of illness, unhappiness, and even poverty. These all come from the same source, which depends on our consciousness.

If we could understand this law, we could change our consciousness of all that surrounds us, and, I have no doubt, could find the key to health, wealth, and happiness.

Everything we see, we must see as part of the whole—only one part of the whole. And we must also see the whole. This is the true holistic way of thinking.

I would like to end this book in humbleness with quotations from my teachers. They are of immense value and encouragement for me eternally.

Illnesses are what we create in our own mind-hearts. The way we live influences the ii energy inside and outside of us. The parts of us that are not aligned with the law of nature disturb that flow of energy and will manifest as illnesses, accidents, or other misfortunes. Such things are valuable messages from the Universe, telling us that we need to improve the way we live (posture of mind-heart). Once we begin to understand this, other aspects of life will change in positive directions.

There are no incurable diseases. As long as your hair and nails grow, your life force is strong enough and you have plenty of your own healing power, which surpasses any medicine. Make your life force stronger in natural ways, not weaker with medicine.
-- Masato Nakagawa I

True yoga is the state of a human being living in complete harmony with nature, constantly changing, constantly balancing, and constantly searching for stability. Ultimately, everything on this planet is led, unified, governed, and guided by one and only one principle. the law of nature.
-- Masahiro Oki

Testimonials

My Eyes

When I visited my ophthalmologist in mid-September, I completely freaked out. He told me I had this "incurable disease" called glaucoma.

I started reading about glaucoma and began to cry. No one in my family has glaucoma, and I'm relatively young to have this disease. In addition, everything I read said that it's incurable: "Either you have it or you don't" and "There is absolutely no cure for this disease." Suddenly, I thought about a friend of mine who broke her ankle. "There's no such thing as an incurable disease," she said. "I'm sure of that. Why don't you call Kazuko sensei and find out what kind of treatment she can offer you?" I called her right a way.

My first three far-infrared sessions with her were quite intensive and painful. I screamed when she applied her Onnetsuki over my kidney and liver areas, to the back of my optic nerve, and to my shoulder areas. It was so piercingly painful, I felt as if boiling water were being poured over me. She kept telling me, "There's no such thing as an incurable disease. It is you who will change for the better."

After six far-infrared sessions, my eye pressure, which was originally measured at 21, came down to between 14 and 16. My ophthalmologist was very pleased, and told me that I don't have to come back to see him in the next three months. I'm sure my kidney and liver are functioning much better than before. I'm no longer hot and tired in my eye area, which caused pain and headaches when I worked at the computer (I used to apply an ice pack several times a day, and my colleagues used to laugh at me). During breaks, I do the eye exercises that Kazuko sensei taught me, and I've begun taking Manda Koso every morning.

In addition, my face has become much clearer. I used to have expensive facials twice a month to pet rid of pimples and red spots. But after receiving Onnetsu treatment and doing *Ki* exercise, those things are pone. I can't believe that during this time three men have declared their love for me!

I still don't know what exactly happened to me. Perhaps it's a combination of everything—meeting with Kazuko, receiving

Shinkiko and Onnetsu, my colleague who helped me a great deal, my far- infrared treatments, my belief that I would be cured, taking Manda Koso. I'm also doing my best to be positive at all times. Mental attitude is everything, and it can be trained and changed. Kazuko sensei's practice of iitoko sagashi—looking for positive things or events—is a great exercise that I'd never been taught before, and which has had a wonderful impact on me.

Lady "A"

In December 1993, I experienced a sharp pain in my chest while bending over to retrieve something from the floor. I found myself choking for air, and suddenly everything went black. A seizure! An MRI indicated that there was a large mass in my brain. This came as a shock, but there was little time to reflect because an immediate surgical intervention was strongly recommended.

The surgeon was unable to resect the entire tumor due to its proximity to the cortex. I was left with a large portion of the tumor intact. Diagnosis: low-grade astrocytoma. Nothing further could be done. I was instructed to monitor it closely by having frequent MRIs...

Six weeks later, I received a devastating pathology report. The tumor had been upgraded to an "unusual and difficult to categorize" genre with properties similar to a glioblastoma, one of the deadliest, most aggressive tumors known.

I returned to New York and began both chemotherapy and radiation two weeks later. Radiation was administered over a six-week period. Chemotherapy continued for months. There was shrinkage, then regrowth, followed by more shrinkage. Seven months later, I was a shell of my former self. My ankles and stomach were swollen to three times their size due to water retention. My face was a mass of angry rashes and cysts. Worst of all was the diarrhea, of such intensity and so constant that I couldn't leave the house. A week in the hospital with a severe case of pneumonia seemed to me the final insult. I was unable to breathe without a respirator.

The turning point was a suggestion by a friend with cancer to consider far-infrared therapy. I had done copious amounts of cancer research yet had never heard of the treatment. It was reassuring to know that it was nontoxic. I had truly reached my threshold with chemotherapy.

The decision to halt the chemotherapy was difficult. Although the side effects were next to intolerable, my tumor was definitely shrinking with the chemo regimen. Numerous professionals expressed concern that it was a bad decision to abandon the standard treatment in favor of the "unproven" far-infrared therapy. I knew I could be making a fatal mistake. The conclusion was to attempt the infrared treatment on a trial basis. It was risky, considering I was uncertain how much time I had. Statistics were not on my side.

The first few months of Dr. Kazuko's treatment were very painful in the area where the cancer was located. However, I was gradually able to tolerate the heat for longer periods of time. The next MRI indicated shrinkage, and the two ensuing MRIs were equally encouraging.

I have noticed remarkable changes since commencing far-infrared therapy. The rashes are gone. The dangerously low lymphocyte levels are advancing to the normal range. My body is no longer swollen. I have excessive amounts of energy, coupled with enthusiasm and a strong, positive will to create a new life for myself while helping others. My family and I are so grateful to Dr. Kazuko. Her persistence and dedication were decisive. She allowed me to imagine that I had a future, whereas other experts predicted a swift downfall. I will never forget.

Professor LIN YUN

Indebted to Your Kindness Om Ma Tri Mu YeSa Le Du
Mantra of Lord Tonpa Shenrad, founder of the Bon tradition

In the summer of 2003, on August 23, I was invited to lecture in Manhattan, New York, upon which occasion I chanced to make the acquaintance of Dr. Kazuko Tatsumura, whose sincerity, altruism, and spirit of compassion deeply moved me. Upon learning that I was suffering from poor health, Dr. Tatsumura offered to treat me at no charge, using the unique method of diagnosis for which she is renowned. The results were remarkable—within seconds she was able to determine that I was suffering from diabetes and diseases of the liver and kidneys. She is truly a miracle worker! But due to commitments back home, I was unable to complete the regimen, and had to fly back to Berkeley to give a series of lectures at the Yun Lin Cultural

Center. Yet after only three sessions, the pain in my waist had disappeared, and my legs now enable me to walk around without any assistance. Mood-wise, I have gone from dispirited to energetic, all thanks to the work of Dr. Tatsumura, to whom I dedicate this piece of calligraphy in red ink, representing the characters "Indebted to Your Kindness." The work is blessed using the mantra of Lord Tonpa Shenrad to wish the owner good fortune, good karma, and wishes come true.

Dragonwake Highlander
Cloudstone Recluse
Jade Garden Descendant
Eccentric Septuagenarian
- *Lin Yun*

Founder of Yun Lin Temple, Lin Yun Monastery, and Yun Shi Jing She. Written in the Violet Room of Rainbow Cottage, Purple Bamboo Grove at Berkeley Mansion, the residence of Crystal Chu Rinpoche.

His Holiness Professor Lin Yun is the Grand Master of the Tibetan Black Sect Tantric Buddhism Feng Shui and Supreme Master of Bon School of Tibetan Buddhism.

About the Authors

Toru Abo, M.D.

Toru Abo, M.D., was born in 1947 and graduated from Tohoku University Medical School. He currently serves as professor of immunology at Nigata University Graduate School. At the frontline of immunology studies, Dr. Abo is in wide demand internationally as a speaker and presenter of his research. His significant studies and discoveries include the creation of a "monoclonal antibody against NK cell antigen CD57" while attending Alabama University in 1980; the discovery of extrathymic T cells (1989); the solution to the mechanism of white cells controlled by the autonomic nerves (1996); and the discovery that extrathymic T cells prevent malaria (1999). His 2000 article on granulocyte theory in the journal Digestive Diseases and Sciences countered the 100-year-old theory that stomach ulcer is caused by acid. Dr. Abo is the author of a number of important texts, including Future Immunology and Illustrated Immunology.

Dr. Kazuko Hillyer Tatsumura, Ph.D., OMD

Dr. Kazuko Hillyer Tatsumura (O.M.D., Ph.D.) has dedicated her life to work in Holistic Health and Philanthropy, especially for unfortunate children worldwide. First an accomplished pianist, then a world-famous cultural impresario in 1970s & 80s producing 2,000 events each year over 100 countries until she retired in 1992. She established a nonprofit organizations Concert Arts Society in 1968, and GAIA Holistic in 2001 in the wake of the tragedy of the World Trade Center. She is a Shinto priest ordained by Shrine Tenkawa Daibenzaiten Jinjya in Nara, Japan. Her tireless lifelong work in Philanthropic field is vast and well-known ranging from Save the Beacon Theater, Save the Boat People, HIV/AIDS children in Africa. Currently she is building nine orphanages in the world modeled on the Manjushree Tibetan orphanage in Tawang, India which she supports. She is a recipient of many medals and honors internationally. She teaches and lectures worldwide and write books.

Printed in France by Amazon
Brétigny-sur-Orge, FR

20088555R00137